CALL ME
RICK
GRACE
IN THE MIDDLE

RICK G. KEE

CALL ME
RICK
GRACE
IN THE MIDDLE

PATRICK G. KELLY

ISBN: 978-1-967375-08-0 (Paperback)

ISBN: 978-1-967375-09-7 (eBook)

Library of Congress Control Number: 2025911009

Printed in the United States of America

Published by:

info@thequippyquill.com
(302) 295-2278

Table of Contents

INTRODUCTION

A name gives birth to a story still unfolding.

Throughout my life, I have been given many names, some tender, some fierce, some cruel.

For years, I sought refuge in a name of my choosing. A name I could control. A name that couldn't be twisted into mockery or shame. I clung to it like armor. But as faith and self-acceptance reshaped me, something shifted. I no longer needed to hide behind a name. I began to embrace the fullness of who I was— every name, every struggle, every story that had shaped me.

Today, I introduce myself with the echo of where I began and a bridge to who I am becoming. And in that, I find something sacred—a whisper of transformation much like Saul becoming the Apostle Paul on the Damascus Road. His name change was not erasure but redemption: an identity refined, realigned with God's will. My own journey mirrors that truth. For the names we are given at birth merely start our journey – a journey of refinement that becomes a testimony to the way God is shaping us through daily trials, struggles, and grace.

Now, before you step into these pages, I owe you an honest warning. You will encounter repetition. In my life as a deaf person, people were constantly repeating words to me to make sure I embraced a concept or direction; therefore, repetition has become a communication mode for me. In my writing, some stories resurface in different chapters, seen from new angles or used to illuminate different truths. Some themes echo and reverberate, not by accident but by design. This is not lazy storytelling. It is the rhythm of my life and the rhythm of my teaching. As a pastor, a coach, and a teacher, I have learned that some truths are too important to say only once. They must be returned to, reframed, remembered, until they move from the page into the bones.

When a story repeats, it does not simply repeat—it deepens. It demonstrates how a single moment can ripple across decades, shaping identity, faith, and calling in ways we cannot predict. If you find yourself thinking, *I've heard this before*, know that the thought is intentional. Life-changing truths rarely arrive only once. They keep showing up until we are ready to listen.

"Call Me Rick: Grace in the Middle" is written in three sections: Discovery, Defined by Differences, and Divine Direction. The first five chapters comprise the Discovery chapter. In these chapters, I share my roots and my experience of growing up in a hearing world. Barriers and the message sent are discussed. My introduction to faith is also highlighted.

Chapters 6 to 10 comprise the Defined by Differences section. In these chapters, differences are described and unpacked within varied environments such as school, home, work, and church. Encounters with sexism, ableism, racism, as well as mental health issues and economic insecurity are also explored.

The final chapters 11 to 16 make up the Divine Direction chapters. In these chapters, I pull from my previous experiences over the years and name the formation and transformation that occurred by divine plan. Like a beautiful stained-glass story created by broken pieces of glass, grace connected the broken pieces of my life to create a witness of how all people are beloved and worth honoring. The book culminates with encouragement and motivation to be one's own true self, no matter what the world says.

The people in my life that I talk about in these pages have not been perfect, but they have been perfectly placed to teach me what to do, what not to do, and to emphasize the truth that we are not God. My sharing about these important figures in my life is in relation to my formation, not to make them be heroes or heroines. Simply imperfect people I love and am thankful for.

This book is not a neat memoir. It is not a simple testimony. It is a tapestry intertwined, at times, with the messy knots of faith, Deafness, football, trauma, and grace, stitched with seams of prophetic imagination and longing for justice. The chapters you will read were not crafted to impress but to bear witness—to the God who meets us in locker rooms and classrooms, in hospital rooms and sanctuaries, in silence and in song.

Inequality in classrooms will emerge where hope seems drained from the walls. The brotherhood of friendship forged across racial divides in locker rooms. Silence of white churches in the face of injustice. The mandate of grace that moves from comfort to action. Experiences of trauma form a resilient cover over a softened heart. The holy restlessness of dreaming bigger than what this world says is possible.

My prayer is that as you move through these pages, you will not only witness my story, but you will encounter your own. That in doubt, you might find courage. In scars, you might glimpse healing. In transformation, you might recognize the quiet, persistent grace already working in you.

So, let me begin the way I've always wanted to:

Hello. My name is Rick.

Welcome to this crazy thing I call my life.

CHAPTER 1

In the Beginning

The power of a name is found in the sacred story called life. A name selected in expectation. A name offered in the face of the unimaginable. A name that titled my story when the purpose was not readily discernible but known only to God. And so that is how it is with my name and my story.

My first moments on this earth were not met with lullabies or laughter, but with the hum of machines and the hurried footfalls of medical staff. My birth, which should have been the joyful beginning of a new chapter in my family's life, was instead written in crisis. There was no time to celebrate. No time for introductions. No time for that first tender skin-to-skin moment that so many parents cherish. Everything moved fast, because it had to.

The delivery room, bright with fluorescent lights and thick with sterile air, became the setting for a different kind of beginning. My tiny body entered this world limp and unresponsive, struggling to take in the breath of life that most babies instinctively grasp. The monitors around me erupted in warning tones. Doctors and nurses worked with practiced urgency. But through it all—amid the flash of machines and the murmurs of concern—there was no sound from me. No first cry to mark my arrival. No declaration of life. Just silence.

Sterile.

Fluorescent.

Silence.

Within minutes, I was swept away from my mother's arms and placed inside an isolette—a high-tech incubator designed to support fragile newborns like me. It was a transparent, temperature-controlled box with small circular portals for gloved hands to reach through. It was designed for survival, not comfort. I would spend the first weeks of my life inside that box, wrapped not in soft cotton but in wires, sensors, and plastic tubing. I was kept alive by the whirring of machines, by the relentless diligence of doctors and nurses, and—though they didn't know it—by something much deeper.

The isolette was not a crib. It was not a cradle. Whispered prayers penetrated the walls of that box that muffled everything, both literally and emotionally. The world outside moved on, but I was doing my best to catch up. Alive—but disconnected from what was perceived as normal. Protected, but still waiting for my parents to hold me. Surviving, but waiting for the verdict on whether I was to stay or go.

It was, in many ways, a sensory desert. For my own good.

Yet, it was not empty.

Even in that unnatural stillness, I believe something sacred was present. I did not have language for it at the time, of course— I was just an infant clinging to life. But now, as I look back, I know that God was there. I believe grace hovered close, even when no one could hold me. I believe the Holy Spirit cupped my body gently when human hands could not.

That plastic box didn't suffocate my spirit. It stirred it awake.

Most babies begin their lives learning to recognize the voices of their parents, the soothing tones of lullabies, and the rhythmic repetition of speech. But I learned something different. I learned to feel the world. I learned through vibration, through flickering light, through the breath of air as it moved across my face. My first language wasn't words. It was present. I felt the world before I could see it. Before I could form memories or understand meaning, I understood stillness. I understood being.

When I was finally discharged from the NICU, when I was brought home and placed in the arms of family, the world outside that box unfolded for me like a field after a long-awaited rain. The air smelled of something new. The light felt different. Even though I could not hear the birds singing or the wind whispering through the trees, I could feel something in the way the world moved. I could sense life in those early years.

I couldn't hear the creak of the old wooden floorboards, but I could feel them shift under my body when my father came home from work. I couldn't hear the roar of engines, but I could feel the low vibrations of a truck passing by as it traveled through the soles of my feet. I couldn't make out the slam of the screen door in the heat of summer, but I could feel its gust echo through the house— shaking the walls, stirring the air, announcing someone's presence like thunder in a quiet sky.

Each of these sensations was more than just a physical stimulus. To me, they were messages. They were sacred signs. My body learned to read them like scripture—line by line, moment by moment.

Later, people would try to tell me that I was missing something. That I had a deficit. That I would need extra help, extra tools, extra grace. They called it hearing loss. They used words like "impaired," "disabled," and "hard-of-hearing." And maybe to them, that's what it was.

I knew the truth, deep down. I was not broken.

I was born listening to a different kind of world.

My Deafness was not a wall that blocked me out. It was a window that opened me up.

Through that window, I saw what others often missed. I saw the way someone's fingers fidgeted when they were afraid. I saw the tension that crept into a person's shoulders before their mouth ever formed a word. I noticed when a smile didn't quite reach the eyes. I learned to read tone in body language, to hear rhythm in movement, to feel joy and grief not in words, but in presence.

The world taught me that listening was something you did with your ears. But God taught me something different. God taught me that listening is about attention. About awareness. About sacred stillness

My ears never gave me the kind of comfort or clarity people spoke of. But my body—my soul—became finely tuned instruments of discernment. I could feel when peace entered a room. I could sense when something holy brushed past. Even as a boy, I began to believe that maybe God whispered loudest in the quiet. That maybe silence wasn't a lack, but a language.

The truth is, I was shaped in stillness. I was formed in silence. It wasn't an empty or frightening silence. It was sacred silence. The kind of silence that hovers. The kind that watches. The kind that sees.

Before I could walk. Before I could speak. Before I could flip through the pages of a Bible or quote a single verse—I knew something true. I knew that the world moves even when no one speaks. That love does not require volume. That presence can speak louder than sound.

Before I ever spoke a word, I listened.

Not with ears, but with skin.

With my ribs.

With the soles of my feet. With the ache of being alone and the miracle of being kept. I did not begin with language. I began with survival. I began with grace.

In that quiet beginning, before the noise and the names and the expectations of the world could define me, I was already learning how to listen. I was learning to listen with wonder.

Hometown as Holy Ground

Delmar was more than a town. It was the first place that ever truly held me.

It is not held in the way people often talk about—full of noise and excitement, busy streets, and fanfare. No, Delmar held me in the way the earth holds a seed. Quietly. Firmly. Steadily. It held me like good soil holds memory, like a riverbank cradles water without ever asking it to stay. It was a place that didn't try to define me but gave me space to grow, to breathe, to listen.

I was raised in a town stitched directly across a state line, one half resting in Delaware, the other half in Maryland. One name. Two states. No division. You could walk down the street and cross an invisible border without ever knowing it. But everyone knew your name. Delmar was small enough to miss if you blinked at the wrong exit sign, but it was big enough to shape a life. People didn't move to Delmar to vanish. They stayed because it reminded them. It was a place that I didn't forget. It was a place where stories were written into the landscape of the heart and mind.

The physical landscape was marked by long stretches of railroad track, worn smooth by time, and storefronts whose peeling paint whispered stories of generations past. The town wasn't loud, but it was alive. And though I couldn't hear it in the way others did, I felt it. I saw it. I lived it. I noticed the steam rising from coffee cups on front porches in the early morning. I watched the way shoulders leaned in during conversation, how people made room for one another. I saw the light change after rain, how it danced in puddles and hung thick in the air like an old hymn.

We didn't have a Wawa or Royal Farms in my earliest memories; we had Cheers.

The store named Cheers was part gas station, part diner, part community bulletin board. It was where the town breathed. Early mornings were full—not loud, but full. I watched men with dirt-caked boots stand shoulder to shoulder at the counter, hands wrapped around coffee cups so hot they fogged their glasses. I could see laughter bloom across their faces before it ever shook the room. A crinkle at the edge of an eye. A head thrown back. A palm slapping the countertop. I didn't need to hear their jokes to know they were funny. I didn't need to understand their stories to know they mattered.

The floor would hum beneath my shoes when trucks idled just outside. A hand on my back, a nod across the room, a quick wave as someone passed by—these were the languages I understood. These were the ways Delmar spoke to me. Not through volume, but through presence. Through texture. Through rhythm.

Just down the road was Delmar Pizza, and you could smell it long before you reached the door. The air around it was thick with the scent of rising dough and sharp tomato sauce. I remember standing at the counter, watching grease bubble on the cheese, the light bouncing off the curved metal of the pizza paddle as it slid under the crust. The smell alone could pull you through the door. But what kept us there was more than food.

Fellowship had a name: after every football or baseball game, we'd pile in—sweaty, grass-stained, and full of joy, brothers, friends, neighbors, and even strangers. I watched my teammates yell and laugh across booths, their hands moving like fire through the air, not with signs but emphasis, reenacting their stories. Every slice burned the roof of my mouth just a little, but it didn't matter. It tasted like victory. Like belonging. Like something only we could understand.

But even pizza, even post-game triumphs, paled in comparison to the memories made with my best friend Chad. He lived one street over, which led to shortcuts over our neighbor's fence and through yards between our houses.

We were wild and unstoppable, wrapped in scraped knees and grit. We weren't just boys, we were explorers, kings, warriors. We rode our bikes like they were stallions, galloping through alleyways and side streets like the town itself had been made for our adventures. We built forts from rotting plywood and stolen cinderblocks. We raced through cornfields until our lungs gave out and the earth blurred beneath us. We stayed out past curfew, past logic, past fear, chasing the last streaks of sunset like they were secrets only we could find.

We shot basketballs, hockey pucks, and soccer balls. The asphalt beneath us was cracked, but it didn't matter. I couldn't hear the bounce of the ball, but I didn't need to. I felt the game in my chest—in the rhythm that pulsed through my legs, in the way the court seemed to speak when the shot was good. We didn't talk much. We didn't need to. Our friendship was rooted in knowing. A shove on the shoulder. A raised eyebrow. A half-smile when the world felt too heavy. He was my brother in every way except blood.

Then, time did what time always does. It moved. Slowly at first, then all at once. The creek between us widened with school, with priorities, with silence. Life carried us in different directions, but I never stopped looking back. I still long for those simpler days when we'd play from sunup to sundown outside and down the streets. Drinking from garden hoses and riding all over town on our bikes. I find myself hoping we could dig up the boyhood we had buried like treasure beneath that sacred dirt.

Now, he wears a badge in Delmar.

He walks the same streets we once ruled with water balloons and toy swords. Sometimes I see him near the school zone, standing tall, eyes scanning the neighborhood. Sometimes I wave. Sometimes I don't. I don't know if he sees me, I feel the thread that still binds us. That invisible line of memory. That sacred bond of boys who once believed the whole world could be found in a backyard fort and a summer breeze.

Delmar still holds that history.

The football field behind the high school is more than a patch of grass. It's where the town gathers—where old rivalries and new hopes rise beneath the floodlights. I couldn't hear the announcer. I couldn't hear the marching band or the cheerleaders chanting their name. But I saw it all. I saw the crowd lean forward like a single body when the ball snapped. I saw the scoreboard lights paint the night with expectation. I felt the bleachers shake beneath my shoes when we scored. I didn't hear the roar. I lived inside it.

That's the thing about holy ground—it doesn't always come with stained glass or choir robes. Sometimes, it comes with cracked sidewalks and the glow of a concession stand. Sometimes, it comes with the smell of popcorn in October, with a hand on your shoulder, with a smile across a parking lot. Holiness lives in the ordinary when the ordinary is full of love.

Delmar wasn't perfect. It had its struggles. Its limits. It's scars. My time in Delmar taught me that silence isn't emptiness. That Deafness isn't the absence of sound—it's the presence of something deeper. It's the way light filters through trees. It's the warmth of a neighbor's wave. It's the memory etched into the pavement outside a pizza shop. It's knowing that you were seen, even when no one said your name out loud.

Delmar gave me more than a hometown.

It gave me rhythm.

It gave me memory.

It gave me wonder.

It gave me holy ground to stand on and sacred soil to come back to.

A Legacy of Faith and Family

Long before I knew how to pray with words, I learned what prayer looked like in motion. In my family, faith was never something set aside for Sunday. It lived in work boots, kitchen tables, steering wheels, and garden rows. It wasn't announced. It was lived out—in quiet habits, repeated rituals, and the rough but faithful ways love tried, failed, and tried again.

My grandfather, Rev. Robert Granville Kelly Sr., was a United Methodist pastor who believed faith should be lived, not just preached. He didn't talk about holiness as something far-off or unreachable. He treated it like something you could hold in your hands—if you were willing to get them dirty.

Every morning, he sat at the kitchen table, same spot, same rhythm. He'd eat a plate of scrapple and eggs, clear his dishes, and then open his Bible and spiral notebook. A pen always rested nearby. He wasn't performing. He was preparing. I watched him underline verses, scribble notes, and pause to listen for God. That table wasn't just where he ate—it was where he worshiped.

He didn't always understand my Deafness. Sometimes he'd speak from across the room, get frustrated when I didn't respond, and fuss when he thought I wasn't paying attention. But his frustration came from care, not cruelty. He wanted to connect. And even when he didn't know how, he kept showing up. That effort left its mark on me.

We rode for hours together in his sedan, the seats worn soft with time, the glove compartment packed with maps and bulletins. We traveled as far south as Crisfield and Snow Hill, Maryland, and as far north as New Holland and Lancaster, Pennsylvania. He pointed out old Methodist campgrounds, country churches, and weathered gravestones. Even when I missed the words, I caught the weight of what he carried. His stories didn't need sound to be sacred.

My Mommom, Ann Bugher Kelly, was strength without spectacle. Her hair was white and always neatly kept, and she moved with purpose. She never raised her voice or wasted motion. She didn't chop wood or seek attention, but her house ran like a clock because she was always in motion—cooking, cleaning, gardening, preparing. She never claimed holiness. She lived it.

Of all my grandparents, Mommom was the most patient with me. She didn't always understand my Deafness, but she didn't let that turn to blame. If I didn't respond, she gently touched my shoulder or waited until I was looking. Her care was quiet, but steady. She adjusted herself to reach me, even if she didn't know that's what she was doing.

On my mother's side were the Prettymans, Joseph and Bettye Jo, my Pepaw and Grandma. Their home in Laurel, Delaware carried a sacredness like a well-loved hymn. It was soft and familiar, with every note in its place. Everything had meaning. Every creak of the floorboards, every dish in the cabinet, every photograph on the wall seemed to hold a story that had been polished by time and touch.

Pepaw worked as a mechanic at DuPont in Seaford for over thirty years. He did not talk much. His long fingers were always busy fixing engines, tinkering with cameras, or repairing whatever needed mending. He spoke less with words than with the quiet solidity of his presence and the way he showed up without needing to announce himself. Later in life, after years of grease and gears, he turned to photography. He had an eye for what most people overlooked, barns at sunset, rusted tractors leaning into the earth, and tree lines dissolving into winter fog. He could take the ordinary and reveal the holy hiding inside it. Looking through his photos felt like walking through his way of seeing the world, a quiet reverence for things that endure and things that fade.

But Pepaw Joseph carried another lifelong love, one few outside the family fully knew, painting. He worked in watercolors and oils, always landscapes and never people. Rolling fields after summer storms. Marsh grass shimmering with tidewater. Faded barns leaning against a horizon of soft light. His paintings carried the depth and warmth of the Impressionist era, blended colors and living brushstrokes that felt alive and almost breathing. He never thought of himself as skilled. He was humble and almost shy, setting down each canvas like it did not matter if the world saw it or not. But I knew better. His art was stunning, rich with the quiet grace he carried in himself.

I never once heard him yell or scold. He could be firm, but he carried a patience I have never seen anywhere else, patience shaped by both discipline and love. He served in the Army, yet even that could not harden him. If anything, it deepened his humility. His strength was quiet and steady, and somehow, you only realized how strong it was when you found how safe you felt near him.

He didn't fully understand my Deafness either. Sometimes he'd talk without making eye contact, and we'd both miss the moment. Nonetheless, he never made me feel like a problem. He simply kept being there. Sometimes that is all a kid needs.

Grandma Bettye Jo was sharp, structured, and full of conviction. She worked first as a paraprofessional, then later as a nurse's assistant—jobs that demanded more strength than most realized. She ran her home with the same loving discipline. Her meals were generous but orderly—stuffed peppers, pork chops, Saturday morning spreads. She expected effort. She valued respect. She didn't soften the truth, but she didn't withhold love either.

She didn't always get my Deafness. She could be stern when I didn't respond, assuming I was ignoring her. "You hear what you want to hear," she'd say. But underneath that was a fierce love—a belief that I was capable, that I mattered, and that she wasn't going to let misunderstanding rob me of responsibility.

My parents came from all of this—formed by faith, forged by work.

My mother, a Special Education teacher, worked late nights, read constantly, and poured herself into her students. She didn't hum while folding laundry or sing in the kitchen. She prayed in preparation. She loved showing up. She didn't always understand the limits of my Deafness. Sometimes she pushed me to speak or respond in ways that cost me more than she realized. But her love was consistent. Her faith was real. Her commitment never wavered.

My father was my hero. He worked without stopping, as if rest was something meant for other men. I remember him always on the phone, answering calls about work, or nodding off in his chair after another long day. The sound of his boots on the floor and the hum of his voice were as much a part of my childhood as the walls of our house. He was a builder by trade, but also a builder of our family's security, a man whose hands shaped more than just wood and concrete.

Some of my favorite memories are the rare moments when I got to go with him to job sites. I can still see the sand and salt air in Ocean City, walking beside him at the Garden of Eden miniature golf course on 18th Street. He let me carry a tool or hold a nail, and in those moments, I felt ten feet tall. Football practices were the same. Watching him coach, hearing his voice cut through the field, I felt like I belonged to something larger than myself. Those were the moments I felt closest to him, the moments when I wanted most to be like him.

I also feared him, not because he ever abused me, but because I never wanted to see disappointment in his eyes. The weight of that look was worse than any punishment. A paddling now and then came for the worst offenses, but it did not shake my admiration for him. I loved him and feared failing him all at once.

As I grew older, I began to see the cracks in the armor I once thought was unbreakable. He had struggles I did not understand as a child, battles that I only began to recognize as an adult. Even now, I am not sure if he was running from something or chasing something, but I know he carried both restlessness and drive inside him. He taught me something I have never forgotten; at the end of the day, we have no one to blame but ourselves. Quitting was never an option.

My father was a builder and a protector. He rarely spoke about feelings, but he mowed the grass before it needed mowing, fixed what was broken before anyone else noticed it was broken, and stood between the world and his family like a wall of quiet strength. He did not always know how to meet me in my silence, but he never turned away from it either.

Then there were my brothers—Randy, Robby, and Joe.

Randy taught me toughness. He didn't baby me. He made sure I knew how to stand up. Robby was the joy-bringer, the one who could lighten the heaviest room with a joke or a look. Joe, the youngest, was closest to me in age and in heart. We didn't always agree, but we always stayed connected. Forged in the same fire. Sharpened by the same household.

We didn't grow up in ease. But we grew up in abundance, the kind of abundance that doesn't show up in money or luxury, but in presence, in faith, in the commitment to keep going even when things were hard.

And I'll be honest: I didn't always see it that way when I was young.

The Flip side of Family Life

Don't misunderstand me, there was love in our house. The kind of love you felt in the way we passed food around the table, in the way laughter sometimes came loud enough to rattle the windows. We were raised to work hard, to pray harder, to keep going no matter what. But love doesn't erase pain, and faith doesn't automatically heal what's breaking underneath. Behind our door, there were shadows we didn't name. We learned early to smile for the neighbors, to nod politely at church, to hide the noise that roared behind closed walls. We became fluent in silence.

My father was my hero from an early age. I saw him in work boots and calloused hands, a man who could fix anything except the ache inside him. As a kid, I didn't see the demons he fought— I just saw the man I wanted to be. As I got older, the cracks showed. His battles weren't born with me; they were older than him. Scars carried from a childhood where pain was swallowed whole because speaking it out loud wasn't an option. Trauma that seeped out in the poor decisions he made, while telling me not to do the same. He taught me strength, but he also taught me unhealthy silence. I loved him fiercely, and I still do. But loving him meant loving someone whose pain sometimes bled onto everyone else.

My mother carried her own battles, though she bore them differently. While my father's struggles roared, hers stayed quiet, buried under the weight of expectations and duty. She was a teacher first, and later a pastor. Everyone saw her as dependable: the woman who showed up to every classroom, every hospital bedside, every Sunday service with a steady smile. At home, she graded papers at the kitchen table long after we'd gone to bed, sermon notes scattered between piles of laundry. She swallowed exhaustion because there was no time to name it. She believed if she held the pieces tightly enough, maybe nothing would break. But I know now it cost her. That silence, that holding-it-all-together, was its own slow bleed by the name of enabling.

There were nights when the quiet in our house felt louder than any argument. I can still see it: the kitchen light buzzing past midnight, my mother hunched over lesson plans with red-rimmed eyes, my father sitting in the driveway with the engine off, keeping his actions and feelings out of sight. Or so he thought. We just didn't talk about it. We just passed each other in the hallways, carrying pieces of each other's pain without ever daring to name it.

My brothers had their own weight to carry. One fought through mild cerebral palsy—a struggle the world barely noticed but that shaped every literal step he took. Another brother's life was changed in an instant by a car and a tree. The night the phone rang, I was sitting in the living room when headlights from the ambulance swept across the wall. Sixty miles per hour into a tree. His face was shattered from the eye socket to the jaw. I remember the antiseptic sting of the hospital air, the click of nurses' shoes on linoleum, my mother's hand trembling in mine. He survived, but survival came with scars—some you could see, others you couldn't.

I didn't handle any of it well. I grabbed anything that dulled the ache—drugs, alcohol, chaos. I became addicted to attention because it distracted me from the noise in my head. Counselors broke my trust. Psychiatrists numbed me with prescriptions. I believed I wouldn't live past twenty-seven, so I lived like it: reckless, angry, burning bridges because I didn't plan to cross back over them. Faith was there, somewhere, but it was fractured prayers whispered through gritted teeth, curses muttered under my breath, wondering if God even listened.

There was abuse too—self-inflicted and toward each other. Words we wish we could unsay. Bruises that never made it to skin but bruised hearts just the same. I don't name these moments to shame us, but to honor what it cost to grow beyond them. Over time, we learned new ways to cope. New ways to navigate life when trouble came our way. We learned to have the conversations we once avoided. It doesn't erase what happened, but it lets us hold it without letting it define us.

My mother and I, our story is maybe the hardest for me to tell. Not to say my father and I did not have conflict, I just had to relearn my father as the man, not the myth. Today, we're close, my mother and I. So, close my brother's joke, I'm "the daughter who calls every day." However, as a teenager, I was cruel to her in ways that haunt me. I slammed doors. I shouted in blame. I threw words at her like knives, not understanding she was the one holding us together when everything else was falling apart. She gave us a home when we could've been under a bridge. She fed us when there was barely enough. She still edits my sermons, still believes in my writing, and still cheers me on. I wish I had seen her sooner. I wish I had loved her better then.

Addiction tore through our extended family like a storm. Aunts, uncles, cousins, we've buried too many and have grown estranged from more. Some still won't speak to me because of the choices I made. I've made peace with their silence, but I still hold out hope. Hope that grace will one day make the introductions we haven't been able to.

Please don't read this as me playing the victim. I am not innocent in this story. I hurt people, good people, people who didn't deserve the pain I caused. To them, I owe more than words. I owe a life lived differently, proof in my actions that I've changed. Change is still a work in progress.

Marriage didn't come easy either. My wife and I have had seasons where we felt like strangers in the same house—nights when we debated quitting, days when love felt like work more than romance. And yet, we stayed. Somehow, we stayed. Her family history is its own story of pain—an abusive mother she hasn't seen in over a decade, a father who floats in and out when it suits him. She carries wounds I can't fix, but I've learned that love sometimes means holding someone without demanding they heal on your timeline.

This is not the story of a polished faith or perfect family. It is the story of scars and second chances. Of grace that kept showing up when I least deserved it. Of people who hurt each other, healed in fits and starts, and are still learning what it means to love fully without pretending we were never broken. Looking back, I didn't recognize how much of a privilege it was to be born into this kind of heritage—an imperfect household of work ethic and love offered by imperfect people doing their best in the messed-up world. At the time, it just felt normal.

This kind of inheritance—faith lived out in grit and grace—is not something everyone receives. And the older I've grown, the more I've realized that what I was given was not just a blessing. It was a lens. A way of seeing how unevenly that blessing is distributed. A way of understanding that what I received as default, others have fought for and still been denied.

It taught me to notice the disparities in access to the very things we often claim as universal values - dignity, belonging, love, purpose. My family gave me those things, not in speech, but in sacrifice. And knowing that has changed the way I see everything.

They didn't always hear me.

They didn't always understand me.

But they never let me go.

That is the legacy I carry.

Not a legacy of perfection—but of persistence.

Of people who kept trying.

Of people who stayed.

It is a legacy I once took for granted.

Now I know better.

It is both a privilege to be grateful for and a calling to live out.

Grace—when received honestly—always turns into responsibility.

Deafness as a Sacred Way of Knowing

As a child, I often carried a quiet, unspoken question in my chest: *Was I born wrong?* It wasn't something I could articulate back then, but it lived in me all the same. That doubt didn't arrive loudly; it crept in through the subtle, shifting expressions on the faces of adults when they learned I was Deaf. It was planted in the softening of voices, the sympathetic smiles, and the whispered questions that passed just beyond my reach. No one came right out and said I was broken, but I could feel it. Their posture stiffened. Their eyes lowered. Their tone changed. I wasn't seen as whole—I was seen as someone to grieve or gently explain away.

After church services, I would often watch people pull my parents aside. Their hands rested gently on shoulders, their voices dropped to a murmur, and their eyes darted toward me like I was a delicate subject they didn't want to name too loudly. They asked questions like, "Was he born like this?" "Did something happen during the pregnancy?" "Is it permanent?" "Does he sign yet?" "Do you think God might restore his hearing someday?" Their words weren't laced with cruelty, but they landed like stones anyway. Each one carried the weight of discomfort and uncertainty, as if my Deafness had interrupted a more acceptable version of who I was supposed to be.

There were moments I can still see clearly. A visitor once pulled my mother aside and asked if there had been sin in our family. They wondered aloud if my Deafness might be God's way of getting someone's attention. Another time, after Sunday school, I stood by the cookie table when a woman patted my head and called me "one of God's special crosses." She meant it as a compliment—her smile was warm, her tone gentle—but I remember holding a napkin sticky with juice and wondering why I had to be a burden someone else was blessed to carry. I didn't have the words to explain the confusion, but I felt the dissonance. Why did people see me as a symbol of suffering when I was just a kid trying to belong?

Again and again, I found myself caught between well-meaning theology and the uneasy silence that followed it. I wasn't yet angry. I didn't have the vocabulary to challenge the stories others wrote about me. I was learning, quietly and consistently, that many people needed my Deafness to mean something. It had to be a punishment, a test, a miracle in waiting, or a lesson for others— but never just what it was. And the more others named it for me, the more I struggled to understand it for myself. I began to wonder: Was I broken? Cursed? Chosen? Punished? Or was I simply a child who wanted to be understood?

Even the environment of the church confused me. I would sit through altar calls where music played softly in the background and the congregation wept openly. Hands lifted. Heads bowed. Voices cracked under the weight of confession or gratitude. Something was clearly happening in the room, something meaningful, something holy—but I couldn't access it. I couldn't hear the invitation or the testimonies. I couldn't follow the melody or the words of the songs. I watched everything from a kind of sacred distance, as if holiness lived just beyond the veil and I had not been given the key.

So I adapted. I watched more than I listened. I paid attention to what people did rather than what they said. I learned to follow the rhythm of the service through the movement of bodies—the sway of the choir, the clapping of hands, the folding of fingers in prayer. I learned to read moods through posture and emotion through expression. I knew when people were performing and when something genuine was breaking open inside them. I didn't need to hear the prayer to know when it came from the gut. I didn't need the lyrics to feel the truth in the tears.

One question haunted me more than any other. It came not from the church pew or the cookie table, but from Scripture itself. I had read that "faith comes by hearing." If that were true, I wondered, where did that leave someone like me? What was I supposed to do with a verse like that? Was I excluded from faith because my ears could not function the way others expected? Or was there more to hearing than sound?

As I read through the stories of Jesus, I began to notice something else. Time and again, he healed people who were blind, lame, or Deaf. And every story seemed to follow a similar arc: the healing came, the crowds rejoiced, and the formerly disabled person was welcomed back into the community. The message felt clear: restoration meant change. Healing meant belonging. Wholeness meant being different than before.

What if the healing never came? What if the body didn't change? What if someone like me remained Deaf—not by accident, but by design? What if we didn't need to be healed to be embraced? What if Deafness wasn't a problem to be solved but a person to be welcomed?

I wanted a story like that. I longed for one. I needed a passage where Jesus met a Deaf person and said, "You're already whole." I wanted to read about someone who wasn't healed, just seen. Someone whose body was not a canvas for transformation but a vessel of belovedness as-is. I wanted that story because it would have changed how I saw myself. It would have reminded me that I wasn't a waiting room for a miracle—I was already the message.

Instead, I was handed story after story that told me I could be loved after I was changed.

Even as I wrestled with this, something else was quietly forming within me. It wasn't anger, though I would come to know anger later. It was something more tender, more open. A kind of sacred curiosity. A hunger for truth. A spiritual ache that kept whispering, *There's more to this story.*

Even though the church kept telling me something was missing, I didn't feel incomplete. Yes, I was different. But different didn't mean defective. It meant I knew how to notice things others ignored. I could walk into a room and feel its energy before anyone spoke. I could tell when someone was lying—not from their words, but from the stiffness in their jaw or the shift in their shoulders. I could spot someone's weariness just by the way they carried their coffee cup. I felt the undercurrents of emotion in the space before they surfaced. And most of all, I knew the difference between kindness and performance—between being loved and being tolerated.

No one told me this was knowledge. No one told me this was sacred.

At the time, I didn't have words like *Deaf Gain*, *disability theology*, or *embodied wisdom*. I didn't know that my experience wasn't a deficit, it was a difference. I didn't know that there was an entire Deaf culture, an entire history of resilience, resistance, and spiritual brilliance behind me. All I had were my questions and the silence they left behind.

Slowly, I began to realize something powerful: my Deafness was not a flaw. It wasn't something to be prayed away or explained to others in whispers. It was a way of being in the world—a legitimate, beautiful, and truth-filled way. It taught me how to attend closely, how to listen with more than ears, how to feel the pulse of holiness in places others overlooked.

God had never been silent with me. God had simply spoken in ways others weren't trained to hear.

God met me through light—through flickering candles and sunbeams across stained glass. God met me through movement—through a hand on my back, a mother's glance across a room, a tremble of emotion that passed between people without words. God spoke to me through presence—through stillness that wrapped itself around me when nothing else made sense. The silence that others feared became the very space where God lived with me.

In time, Deafness became more than something I carried. It became a calling. A way forward. A sacred lens through which to see the world. A reminder that God's voice is not confined to sound, and that holiness does not hinge on healing.

I did not need to be changed to be chosen.

I needed to be seen. And welcomed. And known.

And eventually, I was. But not before I walked through the long silence. Not before I sat with the aching questions. Not before I wondered if there was space for someone like me in the kingdom others described with music I couldn't hear.

It was in that space—lonely, quiet, and holy—that I began to hear God most clearly.

Not in the thunder.

Not in the choir.

But in the stillness that never left me.

The stillness where God had been waiting all along.

Call and Calling: Finding My Voice Without Sound

For much of my life, I believed that being called by God meant sounding a certain way. Not just having faith, or being willing to serve—but actually *sounding* like someone who was chosen. Someone with a voice that commanded a room. A voice that came smooth, confident, and polished. A preacher's voice. A teacher's voice. A coach's voice. A voice that never wavered, never slurred, never stumbled over its own syllables. A voice that fit the mold of what I thought leadership had to sound like.

Because of that belief, I spent years assuming the calling could never be mine.

Yes, I speak. I always have. However, my voice has never moved the way other people's voices seem to. It stutters. It drags. It misfires. It gets caught somewhere between thought and breath. Some days it comes clear and sharp, like stones skipping across calm water. But other days, it falters—gravelly, uncertain, exhausting to push out. Even on my best days, my speech rarely sounds like what people expect when they picture someone standing behind a pulpit, pacing a sideline, or writing on a classroom whiteboard. Because of that, I assumed I wasn't the right person. That someone else—someone easier to understand, someone smoother, someone more impressive—would be the one God used to teach, to preach, to lead.

Then, something unexpected happened.

The call still came.

It didn't crash into my life like lightning. It didn't arrive through visions or dreams. It didn't roar through the rafters or split the sky. It came quietly. It came in moments. It came in nudges too small to be dismissed. The way students looked at me after a lesson made sense to them for the first time. In the way a football player locked eyes with me before the snap, wordlessly saying, "I'm with you." In the way I stood behind a pulpit, palms sweating, voice trembling, and somehow—despite everything—delivered a word that met people where they were.

The call came in the very places I had feared: in classrooms where I worried my voice would fail, in locker rooms where I doubted I'd be understood, in sanctuaries where I questioned whether I belonged. The call came *through* my stutter, not around it. It came *through* the voice I had once considered a liability. The very thing I thought disqualified me became the means through which God called me to speak.

It took time, but I began to realize that God wasn't waiting for me to sound perfect. God was waiting for me to speak anyway.

Over time, I learned something else—something I wish I'd known sooner. Calling is not about performance. It's not about polish. It's not about having the voice that turns heads. It's about presence. And presence doesn't come from sounding good. It comes from showing up.

As a coach, my players don't listen to me because I'm loud, although that does come as a side-effect of deafness. I like to think they listen because I'm real. They've seen me show up. They've watched me explain drills five different ways, using hands, eyes, and instinct to communicate urgency and care. They read the intensity in my stare, the rhythm in my claps, the shift in my shoulders before a big moment. They know my voice cracks when I'm proud, falters when I'm frustrated, and rises when the moment calls for courage. But more than anything, they know I mean it.

As a teacher, I've stood in rooms filled with students who've been told—directly or indirectly—that they are too far behind, too distracted, too broken, or too different to learn. Some of them speak English as a second language. Some are neurodivergent. Some have never trusted a classroom. But what cuts through isn't my eloquence. It's my consistency. It's the way I stay until they get it. It's the way I change my teaching style mid-sentence if something's not clicking. It's the fact that I don't give up. And in that stubborn presence, many of them find their own voice— because someone finally stayed long enough to listen.

As a pastor, perhaps most surprisingly of all, I've watched God move through my halting speech in ways I could never predict. I've preached sermons where I lost my place. I've stumbled over Scripture readings. I've paused too long and fumbled words I practiced for hours. But somehow, even in the imperfection, people have told me they felt the Spirit. That something I said hit home. That's what I shared that helped them make sense of their own story.

I've come to believe this: when I speak, what people hear is not just me—it's the space between the words. It's the vulnerability. It's the Spirit speaking through the cracks, reaching them in the places I could never reach on my own. The power of my voice isn't in its clarity. It's in its honesty.

For years, I was afraid to step forward. I feared the pulpit because I didn't sound like the men I grew up hearing. I feared the classroom because I thought fluency was the only thing that earned trust. I feared the huddle because I thought a booming voice was what built leaders. But slowly, I've discovered that I don't need to sound like anyone else to be called. I just need to sound like myself.

The truth is, my calling doesn't rest on how I speak. It rests on how I live. My voice may stutter, but my presence is steady. My delivery may catch, but my conviction does not. I've been called— not because I'm perfect, but because I'm faithful. Because I've shown up again and again, even when I didn't feel ready. Even when I was afraid.

I've stopped waiting to be smooth. I've stopped waiting to be eloquent. Instead, I speak.

I speak in classrooms, where confusion becomes confidence.

I speak in fields where failure becomes fuel.

I speak in sanctuaries, where Scripture becomes story and trembling words become testimony.

I speak, not because it's easy.

I speak because I've been called.

And every time I do, I am reminded of a truth that now lives in my bones:

My voice is not my weakness.

It's my witness.

Faith Formed in Quiet Spaces

My faith wasn't born in a revival tent or stirred into being by thunderclaps and altar calls. There were no spotlights, no rushing wind, no fire falling from heaven. I didn't have a dramatic moment of conversion; no one prayed me through a breakthrough with hands raised high and music swelling in the background. That wasn't how God found me.

God came softly. Quietly. Piece by piece.

My faith grew slowly, like breath on a windowpane—barely visible at first, but real. Gentle. Spreading over time. It took shape in the quiet corners of my life, in the spaces most people looked past.

A lot of that quiet happened in my bedroom. I spent a lot of time there by myself—not because I was unloved, but because that was our rhythm. My mother never barged in with overbearing questions or emotional displays. She was not the kind of mother who hovered. When I was in my room, I was by myself—left alone, not out of neglect, but by deliberate, loving design. Her love was steady, strong, and always present, but she gave it in ways that built self-sufficiency. She was warm and doting, yes—but she also encouraged independence with the kind of conviction that comes from having had to fight for her own.

She expected me to figure things out, to try before asking for help, and to take ownership of my choices. It wasn't always easy. Sometimes I resented it. But looking back now, I can see how it shaped me in ways I'm only beginning to understand. Her faith was not loud, but it was lived. It showed up in packed lunches, clean clothes, late-night lesson planning, and the strength she carried into every room.

If my mother's love gave me space to grow, my father's presence gave me something to hold onto. He was rarely still—always fixing something, coaching, working, or telling a story. He didn't speak of God in Sunday School tones or through traditional devotions. He never sat me down with a Bible or led prayers at the dinner table. Instead, he spoke of faith through stories—told while sanding wood, while explaining a football play, or while walking with me along the shoreline. Job sites, back roads, and beaches were his pulpits. The world was his sanctuary.

Sometimes he'd point to the grain of wood and say, "God doesn't make mistakes in texture." Or he'd nod toward a perfectly constructed foundation and say, "You build from the bottom if you want it to last." It didn't sound like Scripture, but it was truth. You had to listen closely; he didn't spell it out. But if you paid attention, he was always talking about God.

To this day, I still find myself closest to God in those same spaces, on old country roads, riding with the window cracked and nothing but the wind and my thoughts. I pray best that way. Not in pews or pulpits. Not in formal prayers. But with the rhythm of tires on gravel, the trees leaning overhead, and the familiar silence that says more than words ever could. Those rides, with my father and grandfather, shaped how I understand prayer. Not as recitation, but as rhythm. As presence. As knowing.

Neither of my parents taught me faith in traditional ways, but they both taught it. My mother, through her fierce belief in my capacity to endure and lead. My father, through story, example, and silence. And both of them, in their own ways, showed me that faith is not something to be performed; it is something to be lived. Their lives taught me more than words ever could.

I didn't always recognize this as a gift. In fact, for much of my youth, I thought something was missing. Other kids had rules about devotionals, Bible memory, and family prayer time. We didn't do any of that. And yet, we were steeped in faith. Faith as undercurrent, not headline. It was there in how my parents made decisions, how they treated people, how they carried their responsibilities with honor. I just didn't have the language for it at the time.

It took years before I realized that I had been given something sacred. The quiet of my room. The stories on the job site. The long drives. The woods. The waves. All of it was a curriculum of grace. It was the language God used to speak to me. And though I once envied the flashier signs of spiritual formation in others, I've come to treasure the way mine was formed: gently, steadily, and always close by—even when it felt far.

It was a privilege I did not appreciate until much later—to come from such a heritage, shaped by testimony, resilience, and quiet faithfulness. But that privilege also opened my eyes. It revealed the disparity—how many others never had access to such models of work ethic, service, citizenship, and love. My upbringing was a gift—but it also became a calling. A reminder that those who are poured into must pour back out. That privilege is not meant to be held, but given.

My grandparents echoed the same faith-in-motion. At my Kelly grandparents' house, mornings began with Poppop sitting at the table after breakfast, a Bible open next to his coffee mug. He never explained much; he just read. Slowly. Faithfully. Mommom was always working, always tending, her movements purposeful, her kindness consistent. She didn't always understand my Deafness, but she was patient with me in ways that mattered. She made room for me, even when she didn't have the words.

My Prettyman grandparents, up in Laurel, moved slower but carried the same weight. Pepaw read his Bible in his chair like a man watching for signs in the sky—steady, never hurried. Grandma Bettye Jo folded her faith into linens and pie crusts, offering hospitality as theology. Her hands taught what her words rarely needed to say.

They rarely quoted Scripture out loud. But their lives echoed it.

They didn't preach sermons. They lived them.

I watched. I watched all of it. The quiet strength of my mother. The steady force of my father. The patience of my grandparents. The unspoken witness of people who showed love through presence more than proclamation.

That's how my faith began to grow. Not through noise or spectacle. But through noticing.

I noticed how silence could hold you like a song.

I noticed how a father's story could build trust before the words were even clear.

I noticed how a mother's steadiness could become a shelter.

I noticed how a table set with care could feel like communion.

My Deafness didn't distance me from God. It brought me closer.

It made me pay attention.

To look for meaning in movement.

To feel presence without proof.

To listen—not just with ears, but with my whole body.

Faith doesn't have to be loud to be alive.

It doesn't have to be spoken to be strong.

It doesn't have to be heard to be true.

My faith was formed in the quiet.

In solitude.

In the reliable rhythms of a house filled with people who lived love in motion.

That's where I first met God.

Not in a sermon.

Rather, in the kitchen.

In the hush of a ride down a dirt road.

In the steady, unspoken grace of being raised by people who lived what they believed.

In the stillness that held me long enough to believe I belonged.

Naming Grace in Retrospect

I have lived my life between names.

Some of those names were spoken with tenderness, trust, and hope. They gave me identity when I did not yet know how to claim one for myself. One of the first was Big. That was what most people called me growing up. At first, it referred to my size. I was broad-shouldered and heavy-framed. But as I grew, the meaning shifted. Big came to reflect more than just my physical presence. It meant that I carried weight emotionally and spiritually. It meant I could hold burdens for other people. I could take up space without apologizing for it. I could walk into a room and be felt before I was heard. In many ways, being called Big helped me begin to believe I was allowed to matter.

Then there was Diamond.

That name came from my high school football coach, Coach Vipond, in Loudoun County, Virginia. He was the kind of man who saw deeper than surface impressions. When he looked at me, he did not just see a Deaf player on the edge of a hearing team. He saw potential. He saw resilience. He saw someone being formed under pressure. He gave me that name because he believed in what I could become. Not because I was flashy or refined, but because I was being forged. That name meant something. It meant he saw value in me. And it gave me something solid to hold onto when I wasn't sure who I was becoming.

Later in life, the name Brother became one of the most sacred names I have ever received and one I cherish. On the football field, in the church pew, and among those walking through loss and healing, Brother became a way people chose me. It meant I belonged. It meant someone saw in me not just a teammate or a leader, but family. It meant we were bound together by something deeper than blood. We were bound by commitment.

Not all the names I was given felt like blessings.

I was also called Fat Pat. I was called Retard. I was called "Deafie." I was called Oaf. Some of those names were shouted across locker rooms. Others were whispered behind my back or muttered under the breath of someone who thought I could not hear. Some were written into jokes, scribbled onto desks, or spoken by people who should have known better. They may not have always meant to hurt me, but they did. Those words lived in my skin. They clung to my body like bruises only I could see.

For a long time, I believed the only way to silence those names was to outgrow them. I tried to prove them wrong through performance. I tried to be stronger, faster, smarter, and better than anyone expected. I believed if I achieved enough, those names would fall away on their own. But they did not. Because the names people give us do not disappear until we look at them directly and take back the power they tried to steal.

It was not until I became a man, standing in leadership as a teacher, coach, and pastor, that I realized the truth. The more honestly I looked inward, the more I began to heal. And the more I healed, the more I began to see other people for who they really were. I began to notice the pain they carried, too.

When I started sharing my own story, people started sharing theirs.

I heard stories from people of color who were tired of being followed through stores or pulled over without reason. I heard from women who had spent their entire lives being talked over, silenced, or used. I heard from disabled friends who had been treated like burdens instead of beloved. I heard from LGBTQ friends who carried both faith and fear in their chests because the church had taught them love with conditions. I did not just hear their stories. I felt them. And I recognized something familiar.

Their pain was different from mine, but it was kin to it.

That is what changed everything.

The more I named my own journey—the pain, the misunderstandings, the weight of being called broken—the more I found myself drawn to the margins, where other people were still waiting to be named rightly. I started to see how racism, sexism, ableism, classism, ageism, and all the other forms of exclusion and harm do not live in theory. They live in names. They live in assumptions. They live in the spaces where people stop seeing each other as image-bearers of God.

That realization was the beginning of this book.

This book was not written because I had all the answers. It was written because I could no longer carry the questions alone. It was written to reclaim my own name. Not the ones that were given in mockery, but the one that was written on my spirit by the One who formed me in the quiet.

It was also written for others. For those who have been misnamed, misread, and misunderstood. For those who have been told they were less than, or too much, or never enough. For those still wondering if they will ever be called by something sacred.

This is not just my story. It is a window into what it means to be human.

It is about the grace that showed up before I had words for it.

Grace was there in the locker rooms, where sweat and failure mingled with unspoken hope.

Grace was there on the job sites, where my father's quiet hands taught me more than any sermon.

Grace was there in the classrooms where I stumbled through teaching, only to realize my students understood me better than I understood myself.

Grace was there in the backroads of Delaware and Virginia, where I rode with the window cracked open and the silence filled with God.

I used to think my story began with what I lacked.

Now I know that it begins with what I had.

I have a body that feels what others ignore.

I have a spirit that can interpret silence as sacred.

I have a soul that can hold both pain and possibility at the same time.

I have a God who never needed sound to speak truth.

And I have a name that was never lost. Only waiting to be claimed.

CHAPTER 2

A Childhood in Tension

I walked a tightrope my entire childhood, and in some ways, I still do. Sometimes more gracefully than others.

Not in the circus, of clowns and cotton candy, but in the quiet expanses between sound and silence. Between being understood and being misread. Between what people expected me to be and who I actually was. Imagine a boy suspended high above the world, arms stretched out for balance, toes gripped onto a narrow cable stretched between two tall poles. One end was anchored in the world of the hearing, a world filled with noise and conversations and school announcements. The other was anchored in the world of Deafness, a world of vibrations and gestures and watching lips move without ever hearing their sound. Beneath me, there was a net suspended - woven from threads of family, faith, frustration, and from fierce love.

Yet it wasn't falling that I feared. It was the feeling that every step I took was being watched, every move evaluated by people who didn't understand the path I was walking. Watchers who had already made up their minds about where I would land.

This is not a story about tragedy.

My story is a story about formation. It is about how tension, when it does not break you, can shape you. Tension can make you more aware. It can strengthen your character, deepen your compassion, and sharpen your vision. The right kind of tension, like the right tension on a guitar string, creates music. Too loose, and it buzzes without purpose. Too tight and it snaps. But when the tension is tuned just right, it sings. My childhood was full of that kind of tuning. It did not always feel good. It certainly was not always fair. But it taught me how to listen in ways beyond sound and how to grow in places where I was not planted deeply.

I grew up in a place where people knew the sound of one another's screen doors, where bikes rattled along cracked sidewalks, and where baseballs echoed off aluminum bats on dusty fields. I did not always hear those sounds the way others did, but I felt them. I felt the rhythm of my town in the slam of a locker door, in the vibration of a school bus as it climbed over potholes, in the way a classroom would pause and shift whenever someone said something funny. I felt the sound of the world without always catching all the words. My body learned how to listen and pay attention when my ears could not.

Even the rhythm of my town was fragmented. My life was a crazy quilt of transfers and placements and paperwork that sent me to schools scattered far and wide. While the kids on my block grew up side by side, riding the same bus to the same classrooms and sitting beside the same faces year after year, I was often the outsider. I was sent to different schools, always starting over. I would play sports with one group of kids, then walk into a school building filled with another. I would learn and study beside children who went to churches I had never been inside, who shared inside jokes I never had the chance to hear.

I always felt one step behind and one circle outside.

My friendships were real, but rarely permanent. My life was segmented by zip codes and school districts. I knew how to adapt, but I longed to belong. I carried a backpack full of books and an invisible weight of trying to figure out where I fit. I lived on one side of the county, went to school on another, and worshipped in places still different from both. I never fully belonged anywhere, but I had to learn how to live everywhere.

At home, there was love. Real, steady love. But love did not always translate into understanding. My family did their best. They prayed for me. They fought for me. They believed in me. But they could not always see the world through my eyes. And I could not always explain what I was feeling. I spoke, but not always clearly. I listened, but not always in the ways people expected. I needed something more than words, and for a long time, I didn't know how to ask for it.

I did not always feel Deaf, and I did not always feel hearing. I felt like a translator trying to speak both languages without being fully fluent in either. I stood in the space between, watching both sides, trying to make sense of the conversation no one else seemed to know was happening. I belonged everywhere and nowhere all at once. I was a child of contradiction, a tightrope walker, a boy stretched between the sound of the world and the silence within myself.

Grace held fast, allowing me space to grow.

School Days – Where Belonging Was Negotiated

My first memories of school carry a strange mixture of excitement and confusion. I remember loving the idea of school—being around other kids, sharpening pencils until they were perfect little arrows, holding new crayons that hadn't yet snapped. There was an energy in the hallways, a current I could feel. But even as a child, I sensed I was already playing catch-up in a race where no one had told me the rules.

I started pre-K twice.

Not because I was behind academically, but because my parents were forced into a decision that no family should have to make. The doctors said we had to choose. Either immerse me fully in Deaf culture, give me ASL, and surround me with others like me, or push me entirely into hearing culture and force speech as my only bridge to the world. There was no room in their model for both. No vision for a child who could live between. My parents, both educators, refused to accept that limited choice. They wanted to see where I would thrive. They wanted to let me find my way before the world boxed me in.

So we tried both paths.

The first year, I was placed in a satellite Deaf program. On the surface, it seemed like the right call. The classrooms were designed for Deaf students. Some teachers signed. I was with other kids who also could not hear. And there were benefits. I began to understand that language could live in movement, that communication did not require sound. But we were isolated. We were kept in a self-contained wing of the school, away from the hearing students, away from our same-aged peers. We did not share recess, lunch, or any real community. It felt like we had been put aside. As a child growing up in a hearing family, I recognized this exclusion early. I saw what I was missing. I felt what I had been cut off from.

The next year, I was placed in a public school pre-K with an interpreter—at least, for one hour a day. The other six hours, I was expected to manage on my own. That single hour of access, instead of being a solution, felt more like a quiet reminder of what I did not have. It wasn't even during the most critical lessons. I didn't get to choose. Sometimes it wasn't enough to make a difference. Sometimes it was too little, too late. The system seemed to say, "This is enough for you."

Both settings had strengths. The Deaf program introduced me to a language that felt natural in my body. The public school connected me to the wider world, to the one my family lived in, to the familiar rhythm of life around me. But neither setting met all my needs. One gave me language but kept me isolated. The other gave me proximity but left me unsupported. If there had been a way to bring the best of both together, to build a bridge instead of a wall, maybe my story would have looked different.

Even at that young age, people made assumptions about me. Because I could speak fairly well, because I smiled when they smiled, because I appeared to be "getting by," they thought I must be fine. But I wasn't fine. I was learning how to disappear. I was learning how to fake it. I was learning how to pass. I became skilled at laughing when everyone else laughed, even when I had no idea what had been said. I knew how to nod, how to pretend, how to keep moving so no one would notice how lost I felt.

Teachers rarely faced the class when they spoke. They turned their backs to write on the board. They moved around the room as they talked. They assumed everyone was following. My classmates didn't understand why I didn't answer when they called my name, why I didn't react to their jokes, and why I sometimes stared blankly in conversation. They assumed I was rude. Or slow. Or not paying attention. Some even whispered that I was faking my Deafness. The truth—that I was working twice as hard to understand half as much—was invisible to them.

People often praised my lip-reading. They called it a gift. But lip-reading is not a gift. It is a last resort. It is mental gymnastics, trying to piece together language from partial shapes and facial expressions, and guesswork. It is unreliable and exhausting. It breaks down the moment someone speaks too fast or covers their mouth, or turns their head. And yet, because I could do it "well enough," many assumed I didn't need anything else. But I did. I needed much more than what I received.

I did not receive a certified ASL interpreter until college. From my earliest school days through high school, I had to make do. When support was requested, we were told that certified interpreters were in short supply. That my speech was too good to justify more help. That's what I was getting was "reasonable." But reasonable never felt fair. Reasonable always seemed to mean just enough to avoid legal trouble, never enough to actually help me thrive.

The emotional toll was deep. I began to wonder if the teachers were right when they said I wasn't paying attention. I began to believe the classmates who called me slow. I sat in classrooms filled with people and felt completely alone. I walked down crowded hallways and felt invisible. I was never completely isolated, but I was almost always disconnected.

I remember clearly when I realized I was being treated differently. It was second grade. Another new school. Another new program. I was placed in a Special Education classroom at a public school across the state line in Salisbury, Maryland. The teacher did not believe I was truly Deaf. She told me my speech was too good. She accused me of pretending. Literally grabbed my face and said, "Knock off this Bullshit! You are just desperate for attention." Just like that, I was disqualified. Not because I could hear. But because I didn't fit her definition of what Deaf should look like. That moment taught me that unless I fit into someone else's mold, I would never be fully accepted.

It wasn't until later, in another Deaf-centered setting, that a deeper hurt arrived. A Deaf student assaulted me sexually. A betrayal from someone who should have been part of my community. When I tried to speak up, no one truly heard me, so I did not think anyone would believe me. The interpreter was pulled. Support vanished. My parents found out because they came to pick me up from school, and the simple question of "How was School today?" Made me break down into tears. Eventually, my parents, exhausted and protective, pulled me from the program entirely and enrolled me in a residential Deaf school.

At that school, I was surrounded by other Deaf students. But the cost was high. I lived away from home. I missed my siblings. I missed my neighborhood. I missed the familiar sounds of family, even if I couldn't always hear them clearly. I only came home on weekends. The loneliness was different there, but it was still loneliness.

Later, when I returned to public school, I was given an interpreter again. She was kind and willing, a CODA who tried her best. But she wasn't certified. I wasn't fluent enough in ASL yet to make the most of her help. We struggled through together, doing what we could with what we had. But it still wasn't enough.

Even with all these struggles, there were small moments of grace. A teacher who paused to check if I understood. A coach who made sure I saw his face when he spoke. A classmate who tapped my shoulder instead of shouting my name. These moments didn't fix everything. But they helped me believe I wasn't entirely alone.

School was never easy. But I learned how to move through it. I learned to walk its hallways like a quiet observer, always alert, always scanning, always adapting. Being different wasn't the hardest part. Being unseen was. And over time, I learned how to be seen. Not with words alone. But with presence. With persistence. With the quiet strength that comes from showing up anyway.

Navigating Family Expectations

At home, I was never pitied. I was expected to adapt and rise.

My family did not lower the bar because I was Deaf. They did not soften the rules or offer special treatment. If anything, the expectations were higher. I was taught that no one was coming to rescue me. That the world owed me nothing. That nothing in life comes free. If you want something, you work for it. You keep your head up and press on. That was the rhythm of the house I was raised in.

There were clear rules. You respected your elders. You did your chores. You showed up on time. You paid attention. You worked hard. Whether we were talking about school or sports or just doing what was right, the message was the same. You do what you are supposed to do, and you do it well. If you fall, you get back up. If you do not understand something, you figure it out. That mindset shaped me. It gave me determination. It taught me how to push through when things were hard.

Sometimes being strong and stoic also made things lonely.

Even though I knew I was loved, I did not always feel understood. There were quiet moments when the gap between us felt wide. Moments when I asked someone to repeat what they said and instead heard the words, "Where are your hearing aids?" or worse, "Never mind." Those two words stung more than anyone realized. They sounded like I did not matter enough to be brought back into the moment. After a while, I stopped asking.

It was not that my family lacked compassion. They cared deeply. Nonetheless, caring and understanding are not the same. Communication is more than words. It is about presence and patience and knowing how to make someone feel included. I could not always keep up with the pace of dinner conversations. I missed jokes, stories, teasing between brothers. I remember sitting at the table while everyone else talked, feeling the energy swirl around me like wind I could see but not hear. I was there, but not always part of it. Even then, when I was attending Residential Deaf Schools, even when I did not have to live in the dorm but with family or family friends, I was isolated from the ebbs and flows of life at my own home. Never able to put roots down.

At my youngest age, before speech therapy had taken hold, Joe was the one who understood me. My little brother, still a toddler himself, became my first interpreter. He knew what I was trying to say before the words formed clearly. He listened with his eyes, with his heart. I still remember the way people turned to him and asked, "Joe, what is your brother saying?" And he answered, every time, without hesitation. He knew my world without needing to be trained in it. His understanding made space for me when no one else could.

That early bond meant everything. It told me I was not invisible. It told me I was worth being understood. Even when I lacked the tools to communicate the way others wanted me to, Joe heard me.

The age gaps in my family added another layer. Randy is ten years older than me. Robby is eight years older. Joe is about three years younger. By the time I was forming full memories, my older brothers were already teenagers with jobs and friends and lives of their own. I was the youngest, and I was also the one who left. I was sent away to school, pulled from the rhythm of family life. I came home only on weekends. While my brothers were growing up under one roof, I was learning how to live apart from it.

Even with Joe, who was closer in age, there was distance. Our childhoods unfolded beside each other, but they were not the same. The gap that opened during those early years never fully closed. We love each other deeply, all of us do, but our stories were shaped by different timelines. Different homes. Different kinds of silence.

I often felt like I was living a different life inside the same house.

I would come home from school with new words, new signs, new stories. And no one quite knew what to do with them. My family wanted to understand, but they were living in a world built around sound. They had not walked the same road I was on. I spoke, yes, but not always clearly. When I needed time or when I struggled to express something, it created tension. Not because they loved me any less. But sometimes love alone is not enough to close the gap.

Still, we found ways to stay connected. Through chores. Through quiet mornings. Through shared routines that needed no words. Through the steady bond that family holds, even when the conversations fall short.

My family's expectations taught me how to work hard. How to lead. How to keep going. But being Deaf taught me how to listen differently. It taught me to notice what others miss. It taught me to sit still in a world that rushes past. And even in a house filled with voices, even in moments when I felt alone, I never doubted that I was loved. Even when I was not always heard.

Finding the First Language: Physical Expression

Before I ever mastered the structure of English or became fluent in American Sign Language, I found a language that required neither voice nor vocabulary. I discovered it in motion. In muscle. In breath. I found it on fields, in gyms, on mats, and under the barbell. Sports were never just games to me. They were places where the world finally made sense. For the first time, I could communicate without needing words. I could be seen without having to explain. I could show up and be part of something where my Deafness did not disqualify me. In fact, it became part of what sharpened me.

My connection to sports came naturally and early. Wrestling mats, football fields, baseball diamonds, the weight room, the cheerleading sidelines, and the circle where I threw shot put and discus—these were the places where I found a voice I didn't know I had. In powerlifting, no one cared if I heard the starting call. The only thing that mattered was the weight in my hands and the will to move it. In throwing, rhythm lived in my legs and chest, and shoulders. No words were needed. I felt it. I knew when the throw was right the second it left my fingertips.

I wasn't a phenom. I wasn't a star. But I was relentless. I went to six high schools in four years. From first through eighth grade, I attended eight different schools. Every move meant learning a new system, meeting new teammates, and reintroducing myself to new coaches. I was always the new kid, always the outsider. I rarely had the advantage of familiarity or reputation. I had to earn everything. I wasn't always the starter, but I never let that keep me from giving everything I had. If I were not going to start, then the person ahead of me was going to have to fight like crazy to keep that spot.

I studied the game. Not just the rules, but the patterns. I studied my teammates, my coaches, my opponents. I learned to notice what others missed. I paid attention to formations, tendencies, body positioning, and cadence. I watched for moments when people's habits betrayed their next move. I broke down what each coach emphasized and how each player reacted under pressure. I became a student of strategy, not just survival. I did not wait to be told what to do—I prepared until I could anticipate what was coming before anyone else knew it had arrived.

The body became my first language. A real language. I learned to read subtle shifts in movement, to communicate through instinct and repetition. I was not guessing. I was translating. And the game became the one place where I could do that fluently.

Church didn't always feel that way. Most of the time, I did not feel like faith communities knew what to do with me. People meant well. But they did not understand Deafness. Some would pray for healing without ever asking what kind of help I actually needed. Others assumed my presence was enough to include me, when in truth I was often left sitting quietly, watching the world move around me without access.

Coaches—some of them—saw something more. Not all. Most didn't. For every ten coaches who viewed me as a problem, two or three took the time to see what I brought to the table. Some treated me like a burden. Like I was too much to deal with. Like I was never going to be worth the extra effort. A few made it clear they hoped I would quit. Several even mentally and socially abused me under the guise of toughening me up and hazing, but always being the new kid, I thought it was normal. In my senior year, my cleats were stolen out of my locker. I told my coach, and I was given size 11 cleats to replace them. I wear size 13. My parents were wrapped up in their fresh divorce and I did not want to ask them to spend more money when they had just spent $200 on my cleats the week before. My father was late getting me to practice and the coach tried to convince the players to cut me from the team. A group of about 10 guys proceeded to bully me for the rest of the season until I transferred to live with my mother. What

I thought was tough love at the time, I later recognized as neglect, even cruelty.

Others were different. A few stood out. They adjusted. They slowed down. They made space. They gave me a chance. And it wasn't just my father, though he taught me so much. It was other coaches too. Men and women who saw that I was working twice as hard just to be in the room. Coaches who didn't see my Deafness as a barrier but as part of my resilience. Coaches who knew leadership had nothing to do with hearing and everything to do with heart.

Eventually, some teammates adapted too. They tapped me on the shoulder instead of calling my name. They used hand signals. They looked me in the eye before the play began. And I noticed everything. While others were distracted by the noise of the crowd or the shouting from the sideline, I was locked in. I did not rely on sound. I relied on focus. I watched. I reacted. I executed. Silence, for me, was not a weakness. It was a strength.

When I played at a Deaf school, I saw what it could be like when everyone operated on the same channel. No shouting. No confusion. No wasted communication. We moved in sync. Our opponents were disoriented by the quiet. But we thrived in it. We were not less capable. We were more coordinated. More disciplined. More attuned to the rhythm of the game without needing to hear it.

Sports became more than a way to pass time. They became my identity. My calling. My place of belonging. The field, the gym, the mat—these were sacred spaces. I wasn't just trying to prove something. I was trying to find something. My purpose. My place. My peace.

Even now, as a coach, I carry that with me. I remember what it was like to work twice as hard for half the recognition. I remember what it was like to be misunderstood. And I make it my mission to see the kid others overlooked. To listen with more than ears. To teach with more than words. To make sure every player knows that showing up matters. That effort speaks louder than sound. That presence and persistence still mean something. Sometimes the body says what words never could.

Internal Struggles and Silent Discoveries

Fitting in was never simple. Every new school brought a different set of rules, unfamiliar faces, conversations I could not hear, and moments that passed me by. But the longing that ran deeper than fitting in was the desire to be known. I did not want to disappear into the background or fake my way through the day. I wanted to be seen for who I was, not reduced to a label or pitied as a case to manage. I wanted to belong - fully, freely, and without explanation.

That longing often pulled against another desire I carried just as strongly. I wanted to be myself. But being myself came at a cost. The world I was placed in rewarded those who could blend in. Who could laugh at the right moment. Who could hear instructions the first time. I learned quickly that being different meant being excluded. So, I adapted. I trained myself to respond with a smile even when I was lost. I nodded even when I missed the question. I taught myself to survive, but I didn't know how to thrive.

Underneath the surface, the pressure built. I wrestled with questions I didn't know how to name. I sat in church pews and watched others raise their hands in worship, their faces lit with something I couldn't touch. I wanted to feel that too. I wanted to know that God could hear me even if I could not hear Him. I believed in God, but I didn't know if God believed in me. At least, not in the version of me that the world always seemed to call broken.

There were nights I prayed to be healed. Not because I was ashamed of who I was, but because I was so tired of feeling like I was on the outside. I didn't want to be someone else—I just wanted to feel what others felt. I wanted to talk with my family without missing half the conversation. I wanted to walk through school without having to guess what was going on. I wanted connection, not perfection. I wanted to belong.

I even went to healing services.

I remember the oil on my forehead, the hands pressing down, the voices lifted in prayer and power. People cried. People shouted. They laid their hands on me and asked God to restore what they believed I had lost. I closed my eyes and asked too. I asked God to take my Deafness. Not because I hated it, but because I thought it was the thing keeping me from being included. I thought maybe if I could hear, everything else would fall into place. Maybe if I could hear, I wouldn't be left behind.

The healing never came. Not in the way I asked for it.

Instead, God continued to meet me in silence.

I started noticing something quiet and holy that had been with me all along. God was present, not in the noise of revival, but in the stillness after the crowd went home. God was in the early morning light that stretched across my bed. God was in the way trees swayed outside my window. God was in the rhythm of solitude. I didn't hear a voice, but I felt a presence. I didn't understand it, but I knew it was real. I knew I was not alone.

People do not understand how deep I have to dig just to reach what others call acceptable. They do not see the weight I carry just to keep up with the basics. Every conversation is a calculation. Every classroom is a test. Every interaction comes with the pressure to prove I belong. I am more critical of myself than anyone knows. Not because I want to be better than others, but because I am trying to stay in the room. I am trying to keep pace. I am trying to hold on to something that always feels one step ahead.

I didn't have the language for it then, but now I can see what was happening. God was not waiting for me to become someone else. God was already loving the boy I was becoming.

In the quiet places where no one applauded, in the unseen effort, in the private ache to be understood—there, God whispered. Not with words I could hear, but with peace I could feel. And that whisper stayed with me. Through the struggle. Through the silence. Through the longing. It was the beginning of something holy. A calling I could not yet explain. A truth I carried in my bones even when my mouth could not form the words.

The Unexpected Victories

Not all victories arrive with applause. Some come in silence, unnoticed by the world, but unforgettable to the soul. These were the moments that mattered to me the most - not because they were loud, but because they were real. They were cracks in the wall that had been built around me by low expectations, constant misunderstanding, and the quiet ache of never being fully included.

One of the first victories that changed something in me happened in eighth grade. It wasn't in the gym or on the field. It was in the classroom. We were assigned to write a poem—just a basic assignment in an English class that had mostly been forgettable until then. I wrote what I could. I didn't know if it was good. I didn't even know if it would make sense to anyone else. But I put something true on the page.

When the teacher returned our work, she paused at my desk. She held the paper in her hand and looked me in the eye. Then she said something no one else had ever said to me—not before, and not again for a long time. She said, "You could be a good writer." She didn't say it like she was surprised. She didn't say it with pity or shock. She just said it plainly, like it was already true. And in that moment, something opened. I was a Deaf kid, used to being seen as a disruption or a burden, and here she was naming a gift in me I hadn't yet claimed for myself. That moment stayed with me long after the poem was forgotten. It was the first time I felt like my words—not my speech, not my lip-reading, but my words—had power.

There was also a moment on the football field that I can still feel in my bones. The game was close. The play was tense. I had studied every angle, every opponent, every tendency. I wasn't the strongest or the fastest, but I had prepared for this. I read the play before it happened. I moved before the quarterback had time to change direction. I hit the gap and made the stop. It wasn't flashy, but it changed the game. For a few moments, I was not "the Deaf kid trying to keep up." I was a player. I was a teammate. My name was on their lips, and for once, it was not followed by correction or complaint; it was respect.

Then there was laughter. One of the most underrated victories of my life came not from sports or school but from the soundless space of shared joy. Every so often, I would time it just right. A perfectly placed joke. A comment that cut through the noise and made the room erupt. The surprise on their faces was always the same. People did not expect me to be funny. They did not expect me to jump in. But when they laughed, and I laughed with them, I felt something that tests and trophies could never give me. I felt seen. I felt part of something. I felt like I belonged in the rhythm, even if I moved through the world on a different beat.

Each of these small victories chipped away at the isolation I had come to accept. A poem. A tackle. A moment of laughter. These were not grand achievements in the eyes of the world. But they were holy to me. They were reminders that I was not invisible. That I was not too much or not enough. That I could bring something to the table that no one else could bring. That even in a world that did not always understand me, there was space for me to be known.

They reminded me that God speaks through quiet breakthroughs. That grace does not always come wrapped in a miracle. Sometimes it looks like a teacher's kind words. Sometimes it looks like a game-changing play. Sometimes it looks like shared laughter in a cafeteria full of noise I cannot hear. And each time, something deeper was being built inside me—not a need to prove myself, but the truth that I did not have to.

I was already enough. I just needed someone to say it. And slowly, through these small victories, I began to say it to myself.

The Weight of Representation

There is a kind of weight that is invisible to most people. It does not show up on your back or shoulders, but it presses down on your spirit all the same. It is the weight of being the only one. The only Deaf student in the classroom. The only kid who couldn't join the banter in the locker room or follow the flow of hallway conversations without piecing together fragments and hoping you guessed right. The only person who couldn't just "listen up" or "speak up" without running into a wall. The silence was not what made me feel alone. It was the way people responded to it.

What made it heavier was that I didn't yet understand what it meant to be Deaf. Not really. I didn't grow up knowing about Deaf culture or Deaf history. I didn't know that being Deaf came with community, with pride, with a shared language and story. I only knew I wasn't hearing—and that everyone around me seemed to want me to act like I was. I was expected to perform, to pretend, to smile through the disconnect. I was taught to adapt to others, not the other way around.

In those early years, the pressure to "perform hearing" was constant. If I spoke well, people assumed I was fine. If I missed something, it wasn't just a mistake—it was treated like proof that I didn't belong. I was allowed no margin for error. I had to be exceptional just to be treated as acceptable. I had to go out of my way to make hearing people comfortable, to excuse their ignorance or impatience, to let their missteps slide. But if I made a mistake, even once, it was remembered. It was recorded. It was used to explain why I shouldn't be in the room.

So I learned to adapt. To switch. To shift. I code-switched so often I started to forget what my original voice even sounded like. I wasn't just switching between spoken English and signs—I was switching between versions of myself. One version at school. Another at home. Another in church. Another on the field. I learned to laugh when I was confused. To nod when I didn't understand. To blend in even when I was drowning.

Constant adaptation came with a cost I didn't fully understand until I was older.

The more I performed, the more I lost touch with who I really was. I had learned to be different people in different places—shifting depending on who I was with and what I thought they needed me to be. Eventually, I realized I didn't know how to stop. I didn't know who I was apart from the performance. I was living fragmented. Always watching, adjusting, measuring, recalibrating. Never resting. Never whole.

The world had never given me space to just be myself. So I learned to wear myself in pieces.

But even then, something began to rise in me. A quiet resistance. I began to notice the patterns. I began to ask questions. Why was I always the one expected to change? Why was access treated like a luxury instead of a right? Why did my success surprise people? Why did my mistakes confirm their bias?

That awareness grew slowly, but it grew. And with it came something else—not bitterness, though I had reason to feel it, but purpose. I started to realize that my experience wasn't just mine. There were thousands of others like me, moving through a world that refused to meet them halfway. And if I could find the words, if I could speak the truth of what I was living, maybe I could help others name it too.

That's when the seed of advocacy began to take root.

I didn't know it would one day lead to preaching, to teaching, to writing, to standing in rooms and helping people see what they had ignored. I didn't know I would become a voice for those still caught in the silence. But I did know that I couldn't stay small anymore. That I couldn't keep switching who I was just to make other people more comfortable. That something in me—something holy—was calling me toward truth. Toward wholeness. Toward home.

God was not waiting for a more polished version of me.

God was meeting me exactly where I was—tired, fragmented, pretending. So the Author of my life and my story invited me to come back to myself.

Preparing the Ground for Faith

Even before I understood what faith was, something had already begun to take root. It didn't begin with theology or preaching. It began in the simple and familiar routines of my childhood—in Sunday mornings at church, in whispered prayers over dinner, in the steady presence of people who trusted in something greater than themselves. I could not yet explain it, but I could feel it. Faith was there, humming quietly underneath everything, even when I didn't fully understand what it meant.

Some of my earliest experiences of faith were shaped at St. George's United Methodist Church, a small country church tucked near Bacon Switch. The sanctuary was filled with warm faces and faithful hearts. That community had prayed for me before I could speak. They carried me to the altar, anointed me, and laid hands on me with the hope that God would do something special in my life. My grandfather, Rev. Bob Kelly, had been a respected pastor, and I grew up hearing his name spoken with reverence. His example became a quiet anchor for my understanding of faith. And then there were Sunday School teachers like Ms. Phyllis and Ms. Nancy. They didn't have training in Deaf education. There were no interpreters. But they taught with love, and somehow their care reached me even when their words did not.

Still, the church was a complicated space. It was full of sound—hymns, preaching, amens rising from the pews. I watched people raise their hands, clap with joy, and wipe tears from their eyes. I could feel something powerful happening, but it often felt just out of reach. I could see the movement, but not always the meaning. Sermons passed by like trains I was not fast enough to board. I believed in God, but I wasn't sure God could reach me in the same way He reached everyone else.

So I prayed to be healed. Not because I was ashamed of who I was, but because I wanted to belong. I wanted to be part of the conversation without needing to catch up. I wanted to understand jokes without having them explained. I wanted to hear the sermons, sing the songs, and feel what others felt. I thought if I could just be like everyone else, the door to connection would finally open. I went to healing services. I closed my eyes and believed with all my heart. But I never came home with new ears.

Instead, something quieter began to grow inside me.

God didn't change my hearing. He changed how I saw myself. Slowly, through silence and struggle, through the questions no one could answer and the fatigue I could not name, I started to understand that my Deafness was not a mistake. It was not a problem to be solved. It was part of who I was. And more than that, it was part of how God was choosing to speak into my life.

At first, I didn't recognize it. But the roots were stretching. Faith began to look different than I thought it would. It was not built on emotional worship or perfect understanding. It was built on presence. It was built on persistence. It was built on the belief that God could meet me in the quiet. That God could reach me in a language that didn't depend on sound. That God could be close even when no one else noticed.

Growing up Deaf was not about overcoming disability. It was about learning to live fully in the body and the story God had given me. My identity did not need to be healed. It needed to be honored. And that shift began to prepare the ground for the kind of faith that would carry me forward.

Even when I didn't know who I was, God did. He was shaping me gently, patiently, and faithfully. He was teaching me that I did not have to be someone else to be loved. He was showing me that Deafness was not the opposite of divine calling. Divine calling was embedded in my deafness.

CHAPTER 3

When the World Doesn't Make Room

I remember the locker room.

Not some glossy, airbrushed version you see in recruiting videos. Ours had a kind of rough character, worn down by time and sweat and the weight of a thousand pep talks. The overhead lights buzzed faintly, casting a flat glare across the space, making shadows that stretched across the corners. The lockers were painted but chipped in places where helmets had slammed shut in frustration and celebration. The walls were bold and loud, like the school colors we wore with pride even when the pride didn't quite wear comfortably on us.

The air was thick with the scent of muscle rub, sour laundry, and plastic from cracked mouthguards. Cleats clacked against the concrete floor, echoing under the low ceiling. That floor was always cold, no matter the season, and stained with rings of Gatorade, streaks of red dirt, and sweat-slick footprints that never quite dried.

My nickname was Diamond. It started as a joke, then stuck. I wasn't flashy or fast. I wasn't even in the starting lineup. But they said I was built solid. A grinder. The kind of guy you wanted in a trench, not on a poster. "Diamond in the rough," they said. It was meant to be kind, but most days, it just felt like a reminder that I still had something to prove.

That day, I walked into the locker room already on edge. I had packed my gear with care the night before and triple-checked everything. Helmet, cleats, pads. I replayed Coach's instructions over and over in my head, trying to piece together what I thought I heard as practice ended. He spoke fast, turned his back halfway through the announcement. Everyone else seemed to nod like it was clear. I didn't catch it all. But I caught enough, or so I thought.

"Be in gear tomorrow." That's what I heard. So I brought my full pads. What I didn't bring were the team-issued warm-up shorts. And that was the problem.

As soon as I entered the locker room, I noticed it. Everyone was pulling on their mesh warm-ups and short-sleeve compression shirts. No one had pads. No helmets. Just walk-through gear. I didn't have any of that.

In that moment, I had a choice. I could dig through my bag, try to borrow shorts, and maybe be late getting to the field. Or I could show up on time. I chose on time.

I pulled on my padded girdle and hoped it would be enough. It wasn't designed to be worn alone, but I figured it covered what it needed to. I laced up my cleats, slipped on my compression top, and walked out the door, trying to carry myself like I had everything under control.

The sun was brutal that afternoon. It hung low and heavy in the sky, turning the maize stripes on the field into liquid gold. The turf was gritty underfoot. The air smelled like sunbaked rubber, grass clippings, and anticipation.

The team was already out there, stretching and jawing, tossing the ball around, coaches scribbling on clipboards. They looked relaxed, like they all knew they were doing it right.

Then they saw me. First, it was just a few heads turning. Then came the whispered jeers. Then the full eruption.

"Yo! Diamond forgot his shorts!"

"Man showed up in a girdle!"

"Lookin' like he stepped out of a video game glitch!"

The laughter hit hard and fast, like a blindside block. I tried to laugh too. I fired back jokes of my own. Shrugged like it was no big deal. Like I meant to do it. The truth settled deep in my chest like a bruise.

I had done everything I thought I was supposed to. I showed up. I prepared. I followed the rules, at least the ones I heard. None of that mattered. No one made sure I heard the right message to begin with.

That's what it means when the world doesn't make room. Not just that it forgets you, but that it was never designed to include you in the first place. Not fully. Not clearly. Not without extra effort.

Being Deaf didn't mean I couldn't understand. It just meant I was always playing catch-up with information that was given away casually, like it was nothing, like everyone got the memo, except me.

It wasn't just football. It was school, too. It was church. It was classrooms where teachers said, "I already explained it," and hallways where announcements blurred into noise. It was the moment when you realize you're always half a step behind, not because you're slow, but because the door was closed when the instructions were given.

This chapter isn't about that moment on the field. It's about what it means to carry the weight of showing up when no one expects you to. It's about what happens when survival becomes your second language. It's about the difference between ability and access. I was never the problem.

The problem was a world that made its rules in whispers, then laughed when I got them wrong. Still, I showed up. Grace doesn't need permission to enter the room. It walks through the door with scraped knees, wearing borrowed gear, and holds its head high. Grace doesn't wait for an invitation. It becomes the space no one else made. When the world doesn't make room, grace does.

Educational Inequality: Surviving Systems Not Built for You

I didn't grow up in one school, in one town, with one familiar set of hallways. I grew up in many schools. I was the new kid so often that I stopped bothering to remember my locker combination. I figured I'd be gone before I got too comfortable. Each school had its own flavor, its own code to crack. Some were sprawling brick buildings with wide hallways and classrooms that smelled like floor wax and old pencils. Others were smaller, dimmer, almost claustrophobic, with a single custodian trying to hold it all together and ceilings stained from forgotten leaks.

All that said, it was never the buildings that made those years hard.

It was the feeling that I never quite fit into the blueprints of the system.

In every school, I had to relearn how to survive. Not how to read or write, I had those skills. I had always loved books, loved language, loved stories. I had to relearn how to exist, crack the cultural and pragmatic combination, so to speak. How to track with the teacher when there was no interpreter, or worse, when there was one but they weren't trained, weren't fluent, or didn't seem to care. I had one who texted under the table the whole time. Another who stood way in the back, partially blocked by a tall metal cabinet. I would twist in my seat trying to see her hands, only to be told by the teacher to face forward and pay attention.

Most of my teachers had no Deaf awareness. They'd speak with their backs turned to the board or pace around the room while lecturing, assuming that if their words filled the air, everyone must be absorbing them. Some mumbled. Some rambled. None of them paused to ask if I was catching what they said. Their voices swirled around me like smoke, thick, disorienting, impossible to hold.

There was one class where I tried to answer a question the teacher had written on the board to be completed a compare and contrast essay between two presidents their strengths, weaknesses, policies and notable contributions. I'd read ahead in the books, followed along as best I could, and raised my hand in class when I had questions. I woke so hard on that essay. When I turned the essay in the teacher blinked.

"This is impressive," he said. "Did someone help you?"

I felt like I had been punched in the gut. I wanted to get defensive instead I replied feeling as small as a mouse to the Grand Canyon. "No," I signed, then spoke quietly. "I wrote it by myself."

He shook his head slightly, then said it.

"I just never met a Deaf kid who could write like that. I am going to double check and make sure it really is yours"

He moved on without apology, without reflection. The whole class had heard it. Some smirked. One girl looked at me with wide eyes, like I had just turned into a talking dog. They never meant to be cruel. At least that is what I have tried to tell myself over the years. Regardless, their low expectations were a slow suffocation. A thousand paper cuts of doubt, disbelief, dismissal.

The kids picked up on it too.

In one school, they called me "Diamond." That name stuck for a while, maybe because it sounded tough, maybe because one coach said I had something hidden under the surface. That nickname gave me a little pride, even though many mocked me for it. In every single school I attended hearing or deaf, they called me "Fat Pat". The joke rolled through the halls like thunder, echoing in the cafeteria, in the locker room, in the back of the bus. I tried to laugh it off. Tried to be the funny one. Tried to turn the shame into charm. But inside, I was shrinking.

I didn't just feel alone. I felt disposable. I would usually get in trouble if I retaliated or responded, but the bullies were excused as being kids.

It was almost impossible to make friends. The interpreter, when there was one, stood like a wall between me and the rest of the room. Even when they were well-meaning, their presence turned every interaction into a performance. I wanted to lean over and whisper to a classmate, crack a joke, ask to borrow a pencil. With someone standing over your shoulder, relaying every word in slow, visible motion, intimacy becomes impossible. Everything gets filtered. Every glance, every sentence, every attempt at connection feels exposed.

Then came the meeting.

One of those long, gray-table IEP meetings with mismatched chairs and coffee-stained forms. I was a junior in high school. There were too many adults in the room, case managers, guidance counselors, a teacher or two. All of them talking around me, not to me. They looked at charts, test scores, progress notes.

Then they looked at me.

"You're setting yourself up for failure," one of them said. Her voice was soft, like she thought she was being kind. "You need to be realistic."

I told them I wanted to go to college. Not just any college, I wanted to study education. Maybe even get my master's. Maybe one day, my doctorate. I told them I wanted to become a teacher. A head football coach. I wanted to own a home with some land, open a dog shelter and sanctuary. I told them I wanted to be a pastor.

They chuckled. Not in a mean-spirited way. In a condescending way. The kind of laugh people give when a toddler says they want to be an astronaut or marry a superhero.

"You should consider applying for Social Security Disability," one of them said gently. "You'd probably qualify for Medicaid and food stamps. Maybe a Section 8 apartment. We just don't want you to get your hopes up."

They said "realistic" like it was a gift. Like I should be grateful to have a system waiting to catch me, when that same system had never once taught me how to fly. I left that room shaking. I wasn't just hurt. I was angry. Not because they didn't believe in me, but because part of me had started to believe them.

I started gaining weight. Not just because I stopped moving as much, but because food became a comfort, a mask, a coping mechanism. It was something I could count on. Something that didn't ask questions. I started withdrawing. It got easier to disappear.

Despite I kept showing up. I kept reading ahead, memorizing chapters before they were even assigned. I studied teachers' body language, learned to anticipate their movements like a quarterback reading a defense. I pieced together meaning from fragments. I sat in the back and observed every twitch, every eyebrow raise, every shift in tone. I worked harder just to stay in the same place.

That's what they never saw. The system wasn't just broken. It was never built for me. It wasn't that I couldn't succeed. It was that they never imagined someone like me would even try. I did more than try. I didn't live to prove them wrong. I was not going to dare give them the satisfaction of being right. I lived to make them liars.

The Body Remembers

The body is a library. It keeps perfect records long after the mind tries to forget.

I used to think time would heal everything. That if I ignored the past long enough, it would disappear into the fog. That if I succeeded enough, smiled enough, performed well enough, prayed hard enough, I could rewrite the story from the outside in.

My body remembers.

Not in daylight. Not usually.

But in shadows. In dreams. In the silence of my own chest, when everything else was still.

I don't remember all the details clearly. I wish I did. I wish I could point to every face, every name, every year. I wish I could construct a case file neat enough to make sense of it all. But trauma doesn't file itself in alphabetical order. It comes back like a storm, sudden and uninvited.

I remember cold surfaces. The prick of a bus seat's torn vinyl under my thigh. The squeak of sneakers on hallway floors when I tried to walk away. The rattle of a school locker door slamming shut behind me, echoing off tile. I remember fluorescent lights humming above me like they were trying to warn me. I remember smells: cafeteria grease, deodorant and dirt, that strange mix of metal and sweat in gym locker rooms.

These were not unfamiliar places. These were school properties. Not basements. Not strangers in the night. Buses. Stairwells. Locker rooms. Classrooms left unattended for just long enough. It wasn't always older boys or men. Sometimes it was older women. Sometimes it was kids my own age. Sometimes it was people I thought were my friends.

They laughed in public. They joked with me during the day. But behind closed doors, they stole from me. They didn't ask. They didn't care. They didn't stop. Afterward, they walked away like nothing had happened. Like I was nothing.

That's what stayed with me. Not just the pain, but the emptiness it left behind. The way I disappeared from the story. The way I was made into something less than human. Not someone who mattered. Not someone who could say no. Not someone anyone would believe.

There were no rescue scenes in my story. No adult came crashing through the door. No counselor read between the lines. I walked back into classrooms after being assaulted and turned in my homework on time. I sat at lunch tables while my hands trembled under the tray. I wore my football gear and ran drills in cleats that didn't fit while my body screamed.

Because I thought that's what strength was. Enduring. Silently. Every day. I carried that silence like armor. The worst part?

I thought it was my fault.

I truly believed that something about me invited this. My size. My Deafness. My awkwardness. My desperation to be liked. I thought maybe I had done something, failed to say no the right way, failed to run fast enough, failed to matter enough for someone to care.

The loneliness was a weight I couldn't name.

No one saw it. No one spoke to it. The teachers looked at me and saw a file. The coaches looked at me and saw a project. The students looked at me and saw a target. I don't remember a single adult ever sitting me down and asking, "Are you okay?" Not once. Not in all those years.

So, I stopped asking myself.

I shoved the memories so deep that they only came back in pieces.

Even now, grown, educated, called Pastor by some, Coach by others, they still return. In nightmares. In moments I can't predict. In flashes. In panic attacks. In sounds that transport me without warning. In shame I can't trace, but feel in my gut like a live wire.

My body remembers. I've come to understand this: trauma isn't just about what was done. It's about what wasn't undone. It's about what grows in the silence afterward.

I can tell you one thing aside, something I know in my bones: I have fought like hell to understand my trauma. To name it. To face it. To refuse to let it make a home in me and grow into something I pass on.

Trauma is never just one event. Trauma is the story of pain that runs on auto-pilot, inserting itself into life when you just want to forget.

Even if the person who hurt you never does it again, the wound does. It festers. It leaks into how we love. How we cope.

How we speak to our children. How we trust, or don't trust, our partners. How we medicate. How we eat. How we hide.

It can become alcohol bottles on nightstands. It can become broken bones and screaming matches. It can become pills tucked under pillows and bruises covered with foundation. It can become silent in the name of survival. It becomes cycles.

I have spent my adult life learning that cycles don't break on their own. You have to name them. You have to drag them into the light. You have to look at the mirror and say, "This ends with me."

I say that every single day. I say it when I choose kindness over control. I say it when I hold my tongue instead of repeating what was modeled for me.

I say it when I speak gently to my wife, when I pay keen attention to my students, when I hug my dogs instead of raising my voice, when I show up to preach and tell the truth even when it trembles in my throat.

I say it when I stay. When I love. When I forgive, but never forget. I don't know what they did to me. I am what I did next. And I'm still here. Still fighting. Still rising. Still remembering, not just the pain, but the power that pain tried to bury.

Accessibility Beyond the Classroom

It didn't stop at school. The silence the world offered me was not confined to classrooms, hallways, or IEP meetings. It followed me into every corner of life like a shadow I couldn't outrun. After the final bell rang and the buses pulled away, the barriers I faced didn't disappear; they simply changed form. I carried them with me into church sanctuaries, locker rooms, barns, family outings, movie theaters, and any space where people gathered and assumed we all understood one another.

There was one place my brothers loved more than almost anywhere else: the movie theater. Their eyes would light up whenever a new blockbuster trailer dropped. They planned snack orders days in advance, argued playfully about seat locations, and counted down to Friday night premieres like it was Christmas morning. For them, movie theaters weren't just a pastime. They were cultural hubs, places of memory, ritual, and belonging. We'd even turn movie nights into a family event between the brothers.

I loved movies too. I still do. But I had to love them from the home side of things, not so much the movie theatres.

Inside those darkened auditoriums, I couldn't follow the dialogue in real time. I'd catch a word here or there, just enough to know I was missing something. I'd try to lipread through the shifting shadows of a fast-moving scene, but the angles were inconsistent and the edits too rapid. As explosions roared, music soared, and the audience broke into laughter, I would sit quietly, smiling faintly, pretending I got the joke like everyone else.

So, I waited. I waited until the movie came out on DVD or digital download. I waited until I could turn on captions and, finally, truly understand what I had already seen. But by the time I caught up, the cultural moment had passed. My brothers had moved on. Their conversations referenced inside jokes, iconic lines, and emotional twists, and I stood just outside of those exchanges, nodding along, like a tourist in a country where I once visited the airport but never left the terminal.

I hadn't been excluded on purpose. I was simply never expected. The theater was a rite of passage, a communal memory bank for most of my peers. For me, it was a weekly reminder of how easily I could be present and yet not counted.

Eventually, some theaters introduced "Assistive Technology", captioning devices, rear-window readers, and audio description headsets. They marketed these with pride, as if the mere existence of the device erased the years we had been left out. But when I finally tried them, I found they often created more alienation than access.

The captioning devices were awkward, like a bendable green-lit screen you had to clip to your seat's cupholder. To follow the movie, I had to dart my eyes between the screen and the reader, which felt like reading subtitles from the bottom of a soda can. The captions were often delayed. The timing was off. Jokes landed after the laughter had faded. Emotional nuance was flattened into "[muffled speech]" and "[music playing]." Worse still, I could feel the stares from strangers behind me, whispering, curious about the strange glow in the front row.

It wasn't just about whether the captions worked. It was about what the device symbolized. It said, "You can come in now," but it didn't say, "We see you." It didn't say, "We prepared for you from the beginning." That's the difference between access and welcome. Between inclusion and belonging.

My brothers never intended to leave me behind. They were just swept up in the joy of the theater, unaware that what was a release for them was labor for me. I never wanted to ruin their fun. So, I smiled. Stayed quiet. Waited for captions. Waited for inclusion. Waited for the world to notice. And by the time it did, the magic had gone.

That's what people forget: delayed access is still exclusion. Letting someone into the room after the party has ended doesn't erase the memory of standing outside alone.

Yet, I kept loving movies. Because stories saved me. Because cinema was one of the only places I could imagine people like me existing, even if I had to wait to understand them. Maybe that's why I fight so hard for access now, not just in theaters, but in life.

Because I know what it's like to sit in the dark while everyone else laughs.

To feel the vibration of joy in the room but not be part of it.

To love something deeply that doesn't fully love you back.

But I also know what it's like when someone makes room, not as an afterthought, but from the beginning. For example, music. For most of my childhood, Music TV was faster than captions, Radios had nice bass, and I could recognize a beat like a fingerprint to a song. Lyrics are just beat with English translation. It was not until YouTube lyric videos started being made, and more recently, when Spotify included synced Lyrics to the music in their apps, allowing me to enjoy more than the bass drop and music. What would happen if this sort of consideration were put into our world around us?

I learned early on that most churches were built for hearing people. The sermons came without captions. The hymns without lyrics I could follow. The prayers were full of meaning but empty of explanation. Pastors would turn their backs to pray, their words fading into a space I couldn't reach. Sometimes they spoke so quickly and emotionally that lipreading became impossible.

There were no interpreters.

Rarely any truly helpful visual aids.

Just the assumption that if you were in the pew, you were receiving the Word.

I remember sitting in a packed sanctuary one Easter Sunday beside my mom. The choir began to sing. The congregation lifted their hands. The pastor shouted, "He is risen!" and the room exploded in response. I stood among them, smiling.

Silent.

Pretending.

It wasn't that I didn't believe. I did. I just couldn't follow.

And no one noticed. No one asked. No one offered an outline or a copy of the sermon. I was worshiping a God who heard everything, while I couldn't hear anything at all.

It wasn't just church, either.

It was football. Huddles were brutal. Coaches barked plays at warp speed while whistles blew and helmets clashed. I tried to catch the gist by watching mouths or asking teammates, but often I had to guess. Sometimes I got it right. Other times, I blew the play and got benched, not for lack of effort, but for lack of access.

That's the part most people never see. Inaccessibility doesn't always mean being told "no." Sometimes it just means no one thought to say "yes." It means everyone else gets instructions while you're still trying to figure out if this is a pass or a run. It means being called lazy when you're actually surviving.

Outside of school, I avoided jobs where I had to interact with people too much. Not because I didn't want to work, but because I was tired. Tired of having to explain myself. Tired of teaching every boss, every coworker, every customer how to communicate with me. Tired of being "inspiring" for just existing.

So, I worked the land.

I worked on horse farms.

I worked on Christmas tree farms.

The trees never asked me to repeat myself. The horses didn't judge my voice. The soil never corrected my grammar. There was something sacred about that labor, something beautifully honest about pulling a halter over a restless mare, dragging trees through wet ground, loading bales of hay under a rising sun.

Even in those wide-open spaces, the Blackbird Forest and Creek in Delaware or in the foothills of the Shenandoah Valley near Middleburg, Virginia, the world found ways to remind me I was different.

Supervisors yelled instructions from across the field. I'd miss them. They'd get impatient. Coworkers told jokes I couldn't track. I'd laugh too late or not at all, and the distance would grow again. I would get accused of disrespect and ignorance when I simply was unaware.

Even with your hands in the dirt, you can still feel invisible.

In every space, I bore the weight of being the one who had to explain. The one who had to teach. The one who had to carry everyone else's assumptions, confusion, and inconvenience like a second pair of boots.

There's a special kind of exhaustion that comes from having to make yourself legible to people who were never taught to read someone like you.

I didn't get to just show up. I had to accommodate everyone else so they wouldn't feel uncomfortable around me. Always prepping my mask and trying to calm my nerves before having to go anywhere outside of my home.

Yet, I keep showing up. Still hoping someone would meet me halfway. Occasionally, some do.

I remember like yesterday, a new high school semester. A new classroom. That familiar tightening in my chest, wondering if this would be another space where I had to fight to belong.

Before class even began, Mr. Hyland approached me, not loudly, not pityingly, and said, "I read your file. I saw that you signed. I'm learning fingerspelling. Would you help me get better?" He didn't make a show of it. He didn't apologize. He didn't ask me to adapt to him. He came toward me, with humility, with sincerity, with care.

That semester, he made small changes. He faced the class when he spoke. He added visuals. He gave me notes early. It wasn't perfect, but it was intentional. He didn't lower the bar; he raised it. For the first time in a long time, I didn't feel like a burden. I felt seen. He even worked out with me to get me ready to play college ball in the fall. He is now, as an adult, a teacher in the same school I teach at and a friend.

That's what real access is. It's not a favor or an exception. It's not a formality. It's not charity. It's design. It's someone saying, "You belong here, and I'm going to act like it." And in that space? I started to believe it, too.

Early Spiritual Confusion and Church Silence

I believed in God before I had the language for belief.

Not because someone handed me a neat theology or because I had all the answers figured out. I believed because my grandfather prayed like someone was truly listening. I believed because my mother folded Scripture into the rhythms of our daily life, tucking faith between packed lunches and bedtime prayers, as if it were as ordinary and essential as breath. I believed because something deep inside me needed to believe that beyond the confusion, beyond the chaos and silence, there was someone bigger holding it all together.

Belief does not always come with clarity. Faith, as it was taught to me, was wrapped tightly in sound. Whereas, I lived in silence.

From the time I was a child, people in church would tell me to listen for God's voice. Be still and know. Close your eyes and hear Him speak. God is always talking, they said. You just have to be quiet enough to hear. They said it like a promise. Like something simple and universal. However, no one ever explained what it meant for someone who could not hear.

I would sit in church, spine straight as I could with the occasional affliction of the wiggles, eyes closed like the others, trying to mimic what I thought prayer was supposed to look like. I would bow my head and wait. I wanted so badly to experience whatever they were experiencing. I longed for the voice they swore would come in the stillness. All I heard was more silence. Not the holy, peaceful kind people preached about, but the heavy kind. The kind that makes you feel like maybe you are the only one God forgot to include.

No one ever said what God's voice sounded like for someone like me. Was it a whisper? A gut feeling? A flicker of light behind the eyes? Or was it something entirely different, something meant for others but not for me?

What did it mean if I could not hear Him at all?

Was I disqualified from real faith? Was I missing something everyone else got to have?

The church did not give me answers to those questions. If anything, it added more.

Healing services, in particular, were the most confusing. I remember altar calls where people wept and collapsed under the weight of emotion. People danced. People shouted. People placed their hands on my ears and declared me healed in Jesus' name. They said the right words. They had all the faith in the world. I stood there, eyes closed, hoping with everything in me that this would be the moment. This time, I would leave differently.

I never did.

Every time I walked back to my seat with the same Deafness I arrived with, I felt a little smaller. A little more broken. A little more like God had passed me over again.

No one ever said it directly, but the message was clear. If I had more faith, I would be healed. If I were not healed, the problem must be mine.

So I started to wonder if I had failed God. If I was not enough. If I were not worthy of the miracle. If I were not trying hard enough, praying correctly, believing the right way.

Then I read Romans 10:17. "So then faith comes by hearing, and hearing by the word of God." I stared at that verse like it had been written to exclude me.

Faith comes by hearing.

What if you could not hear?

What if you never could?

Did that mean I could not have faith? Did that mean God's word was inaccessible to me?

I did not understand Greek. I did not know the historical context. I did not yet understand that "hearing" in that verse could mean "understanding" or "receiving." I just read it and saw the door close in my face. I saw a verse that felt like it told me I did not belong.

Nobody talked about what it meant to be Deaf and Christian. Nobody taught me how to pray in silence, how to hear God without ears, how to worship when the music did not reach you. Nobody gave me a framework for sacred embodiment that included my Deafness. So, I created my own theology, quietly, painfully, slowly.

Still, I kept showing up.

That was my rebellion.

Not a loud, dramatic rebellion. But the kind that sits in the pews anyway. The kind that keeps showing up to Sunday school with questions you are too scared to ask. The kind that keeps serving communion even when you have not felt communion yourself in weeks. The kind that says, I do not understand, but I am still here.

I stayed when it did not make sense.

I stayed when my prayers were met with silence.

I stayed when the Word felt like a foreign language.

I signed prayers into the night air. I flipped through my Bible, hoping something, anything, would leap off the page and hold me. I kept hoping that one day a pastor would look at me, speak with his whole body, and say something that told me I was not invisible.

Truth is, there were long stretches when I did not pray at all. If I did, it was not with words I would repeat in a prayer circle.

There were seasons when my prayers were laced with expletives. My rage took center stage. I yelled in the quiet of my room, fists clenched, eyes burning, mouthing words like Where are You? Why won't You speak to me? Why did You make me this way and then hide?

My prayers were not poetic. They were not clean. They were born of frustration, confusion, and grief.

They were real.

I never stopped believing. However, I did not always want to talk to God.

Even in those seasons, I never stopped serving. I showed up. I worked. I volunteered. I opened doors for others walking into sanctuaries that I still was not sure had room for me. I smiled when I was breaking inside. I carried burdens, cleaned up after events, and stood at the back of the sanctuary hoping to hear something, even if it was not audible. I have come to believe that all of that was a form of worship, too.

All of that counted.

God never asked for performance, only presence.

Looking back now, I do not think God was silent. I think He was sitting in the silence with me. I think He held my questions, my anger, my aching belief. I think He honored the tears I could not explain. I think He received the expletives like psalms and held space for me when I did not know how to hold space for myself.

Slowly, through the confusion and pain, I started to unlearn the belief that I had to be healed to be holy. I started to see that

Deafness was not a punishment or a barrier. It was a way of being. A sacred, embodied witness to the fact that God speaks in more than one voice. That His Word is bigger than sound. That His presence is not bound by hearing.

I still have days when I do not know what to say to Him.

But I no longer believe that silence disqualifies me.

Because God lives in the silence, too.

And He hears even the words I cannot speak.

Grit and Grace – What Got You Through

There were more than a few moments when quitting would have made perfect sense. When the loneliness, the exclusion, the exhaustion of constantly having to prove I belonged could have driven me to disappear. When the silence didn't feel sacred, it felt suffocating. And yet, something in me kept going. I didn't know it at the time, but that "something" was grace. Not the kind of grace that floats in with soft music and easy comfort, but the kind with dirt under its fingernails. The kind that limps forward when everything aches. The kind that chooses to hold on, even when it doesn't know how much longer it can last.

Much of that perseverance was shaped by the people who raised me. My mother was a special education teacher for most of my childhood. I watched her advocate fiercely for students that other educators overlooked. She knew what it was to be dismissed, and she refused to let her students face the same. She taught with both conviction and compassion, modeling what it meant to fight for someone else's dignity when they couldn't speak for themselves. Then, during my high school years, she answered a different kind of calling. She left the classroom and entered ministry, eventually becoming an ordained elder in the Methodist tradition. I didn't understand the full weight of that shift at the time, but looking back now, I see how she carried her teaching spirit into her preaching life. She continued to make space for people the world often forgets. And in some unspoken way, she kept making space for me, too.

My father's path was formative in its own way. He was a Technology Education teacher, a shop teacher, who found beauty in functionality and meaning in manual labor. He taught generations of students how to build, to measure, to plan, to trust the process. After I graduated from high school, he returned to his roots in construction. He shifted from residential to commercial work, focusing on bigger projects with bigger blueprints. Yet no matter what he built, it was never just about the structure. It was about doing the job with integrity. He approached every project, whether a house frame or a life, with an ethic of care and excellence.

What people did not see behind his strength was the fragility he was also carrying. My dad has faced multiple major health scares, including cancer, more than once. There were nights I went to sleep unsure if he would make it through the next day. Seasons when the word "terminal" hovered in the background like a shadow we weren't allowed to speak aloud. His body has been to the brink of death and back. And yet, he is still here. Still stubborn. Still sharp. Still teaching me how to keep hammering forward even when your breath is short and your hands are shaking.

After the divorce and separation when I was a Junior and Senior in High School, both of my parents walked through their own private wilderness. It was messy in many ways. There were financial setbacks. Emotional wounds. Spiritual questions. Yet, in their own ways, they each found their footing again. They landed on their feet, not perfectly, not without scars, but with grace. They never once blamed me for what happened. In fact, they went out of their way to reassure me that I was not the cause. They told me over and over again that their divorce was about their story, not mine. That they loved me. That I was not a burden.

Still, I carry a weight I've never been able to fully put down.

There's this quiet part of me that wonders, what if the complications of my childhood, the endless meetings, the stress of navigating IEPs and miscommunication, and all the invisible grief of raising a Deaf child in an inaccessible world... what if that played a role? What if the load was too heavy? What if they had to be strong in public for so long that something cracked in private?

I know what they said. I believe them when they told me it wasn't my fault.

Part of grace is learning to name the parts of ourselves that still feel broken. And this is one of mine.

Still, even in their own pain, my parents never stopped showing up for me. They never made me feel like I had to apologize for being who I was. They never let their disappointment, if they had any, be louder than their love. That kind of love is its own kind of miracle. A quiet, steady grace that does not always rescue you from your pain, but gives you the strength to walk through it without being consumed.

The rest of my strength came from the places I least expected it.

Sports became the place where my body learned to speak when words failed. On the football field, I didn't need to hear, I needed to feel. Feel the rhythm of the snap, the shift in the line, the tension in the air just before the play broke open. While others listened, I watched. While others yelled, I read motion. I became fluent in footwork, in glances, in the language of the game. Deafness became not just manageable, but powerful. My silence became a strategy. My difference became my edge.

Still, none of that would have been enough without the rare people who chose to see me.

A few sacred teachers and coaches who did more than tolerate me, they adapted without being asked. A coach who faced me when giving instructions. A teacher who gave me notes ahead of class and took the time to learn a little fingerspelling. A pastor who sat beside me instead of standing above me. These people did not fix my problems, but they did something even more holy: they saw me as worthy of their effort.

Slowly, I began to see it too.

That is where the deeper truth of this story begins to emerge. Grace does not always look like rescue. Sometimes grace looks like grit. It looks like staying in the game when your jersey is soaked with tears. It looks like walking into school again after being misunderstood a hundred times. It looks like waking up on a hospital floor, waiting for your father to wake up. It looks like serving in a church even when your own prayers are silent or angry or half-formed.

God was never absent from my story. He did not speak in the ways others said He would. I did not find Him in thunder or revival services or neon miracles. I found Him in the quiet places. In the slow recovery of a man who should have died. In the strength of a mother who answered her call even while holding a thousand invisible burdens. In my own heartbeat, even when I wanted to give up. In the people who stayed. In the grit that kept me going.

That is grace too.

Grace is not always soft. It does not always rescue. Sometimes, grace gets down in the dirt with you, hands bloodied, breath ragged, and says, "Let's keep going." Sometimes, grace looks like you, banged up, emotionally tired, full of questions, and still standing.

Still showing up.

Still here.

Seeds of Advocacy and Identity

Identity begins with awareness beyond self.

Not in a flash of glory or a lightning bolt moment, but in the slow, quiet discomfort of being left out. In the hallways, in the classrooms, in the locker rooms where I stood half-in and half-out of conversations I couldn't fully follow. In churches where I smiled along while others sang with abandon. In football huddles where I watched lips move and guessed at the plays. It started in the ache of pretending to understand, in the head nods and delayed laughter, in the way people's eyes flicked past me when I paused too long to respond.

At first, I only knew that something felt wrong. I couldn't explain it. I didn't have the words for injustice or systemic failure. I just knew what it felt like to be invisible. To be seen as extra work. To have my differences framed as obstacles. I knew what it was to work twice as hard to get half as far. I carried the weight of silence before I ever learned to name it.

Eventually, I started to look around. I saw others, kids in similar positions, people made to feel like liabilities because they needed support, because they learned differently, moved differently, communicated differently, loved differently. They were too loud, too quiet, too poor, too brown, too queer, too Deaf, too something. And I recognized that look in their eyes, the same one I had seen in the mirror. The mix of weariness and defiance. The quiet hope that someone might see them and not look away.

That recognition planted something deep in me.

At first, all I wanted was to survive. To make it out. To find a way forward in a world that kept trying to push me aside. But somewhere along the way, survival wasn't enough. My pain started to feel like a lens. My struggle, a language. And my silence, once forced, became a choice. I didn't just want to make it out. I wanted to make it better. Not just for me. For everyone who had been told they didn't belong.

The first time I stood up for someone else, it wasn't some big heroic moment. It was subtle. Quiet. Someone was being dismissed by a teacher who had already made up their mind about them. The look on their face, the defeated slump of their shoulders, and the way they avoided eye contact reminded me of myself. I felt the anger rise before I even knew what to do with it. So, I spoke. Nervously. But clearly. I said what needed to be said. I did what I wished someone had done for me.

That was the beginning.

That was when the shift happened, from surviving to witnessing. From internal fight to outward action. From getting through to giving back.

It didn't mean I suddenly had it all figured out. I still struggled. Still felt unsure. Still had moments where I wanted to disappear. But the more I noticed others, the more I realized that my pain had given me a kind of sight. I could see who was being left behind. I could see the cracks in the system. I could see how change wasn't going to come from waiting for someone else to fix it. It had to start with those of us who knew what it meant to be forgotten.

That's when identity started to take root, not just as something to protect, but as something to offer.

Being Deaf wasn't just a part of my story. It became a way to connect. To advocate. To challenge the norm. I began to see the beauty in difference. The holiness in struggle. The sacredness of the stories that don't get told in the center of the room. I stopped apologizing for what I needed. I stopped shrinking to make other people comfortable. And I started believing that I could use my life to make space for others to show up fully as themselves, too.

That is where advocacy was born. Not in anger. But in clarity. In compassion. In the conviction that I wasn't the only one who deserved better.

The Barrier Became the Bridge

All those closed doors. All the times I was left out, misjudged, or misunderstood, they became my training ground. Every time I was denied access, I learned to pay closer attention to who else was being excluded. Every time I was told to wait my turn, I learned how to open doors instead of waiting for permission. What once felt like rejection started to feel like preparation. Pain didn't just scar me. It shaped me.

What broke my heart also built my calling.

Somewhere along the way, I stopped seeing myself as the end of the story. I started asking new questions. Who else hasn't been heard? Who else is being left out of the conversation? How can I make space that isn't just accessible, but welcoming? How can I be the voice that helps someone else find their own?

I stopped measuring success by how many rooms I got into and started measuring it by how many people I could bring with me.

Every closed door taught me how to build open tables. Every shut window taught me how to carve out new paths. Every injustice I survived deepened my desire for justice not just in theory, but in practice, in classrooms, in churches, in sports, in leadership, in policy, and in community.

God never wasted my struggle. Even when I didn't know He was working. Even when I didn't feel holy. Even when I didn't want to be seen. God kept showing up in the quiet. Kept making a way through the mess. Kept giving me the strength to climb. And somewhere in that climbing, I realized this was never just about me.

The world kept throwing up walls. God kept showing a way through, even when I didn't know it was God.

Somewhere in the climbing, I realized, I wasn't just making space for me. Rather to climb, and pull everyone up as I went. I was paving a path for someone else.

CHAPTER 4

Between the Whistle and the Silence

There is a moment just before the snap, right after the quarterback's fingers twitch and before the chaos begins, when the whole world holds its breath. For most players, that is the moment they tune into cadence or crowd noise. But for me, Deaf as I am and have always been, it was the moment I felt most alive. Not because I heard anything, but because I felt everything. The crowd did not roar for me in sound. It roared through vibration. The bleachers shook with every stomp, and that rumble traveled up through my cleats, into my legs, and settled in my chest like thunder in the bones. The stadium's rhythm beat inside me. And then, in the space between the whistle and the collision, before the lineman fired out, before the linebackers rushed, before the pain and power and prayer of it all, there was silence. Not a lack of sound, but a fullness of presence. A sacred pause. A quiet only God and I knew how to name.

That moment, between the whistle and the silence, is where football became more than a game for me. It was my sanctuary. My proving ground. My sacred classroom. It was where I learned to translate the world through feel, through vision, through trust in something deeper than sound. I started playing when I was just four years old, still small enough that the pads swallowed me whole. Back then, it was forgotten fields and hand-me-down helmets. The love was real, even then. I kept playing all the way through nineteen. Over a decade of sweat, of learning the difference between playing hurt and playing injured, of cracking helmets, of forming brotherhoods forged in early morning practices and bus rides that smelled like cleats and fast food.

I could not hear the quarterback's voice bark the play, but I read the signal in his eyes, felt his hand lift when I played center. I could not catch the snap count, but I watched the Nosetackle's fingers, the twitch in his knuckles, the breath in his chest. What others listened for, I saw. What others shouted, I absorbed through timing and trust. Deafness did not limit me. It sharpened me. It taught me how to notice the small things. How to read the body language of a pulling guard or blitzing linebacker like scripture. How to respond to rhythm without needing to hear it. Football gave me fluency not in noise, but in presence. In a world that often mistook my silence for absence, the field was the first place that understood me.

Even when I stopped playing, I could never walk away. I began coaching Pop Warner and American Youth Football. I found myself teaching what I had once fought so hard to learn: stance, leverage, pursuit angles, responsibility, and poise. Later, I put on the stripes and served as an official for youth, middle school, and high school games. I saw the game from another angle, standing in the middle of it, calling it fair, watching it unfold play by play through a lens of discipline and dignity. Officiating taught me things no coach ever could. It gave me reverence for the rules, for timing, for structure, for the heartbeat of the game. Eventually, I returned to the sideline where I now coach again at the high school level, pouring into young players the same love of the game that was once poured into me. I have been a player. A coach. An official. And I still carry the game in my body and bones.

The practices were never easy. I still remember the sting of the late-summer sun on my neck, the sour smell of shoulder pads soaked with days of sweat, the tight pinch of tape around my wrists where my father, my first coach, scrawled the words "GO BIG!!" before every game. I remember cleats that were too small, helmets that were too heavy, knees that screamed in protest as I crawled out of bed after a Friday night fight in the trenches. I remember breathing through my nose because my mouth was busy holding a mouthguard, blood, or words I never spoke aloud. There were no shortcuts. Just film sessions in the dark, drills repeated until my legs collapsed, weights lifted until my shoulders ached. But those routines built more than muscle. They built a gospel in me. A quiet, stubborn faith that said, Show up. Get up. Keep going. That was football's altar, and those were my offerings. Effort. Endurance. Grace.

I was often underestimated. Coaches, players, opponents, they all looked at me and saw a Deaf kid. They saw my hearing aids. They saw my silence. They did not know how to coach me. They did not know if I could understand the plays, follow the cues, or keep up with the noise. However, the moment the pads cracked, the moment I lowered my shoulder and drove through the man in front of me, the questions stopped. I earned my place not by yelling, but by hitting harder, working longer, and reading the game in ways others could not. I saw what others missed. The tilt in a lineman's foot before he pulled. The blink of hesitation in a corner's stance. Every game was a sermon. Every block, a declaration. I did not need to talk to preach. My actions said it all.

My father understood this better than anyone. He never asked me to hear the game like others did. He taught me to see it. He taught me to own my silence, not as a flaw, but as a form of wisdom. He would sit with me late at night, breaking down film, helping me find the angles, the tendencies, the timing. He coached with conviction and kindness, with strength and presence. He knew how to push without breaking. Before every game, when he taped my wrists and wrote "GO BIG!!," it was not just a phrase. It was a blessing. It meant, Do not play small. Do not shrink back. You belong here. Your Deafness does not disqualify you. It dignifies you. It makes you different, and that difference is divine.

For readers who never played football, it might be hard to imagine what the game really feels like. It is not just touchdowns and trophies. It is dirt and repetition. It is pain in your ankles, knees, and shoulders before school starts. It is jerseys that reek of old blood and new sweat. It is the sting of insult and the thrill of making someone eat their words. It is long bus rides home in silence, wondering if the bruise on your rib is broken or just deep enough to keep you honest. Football is faith on the ground level. It is a community forged in fire. It is a discipline of presence, of motion, of brotherhood. For me, it was Deafness translated into power. Not dominance over others, but belonging with them.

When my time as a player ended, I thought I had lost something. It was my final game at Gallaudet University. I remember crying in the hallway after the game. I felt like I missed my shot or that I did not get a fair shot. When your number is up, it is over. What football gave me, it never took back. It stayed in my muscles. It stayed in my bones. It stayed in the way I lead now. As a pastor. As a teacher. As a coach. As someone who once wore the pads, taped up, and dedicated some part of every day for 15 years to preparing my mind, body, and spirit. The field is gone, but the power in the silence I found is not. I still find it, just before I preach, when I stand before a congregation and let the Spirit move through me. I still find it in the classroom, before the bell rings, when I feel the weight of the day ahead. I still find it in the locker room, before a game, when I look a young player in the eyes and remind him, You belong.

That sacred second between the silence and the whistle is not gone. It lives in me. It reminds me every day that grace is not always loud. Sometimes grace comes quietly, wrapped in tape, forged in dirt, and spoken in the language of endurance. Sometimes grace looks like a Deaf boy on a football field, waiting for the world to move, and already knowing deep in his bones that God is there in the stillness.

The First Jersey: Football as Language

Before I ever held a pencil in a classroom or learned how to spell my own name, I held a football. Or more truthfully, it held me.

When I was born, my body was fragile. My heart was weak, my lungs uncertain. Doctors placed me in a medically induced coma to keep me alive. I was deprived of sound, light, and touch in the most critical hours of my beginning. My parents were allowed to leave just one item with me in that sterile space. They chose a small plastic football, a souvenir from the recent Homecoming game at Delmar High School, where both of them taught, and where my father was the Defensive Coordinator. That little ball sat next to me in the NICU, a silent companion in the dark. Long before I could run, speak, or even breathe on my own, football was already in the room. It became the first symbol of presence, the first reminder that I was not alone, the first language written beside me when no other words could be spoken.

By the time I was four years old, that symbol had become something I could hold. I was standing on the sun-dried fields behind the Salvation Army in Salisbury, Maryland, suiting up for the Green Terrors. The helmet felt like a bucket on my head. The pads are too stiff. The chinstrap is too tight. But none of that mattered. The moment the ball snapped, I felt something unlock inside me. Not just adrenaline, but awareness. There was no need for words. No need for an interpreter. No need to explain myself. It was movement, rhythm, and instinct. On that field, Deafness was not something to be overcome; it was something that made me different in a way that mattered.

Football was the first language I truly understood. It spoke in gestures, glances, alignments, and angles. It moved at the speed of vision. My eyes became my ears. Where others listened to the quarterback's cadence, I watched the twitch of his hands. Where others waited to hear the linebacker call a shift, I read the shifting stances, the small tilts of the shoulders, the clenching of fists. Deafness did not isolate me in this world; it trained me. I became fluent in a vocabulary of motion and force, precision and timing. Technique and football IQ mattered more than noise. That was my dialect.

From Salisbury to Delaware, from Maryland to Virginia, I wore many jerseys. I played with legends, kids who were already giants in their communities and coaches who demanded more than hustle. They demanded heart. My sophomore season in Loudoun County remains my favorite. We only stayed four months before we were forced to move because the Deaf program was housed at another school, and no one wanted to give me an interpreter where I was. But for those four months, I belonged. I was not "the Deaf kid" who needed help. I was a football player who knew how to read a defense and explode through the B-gap when the guard leaned a half-inch too far forward.

In school, I was often left behind, sometimes literally left out. Teachers would speak with their backs turned. Notes were missed. Conversations happened over my head. But on the football field, there was no back to turn. Everyone faced the same direction.

Everyone followed the same play. The rules were clear, and the field was level. Football invited me into the game. It never asked me to prove I belonged.

My last official snap came a few years later at Gallaudet University, under the leadership of Coach Chuck Goldstein. I have lived many football lives. I have been a player. I have been a coach in Pop Warner and American Youth Football. I have even put on the black and white stripes to officiate youth, middle school, and high school games. I have tried to walk away from the game more than once. I never could. Even now, I coach on a high school football team. The whistle still calls to me.

At Gallaudet, the field meant something more. It was not just the place where plays were run; it was a sanctuary of Deaf pride. On that field, Deaf culture was not a hurdle to clear but a cornerstone to build on. Most of the game was visual by nature anyway. So, we leaned in. We communicated better, anticipated quicker, and focused deeper. While other teams shouted through the roar of the crowd, we watched the subtle cues. Our silence was not a disadvantage; it was our edge.

Even among Deaf players, my voice set me apart. I was verbal. That meant some players saw me as too hearing, while the hearing world saw me as too Deaf. But on the field, those lines blurred. Every jersey I ever wore stitched together a part of me. The Green Terrors. The team in Loudoun County. The boys from Delmar. The Bison at Gallaudet. None of them spoke the same way, but they all spoke football. And so did I.

The classroom often made me feel like I had to fight to be understood. But the field was different. It was my first sanctuary. It was a proving ground. A sacred classroom where I learned grit, grace, resilience, and identity. It gave me something precious: a sense of being part of something greater, where I did not have to pretend to be less or prove I was more. The first jersey I ever wore was not just a piece of fabric. It was a declaration. A language. A home.

Deafness on the Field: Advantage and Alienation

Being Deaf on the football field was like playing a game whose rules I could master but whose referees often refused to see me. The gridiron was both sanctuary and battlefield. It was a space where I could thrive, but only after first being tested, overlooked, and too often misunderstood. Coaches barked commands without facing me, expecting auditory compliance in a world where I read cues, not voices. Teammates questioned my toughness, mistaking silence for softness, not knowing that my silence came not from timidity, but from tuning into a different frequency. One that required me to study every nuance of body language, every twitch of a finger, every lean of a lineman's stance. Deafness did not make the game easier. It made the stakes higher and the margin for error smaller.

There were coaches who never even tried to understand me. One in particular refused to learn a single sign or gesture. Instead, he treated me like a liability, assuming that if I could not hear the snap count or a mid-play adjustment, I could not play. He called it a disadvantage. I called it a lack of imagination. He didn't see that I had been reading the game since I was four years old, long before most kids could even spell "defense." He didn't understand that Deafness had trained me to anticipate what others only reacted to. That it sharpened my senses, made me more aware of space, angle, pressure, and timing. That I wasn't distracted by crowd noise or shaken by sideline yelling, I was locked in, focused, calm in the chaos. But he never looked that deep. He just saw what I wasn't.

Then there was the teammate who couldn't read my silence. He assumed I was aloof, disinterested, or worse, arrogant. He mistook my quiet presence in the locker room as distance, when really, I was always listening. Just not the way he expected. He jabbed at me with jokes, trying to provoke a reaction, and when I didn't respond in kind, he wrote me off. It wasn't until a midseason game, when I made a game-saving tackle by reading a pulling guard and slipping under the block before the quarterback could even plant his back foot, that his perception shifted. After the game, he slapped me on the back and said, "Yo, you different, man. You see stuff we don't." He finally realized that my silence wasn't emptiness, it was presence. A heightened kind of focus that let me notice what others missed.

There were still many games where missed cues turned into missed opportunities. A coach might shift a formation at the last second, and I'd be left chasing a play I never heard called. Or worse, I'd be blamed for a mistake I couldn't have prevented without a visual signal. These moments wore on me. I had to work twice as hard to earn half the trust. I had to dominate just to be seen as competent. My Deafness became something I had to outperform. That is, until the field flipped, and I stopped trying to play hearing.

It was at Gallaudet University where Deafness stopped being a deficit and started being a gift. There, we did not try to keep up with the hearing world. We made our own rhythm. Every call was visual. Every checkdown is a gesture. We were in sync not because we could hear each other, but because we watched each other. That season, I learned the power of a shared visual language. I played not as an exception to the team, but as one of its fluent contributors. Deafness was not a hurdle to be overcome; it was the system. And for the first time, I saw what the game could look like when designed for players like me.

Still, even there, I stood in a strange in-between space. I was a verbal Deaf person. Some teammates saw me as too hearing to be fully Deaf. Others outside the Deaf community thought I was too Deaf to be fully hearing. I lived in that tension, learning how to belong without erasing myself. Football was where those lines blurred. It became a mirror, not just of my skill set, but of my journey through identity and acceptance.

Years later, as a coach, I now teach the game with a different kind of urgency. I teach my players, hearing and Deaf alike, to value what they see as much as what they hear. I introduce hand signals not as special accommodations but as tools of precision. I talk about eye discipline, not just as a strategy, but as a language. Because for me, that's what football has always been: a language that spoke where the world fell silent. And while the world often underestimated me, the field revealed the truth. Deafness, in all its complexity, was never the reason I couldn't succeed. It was the reason I did.

The Locker Room and Identity Formation

The field was sacred, but the locker room was another battlefield altogether. Off the turf, where helmets came off and the noise died down, I found myself stepping into a world that was loud in a different way. It was a place where jokes bounced around like stray footballs and where misunderstanding was almost a daily ritual. I never quite fit the mold of what most people expected in that space. My silence was interpreted as arrogance or awkwardness. I would laugh at jokes I barely understood and nod at conversations I couldn't fully follow, all while trying to decipher the maze of facial expressions, slang, and subtle social cues that buzzed around me like static. It was more than hearing loss. It was cultural dislocation. And so, I code-switched constantly, contorting myself to fit the space. I tried to "hear" enough to survive. Enough to seem normal.

In that environment, my body became the only language I could fully control. If I couldn't talk like them, I would train harder than they do. If I couldn't follow every word, I would lift more, run longer, and hit harder. I didn't just want to be accepted; I wanted to be undeniable. But behind the bravado, behind the long hours in the weight room and the exaggerated tough guy act, I was holding back a well of questions, emotions, and vulnerability that had no safe place to go. Football culture expected stoicism, a kind of armored masculinity that prized grit and grind over gentleness or honesty. We partied hard and worked harder, and I often pretended that the partying was fun. The truth was it wasn't about fun. It was about belonging. It was about trying way too hard to prove that I could be one of the guys.

There were nights I sat on the edge of my bed, staring at the floor, wondering if anyone really saw me, beyond the weight room stats or the pancake blocks or the exaggerated baritone I used to mask the stutter in my speech. I remember the sting of being called lazy when I was really just tired from trying to translate a world not built for me. I remember being labeled soft when I was wrestling silently with thoughts about God, pain, and purpose. In that locker room, I learned that being big and strong would get you a seat at the table, but being emotionally honest might get you pushed off the bench. I had to learn to compartmentalize, grit here, grace later. But it was lonely work.

And still, I kept showing up. Because even in isolation, football gave me something solid to hold onto. When I strapped on my pads, I knew who I was. I knew my job. I knew my worth. The cleats grounded me when nothing else did. The jersey covered the bruises, both physical and otherwise. In the chaos of the locker room, I did not always belong, but on the field, I knew exactly where I stood.

The deeper truth I later learned is this: the strength I was trying so hard to prove was never in my bench press or in the fake confidence I tried to wear like a uniform. It was in the vulnerability I carried quietly, in the emotions I never voiced but felt deeply. It was in the tension of living between worlds, learning to speak multiple languages, spoken, signed, and bodily, all without being fluent in any of them. The locker room was a crucible. It did not refine me gently. But it did teach me who I was. Or maybe more importantly, it revealed who I was not. And somewhere between the smell of sweat, the clatter of cleats on tile, and the moments when I felt most alone, I began to understand that belonging, real belonging, would never come from pretending to be someone else. It would come from learning to carry my full self, Deafness and all, into the world without apology.

Gallaudet and the Brotherhood of Difference

Before I ever stepped onto the field at Gallaudet, I carried the weight of another field, one I had left behind with both pride and pain. As a junior in high school, I transferred to the Maryland School for the Deaf in Frederick. For the first time in my life, I was surrounded by teammates who experienced the world the way I did. We signed in the locker room. We read each other without sound. The huddle didn't exclude me, it invited me. For the first time, I didn't have to fight to keep up. I just played. And I played under one of the best coaches in the game, hearing or Deaf. He ran a tight ship, demanded excellence, and built warriors in cleats. That season became one of the most affirming and transformative of my life, not because of wins or stats, but because it was the only time I had ever felt what it meant to be truly *with* others like me, not alone on an island of isolation, trying to translate the hearing world through silence.

By the end of the year, I had been named a team captain for the next season despite only having played four games and two scrimmages before being out for the season due to heart issues. A medical concern dealing with one's heart was no small thing. The bottom fell out of my life in November that year, only seemed to continue to devolve. My parents' marriage crumbled. My own heart, literally and figuratively, gave out again. I suffered a heart attack while still a teenager. And then came the choices, the heavy, regretful, reactionary ones that teenage boys make when pain and shame take the wheel. I left. Not in strength. Not in triumph. But in survival. I transferred away from something sacred because I didn't know how to stay. That departure haunted me for a long time.

When I arrived at Gallaudet University two years later as a College Freshman, I didn't just step onto a campus, I stepped into a legacy. Gallaudet wasn't a second chance. It was a sacred place waiting for me, even before I knew I needed it. And just like Maryland School for the Deaf, it became one of the only places in my life where I wasn't the only Deaf player on the team. That truth still hits me. Across all the years I played, from four years old through youth leagues, public school teams in Delaware, Maryland, and Virginia, all the way to high school and into adulthood, those two chapters were the only times I shared the field with others who signed, who saw the world the way I did, who lived in the tension between presence and misunderstanding, silence and power.

I wasn't a starter at Gallaudet. But I was proud to wear the jersey. I played under Coach Chuck Goldstein, a man who understood both football and Deaf culture, and who carried the weight of both with quiet strength. Being part of that team meant being part of something much bigger than myself. Deaf players had been playing this game for generations, long before society ever gave them credit. Gallaudet's football program wasn't known for national titles, but it was known for tenacity, for trailblazing, and for community. It represented not only Deaf athletes, but Deaf identity. That mattered more to me than any trophy.

The paradox was powerful. At Gallaudet, I was no longer "the Deaf kid on the team." I was one of many. For the first time since Maryland, Deafness wasn't my distinction; it was our foundation. And yet, even within that shared identity, I found myself still growing. I was verbal, which meant I sometimes walked in both worlds. That was confusing for others, and sometimes for me. I didn't always sign fluently enough for Deaf peers, and I was too Deaf for the hearing world. But on the field, those lines blurred. In motion, in silence, in strategy and execution, we understood each other. We played our language.

Our practices were visual, precise, and built on mutual trust. Every cue was a glance. Every call, a sign. We didn't need noise to build momentum; we built it through movement, through execution, through knowing without asking. Playing on that team reminded me that Deafness wasn't something to hide or overcome. It was the strategy. It was the culture. It was the identity. The bond between us wasn't forged in speech; it was shaped in silence and sharpened in sweat.

I often think about the players who came before me, Deaf athletes who broke barriers and challenged every assumption placed on their bodies. They played in decades where interpreters weren't offered, when coaches yelled blindly, and when no accommodations were made. And still, they played. Still, they showed up. Still, they built something. Gallaudet's program wasn't just a team. It was a witness. A form of protest. A declaration that Deaf people belong on the field, not in spite of their identity, but because of it.

Even when I had to leave, again, too soon, too young, I did not leave empty-handed. I carried those teammates with me. That brotherhood. That sacred tradition. I carried the lessons of Maryland and Gallaudet into every locker room, every sermon, every huddle I've stood in since. And while the world still too often sees Deafness as a barrier, I know better. I've lived something different. I've played something different. I've bled beside men who knew the weight of silence and the power of showing up anyway. Those were the only two times I ever played with other Deaf athletes. They were enough to change my life forever.

Lessons from the Line of Scrimmage

Football didn't just teach me how to move. It taught me how to live.

Every inch of grass, every aching tendon, every long-practice sunrise became part of a language that shaped my character. The field was a classroom where lessons weren't delivered in lectures or textbooks but in sweat, in contact, in repetition. And though it would take me years to fully understand it, that chalk-lined space taught me some of the deepest truths I have ever carried into my faith, my family, my failures, and my calling.

I used to think I wasn't a leader because I wasn't always understood. But looking back, I was often the loudest voice in the locker room. Not because I wanted to be. Not because I was trying to prove something. I was just loud, so loud I didn't know I was. Deafness made it hard to gauge my volume. I didn't hear myself the way others did. My voice came out in bursts of thunder, sometimes clumsy, sometimes raw. But the volume was never just noise. It was urgent. It was truth trying to find its way out. I was loud because I had something to say, even when I didn't yet have the words. And in time, that voice became a kind of leadership all its own, not polished, but persistent. Not rehearsed, but real.

The first thing football taught me was discipline. Not the kind that shows up on motivational posters, but the kind you learn when it's 5:00 a.m. and your bones ache and no one else is watching. Football taught me that discipline is doing it anyway. Running the extra lap. Getting back in your stance after a false start. Owning the mistake without blaming your teammate. There were no shortcuts, no magic schemes, no excuses. Either you prepared or you didn't. Either you showed up or you didn't. And if you didn't, the game would show you real quick who did.

And football didn't just teach discipline, it taught me how to suffer well. That's what resilience really is. Not just pushing through pain, but understanding what the pain is there to teach you. I played through a broken hand, worn-out cleats, cracked ribs, and countless injuries that would have sidelined me if I had believed comfort was the point. I learned that pain wasn't punishment. It was part of the price. Every bruise was proof that I hadn't quit. And those physical lessons became spiritual truths. Storms don't always mean you're off track. That sometimes pain is the confirmation, not the contradiction, of calling. You don't get through life without pain. But if you let it, pain will teach you what applause never can.

Football also taught me about people, about trust, about teamwork, and about community. That was hard for me. As a Deaf player, I always had to read more than I heard. I missed calls. Missed jokes. Missed cues. I had to anticipate what others could ask for out loud. And when I didn't get it right, I felt the weight of it, felt the isolation, the frustration of being seen as too slow or too different. But I also learned to adapt. I learned to read shoulders and eyes, and breath. I learned to play the game with all five senses sharpened by necessity. And I learned that communication isn't about volume, it's about connection. Even when I couldn't understand the words, I could understand the intention. I knew when a teammate was angry. I knew when a coach was disappointed. I knew when a locker room was grieving a loss or celebrating a win. My silence became a way of listening to others who didn't know how to access.

Leadership came in strange forms. I didn't have the smooth speech of a team captain giving pregame hype talks. I had stutters. I had slurred words. I had a voice that sometimes made people lean in awkwardly. But I also had presence. I showed up. I outworked. I stayed when others left. And when the team saw that, they listened. Not because I was the most eloquent, but because I was consistent. That's a lesson I've carried into every other place I've ever been asked to lead. Whether in a church pulpit or a classroom, leadership isn't about charisma. It's about character. It's not the volume of your voice that changes lives, it's the weight of your presence.

But the greatest lesson the line of scrimmage ever gave me was about faith.

Because football taught me to trust the process.

There were times I practiced harder than ever and still didn't start. Times I followed every instruction and still lost. Times I gave my all and still got overlooked. But football taught me that preparation is never wasted. That character formed in the dark shows up under the lights. That you don't always get the outcome you want, but you can still be proud of the way you showed up. And that's what walking with God is like. Sometimes you don't see the fruit right away. Sometimes the healing takes longer than you expected. Sometimes the vision God gave you looks nothing like the season you're standing in. But you trust anyway. You keep lining up. You run the next play. You believe the Coach sees something in you can't yet see in yourself.

I don't know what your field is. Maybe it's not football. Maybe it's parenthood. Or recovery. Or surviving systems that don't understand you. But I do know this: what you learn in the dirt, in the discipline, in the pain, it will not return void. There are no wasted reps in the Kingdom of God. Every down matters. Every yard counts. And sometimes the biggest victories don't come with celebration. Sometimes they come with quiet faithfulness, when you rise up, battered but unbroken, and take your place again.

That's what the line of scrimmage taught me. That life is a contact sport. That grace has grit. And that sometimes, the loudest people in the room are the ones who never meant to be heard, but needed to be seen.

The Spirituality of the Game

There are places in this world where the line between the sacred and the ordinary disappears. For me, one of those places was the football field.

Not because it was quiet and reverent, it wasn't. Not because it was clean or holy by anyone's definition. But because it was real. It was raw. It was human. And God always shows up in the most human places.

The field was a sacred text written in grass and blood, in chalk and bruises. It was where I first learned about discipline, yes, but also about grace. Where I first came to understand what it means to belong to something bigger than yourself. Where I first tasted the pain of failure, the quiet dignity of second-string roles, the longing to lead, and the freedom that comes when you no longer have anything to prove. The spirituality of football was not handed to me in a pre-game prayer. It was forged in the fire of repetition, in the silence between the whistles, and in the breathless space between the huddle and the snap.

The huddle, to me, was never just strategy. It was sacred. It was where chaos met clarity. Where eleven individuals bowed their heads toward the center, not in worship, but in unity. In that tight circle, you had to listen with your body. You had to read each other's energy, feel the pulse of the play, believe in what came next. For me, a Deaf player who couldn't always hear the cadence or the chatter, the huddle became a holy classroom. It was a place of trust. We didn't all speak the same way, but we shared the same goal. We drew close, created silence inside the storm, and prepared to move together. That is sacred. That is the church. That is Acts 2 in shoulder pads and cleats.

And then came the snap. The instant when everything exploded into motion. There is no time for hesitation at the line of scrimmage. Once the ball moves, you go. That moment is a leap of faith. You may not see where the block is developing. You may not know if the quarterback will find the open receiver. You move because the play depends on trust. That's faith in motion, Hebrews

11:1 lived out in cleats. "Now faith is the substance of things hoped for, the evidence of things not seen." The play is invisible when you begin. But you run it anyway.

I can't count the number of times I lined up with doubt in my gut. Will I miss the read? Will I hear the check? Will my teammates trust me? Will the coach notice if I get it right, or only if I mess up? But the snap didn't wait for my confidence. It came anyway. And in that moment, you either trust your preparation or you panic. Football taught me how to trust the work. How to keep moving even when fear whispered louder than faith.

The grind, that endless cycle of practice, weights, film study, drills, and do-it-again reps, was its own kind of spiritual formation. It was not glamorous. It was not Instagram-worthy. It was hot, exhausting, painful, and often unrewarded. But it taught me how to show up when I didn't feel like it. How to do the hard things when no one is clapping. How to do it right after I did it wrong. That is spiritual growth. That is the wilderness. That is what Jesus did in the desert. Forty days. No crowd. No miracles. Just preparation. Just presence. Just hunger. Football trained my body, but even more, it trained my spirit. To endure. To persevere. To obey.

I often think of Paul's letters when I think about this part of the game. In 1 Corinthians 9:24, he writes, "Do you not know that in a race all the runners run, but only one gets the prize? Run in such a way as to get the prize." And in Hebrews 12:1, we are exhorted to "run the race with endurance." There are moments on the field that feel exactly like that, a race you're not sure you're equipped to run. But endurance is not born in victory. It is born in failure. In missed tackles. In watching from the sideline while someone else gets the reps. In grinding through the week and getting zero snaps on Friday night. And still showing up on Monday.

Spiritual warfare? I lived it long before I had words for it. Every time I was underestimated because of my Deafness, every time I was called too loud or too slow or too much of a liability. Every time I was given broken equipment, while others got new gear. Every time I got blamed for missing a call, I couldn't hear. That was warfare. Not of flesh and blood, but of identity and dignity. Ephesians 6 tells us to "put on the full armor of God." I used to put on pads and cleats. Now I suit up in truth and grace. But it's the same discipline. It's the same readiness. Stand firm. Stand tall. And when you've done everything, stand.

And grace? It did not show up only in the highlight reel. It showed up in the fumbles. In the time I got put on second string, and felt invisible. In the games I never played but cheered anyway. In the games I played injured and couldn't make an impact. Grace came in the tap on the shoulder from a coach who still believed in me. In the quiet words from a teammate who said, "We need you." It came when I watched the game film and saw my own failure in slow motion, but I knew I'd get another chance next week.

I didn't win many awards. I was not a star. I played at Maryland School for the Deaf, and for one season at Gallaudet under Coach Chuck Goldstein. I was often the loudest person on the field, not out of arrogance, but because I didn't know how loud I was. I was trying to belong. Trying to communicate. Trying to be seen. I was loud because I had something to say, even if it came out messy. And grace met me there too.

It's easy to talk about touchdowns and trophies. But most of football, like most of faith, is not lived in the end zone. It's lived in the trenches. In the bruises. In the losing seasons. In the cold practices where you wonder why you're even doing this. That's where character is built. That's where identity is forged. And that's where God most often meets us, not in the win, but in the weakness.

I know now that football was never just a game. It was liturgy. It was a lament. It was calling. And in those moments when I doubted everything about myself, my voice, my body, my Deafness, my value, it reminded me: you are not what they call you. You are what you persist in becoming. And that is grace in the middle.

Not a Star, But Still Chosen

I was never the star of the team. I was not the one they built the offense around. My name wasn't called in post-game interviews, and I didn't walk off the field with trophies or attention. I wasn't the MVP, and I didn't receive offers from big-name schools. I didn't have the stats, the headlines, or the spotlight. But I had something else. I had grit. I had presence. I had a purpose that was still unfolding.

I was not a receiver, so I never dropped a pass. But I was the center, and I made bad snaps. I made the kind of mistakes that stopped a drive before it began, the kind that made the quarterback glare back in frustration. I knew the feeling of snapping the ball too high, too low, too soon. And I knew what it felt like to carry the weight of those moments long after the play had ended. The world may not remember the center, but the center remembers every mistake. Still, I returned to the line each time. That, I learned, was grace. Not the grace of success, but the grace of repetition. The grace of doing it again.

I never needed to be the star because I was becoming something deeper. I was being shaped in silence, in repetition, in the spaces between applause. I was being formed into a leader, not the kind who shouts instructions from a podium, but the kind who shows up early, stays late, and keeps doing the hard things even when nobody notices. I was becoming a voice, not loud by choice, but loud because I could not hear my own volume. I was becoming a minister, not from the mountaintop, but from the muddy, cleat-churned trenches of daily struggle.

Football taught me to lead from the middle. I wasn't the tallest, fastest, or strongest. But I was the one who came back after failure. I was the one who knew what it felt like to be overlooked. That became my strength. I became the player who encouraged the backup and thanked the equipment guy. I knew what it meant to be unseen, and so I made it my mission to see others.

God never used football to make me famous. He used it to make me faithful. He did not give me the spotlight. He gave me the responsibility of showing up. Every time I was benched, every time I was second-string, every time I was asked to do something unnoticed or unglamorous, I was being shaped. The Lord was teaching me obedience. He was teaching me how to be consistent when applause was absent and affirmation was scarce. He was preparing me for the kind of ministry that is rooted in service, not recognition.

In the weight room, I learned to push past what I thought were my limits. In the film room, I learned to study details that others ignored. On the sideline, I learned how to watch and support when I wanted to be on the field. And in those small, silent moments, I came to understand that God does not only work through victories. He speaks through the losses, through the missteps, and through the second chances.

I think of the times I stayed on the field after everyone left, replaying the mistakes in my mind. I think of the games I watched from the sideline, knowing I had more to give but not yet being called. I think of the bruises that faded and the lessons that did not. And I thank God that He was there in all of it. He did not waste a single play. He did not overlook a single effort. He used every ounce of it to teach me trust.

Football trained me for the calling I now carry. It prepared me to be a pastor, a husband, a father, a coach, and a teacher. It gave me a foundation of discipline, endurance, and resilience. It taught me how to lead without needing to be in charge. It showed me how to serve with quiet strength. And it reminded me, day after day, that I was not forgotten.

I was not the star of the team. But I was chosen. Not by a coach. Not by a recruiter. But by a God who saw the long view. He saw who I could become, not just what I could achieve. And in every snap, every misstep, and every moment of silence, He was shaping me.

I never held the trophy. But I held the line. I held my ground. I held the faith.

The Field as Altar

There were no stained-glass windows. No velvet-draped pulpits. No trained choirs lining the sidelines. But there was a sanctuary.

It was not made of bricks and mortar. It was lined in chalk. Worn by cleats. Bled on. Cried over. Baptized by sweat and made holy by every breath that came up from heaving lungs in the fourth quarter, when everything hurt but quitting was not an option.

The football field was my first altar.

Long before I stood behind a pulpit, I knelt in the grass. Not in silence but in exhaustion. Not in hymns but in grunts and pads cracking under pressure. Not in robes but in shoulder pads and a jersey soaked in effort. It was on that field I first learned how to pray, not with eloquent words, but with aching muscles and grit in my teeth. With a bad snap and a second chance. With dirt in my eye and hope in my chest.

Football did not teach me how to perform. It taught me how to endure.

It taught me that some of the holiest moments come when nobody is watching. That grace shows up not at the trophy ceremony, but when you miss the block and have to face your teammates anyway. When you walk to the sideline after blowing the snap and hear the coach's voice, not with condemnation, but with trust that you'll get it right next time. That is grace. That is the church.

For me, the sacred ground was always sixty yards wide and a hundred yards long. It was where I was most alive. Most exposed. Most human.

And it was loud.

So loud I did not realize how loud I was.

That might sound funny to someone else. But I didn't know. I was Deaf, and when I yelled, I didn't always hear it. I could feel it, though, the vibrations in my chest, the tension in the huddle, the way people turned when I spoke from somewhere deeper than sound. I wasn't trying to be the loudest one on the field. I just was. It wasn't bravado. It was survival. It was present. It was how I made sure I wasn't invisible.

In most of the world, I was asked to quiet down. On the field, I was told to speak up.

And when I did, when I stood over the ball as center, hands shaking from the weight of the game, body aching from collision after collision, I learned what it meant to carry something. To snap that ball clean. To be trusted with the first movement of the play. To know that the whole team was waiting on me, watching me. And if I got it wrong, we all paid for it. And still, still, I was chosen to try again.

I was never the MVP. I was never recruited by the big schools. I didn't make it to D1. I never held the ball in the end zone, and never heard the crowd chant my name. But I was there. I was in the trenches. I was the one fighting for inches when no one noticed. I was a center, sometimes guard, and on Defense nose-tackle, but not a star.

But I was chosen.

Chosen to learn that sometimes victory doesn't look like celebration, it looks like consistency. Like getting up when your body says stay down. Like holding the line so someone else can run the ball. Like showing up every day, even when the world has already counted you out.

I was never just playing a game. I was learning a language. A sacred, unspoken gospel of dirt and devotion. The field was where God met me in my Deafness, not despite it. Where I didn't have to hear the cadence to feel the rhythm. Where I didn't need to speak to be understood.

And now, as a coach, a pastor, and a father, I still walk onto fields with reverence. I still whisper the same prayer I learned as a teenager with taped wrists and trembling knees:

Lord, let me do this with all my heart. Because the field is still holy.

The gridiron didn't just teach me how to play. It taught me how to pray. It taught me that strength isn't about volume. It's about presence. And grace? Grace is not waiting in the end zone. Grace is found in the chaos. In the broken plays. In the huddle after a mistake. Grace is what waits for us at the line of scrimmage, again and again and again.

The field was my altar. The whistle was my call to worship. The huddle was my fellowship. And every inch gained or lost was part of a bigger liturgy I could not yet name.

CHAPTER 5

"I Am Here!"

Marriage didn't start with clarity. Parenting didn't start with peace. Adulting started with chaos.

The baby had been screaming for hours. Veronica was walking laps around her apartment, bouncing her gently, whispering lullabies through clenched teeth and dry lips. I stood in the kitchen with a bottle I'd already reheated twice, unsure if it was the right temperature, unsure if I was even helping. We hadn't spoken in over an hour. Not because we were angry, but because we were too tired to speak. There's a silence that comes with exhaustion, a silence that's heavier than rage.

And it wasn't just one bad night. It was the accumulation of a thousand little weights we'd carried into that moment: overdue bills, inconsistent work schedules, sleepless nights, formula cans that seemed to vanish too fast, and the gnawing feeling that everyone else had figured life out except us.

I couldn't hear the crying unless I was looking. The pitch and frequency of a baby's wail often escape my range. I depended on Veronica's cues, the way her face tightened or her pace quickened. I read her frustration like I read lips, trying to piece together the fullness of what I missed. And every time I misunderstood, every time I hesitated too long or fumbled with the bottle, I felt the creeping sting of inadequacy.

Not just as a father.

As a man. As a husband. As a Deaf adult in a hearing world that rarely slowed down enough to let me catch up.

Earlier that week, we had rushed one of our children to the ER. A Virus. The wheezing started just before dinner, and by the time we buckled the car seat, their chest looked like it was caving in with each breath. I drove like a man possessed. And once we got there, I sat frozen in the corner of the exam room while nurses barked questions I couldn't fully process, alarms rang that I couldn't hear, and Veronica translated through tears and panic.

I wanted to help. I needed to help. But I didn't know how. I had no idea if the nurse had said "code yellow" or "code blue." I couldn't tell whether the monitor was beeping from crisis or just routine. I couldn't even hear the crying that echoed through the halls. I just saw it all on her face.

That's the kind of moment that can break a man, not because he doesn't love his family, but because he does. And love without clarity, without tools, without language, hurts.

So here I was: working night shifts, stocking retail shelves, unable to hear the store radio or the supervisor's announcements. Taking shifts as a nurse's aide, unable to hear call bells or the cracking voice of an elderly person in need. Briefly operating machinery on a grain farm, trying to read the rhythm of a team that ran on instinct and sound, while I lived by visual guesswork.

I admired the people I worked with deeply, honest, hardworking, decent folks. Many of them went out of their way to help me feel included. But even their grace couldn't erase my inner disorientation. I didn't know how to operate, not just the machines or the routines, but my own identity.

I was still trying to figure out how to be a man in a world that kept changing the definition. I was learning how to be a father in the deep end without a float. I was stumbling my way through marriage, desperately in love with a woman who had been through more with me than most people go through in a lifetime. And yet, I kept making mistakes, mistakes that had nothing to do with Deafness and everything to do with pride, impatience, and fear.

I wasn't making wise financial decisions. I was saying yes to jobs I couldn't sustain, no to help I actually needed, and pretending like I was fine because asking for grace felt like failure. I didn't feel strong. I didn't feel ready. I felt like a disappointment wrapped in good intentions.

And then, in one of those blurry moments between bottle-warming and car-seat buckling, something happened.

I looked up.

I don't know why. Nothing magical drew my gaze. There wasn't a bright light or a voice from heaven. But I looked up, and I saw Veronica rocking the baby with tired arms and unfailing love. I saw the hallway light spilling into the living room like a soft whisper. I saw the mess of bottles, blankets, bills, and worry, and I felt the stillness settle like a blanket over the noise.

God was already there.

I hadn't arrived at clarity. I hadn't earned understanding. I hadn't even prayed.

But He was there.

In the sleepless night.

In the ER waiting room.

In the cereal aisle following the graveyard shift.

In the back corner of the grain silo.

Not offering easy answers. Not waving away the struggle. Just... being. Present. Still.

A quiet voice that didn't depend on volume: "I am here."

Not, "You've got this."

Not, "You're doing great."

Not, "Be strong and courageous."

Just that ancient promise, whispered across the clutter and chaos of my life:

"I am here."

And in that moment, mid-mess, mid-failure, mid-exhaustion, I realized something holy had stirred not because I had figured it all out... but because I had finally stopped pretending I could.

Steadying Grace in the Storm

I didn't walk into that creative writing class expecting to meet anyone, let alone the woman who would one day become my wife. It was senior year, and I had just transferred schools, midstream, mid-chaos, mid-heartache. I had moved from my dad's house to my mom's, trying to start fresh after football season ended, but everything still felt unsettled. I was the new kid, again. The halls buzzed with rhythms I didn't know. The routines were unfamiliar. I kept my head down and my hopes low.

And then I saw her.

Veronica sat at the front of my row. Calm. Confident. Radiant, but not flashy. There was a seriousness to her, a focus that made it clear she didn't have time for games. She wasn't just present; she belonged. And that terrified me. I didn't know how to talk to a girl like that. So instead, I came up with a plan that was equal parts bold and foolish.

I pretended to ask the teacher a question. I leaned in toward the desk, glanced at the seating chart with just enough intention to look casual, and located her name, Veronica. My heart was pounding like I was lining up for a fourth-and-goal. I walked back to my seat and wrote her a note, not a flirtation, not a joke, but a declaration. A goofy, over-the-top, heart-on-sleeve kind of note that said, in essence, "I'm going to marry you one day."

I figured if I was going to crash and burn, I might as well do it with poetic flair.

There was a reason I chose to write before I spoke. I wanted her to know my heart before she encountered my baggage. Before she heard my speech or saw the hearing aids or figured out I was Deaf. I wanted her to fall in love with the deepest part of me, the words, the soul, the longing to be known, before the world got in the way with its assumptions and filters. Writing gave me the chance to be heard without interruption. It gave me the courage to say things my mouth was too clumsy to form.

To my shock, she didn't throw the note away.

She didn't laugh or walk past me with a smirk.

She read it. She smiled.

And in that moment, something in the universe shifted.

From the beginning, Veronica saw me, not just the surface me, not just the performative or protective layers I carried into every new environment. She saw through the noise. Through the pride and the uncertainty and the ache. And she didn't turn away. She leaned in.

She became, even then, a kind of grace I didn't know how to pray for.

Veronica didn't ignore my Deafness. But she also didn't treat it like it was my whole story. She challenged my self-pity without ever denying my pain. She stood beside me without trying to fix me. She held my contradictions, my tenderness and my temper, my ambition and my fear, with a strength that stunned me. Even in those early days, when we were just two kids exchanging scribbled notes and nervous glances, I could feel it: she was steady in a way I wasn't. Rooted in something I hadn't yet found.

Her faith wasn't showy. It was forged in private. But it flowed through her words, her decisions, her presence. When I wavered, she didn't preach. She simply was. Her discernment was sharp, her prayers consistent, her loyalty unshakable. I had never known anyone who could look directly at my mess and not flinch. She didn't try to rescue me. She chose to walk with me. That's what love is.

That's what grace does.

I didn't need a savior. I needed a companion. And God sent her, through a classroom door, a seating chart, a scribbled note, and a smile that still steadies me today.

Fatherhood: Terrifying, Tender, Transforming

There was no orchestra swelling in the background, no slow-motion montage, no movie-moment glow when I learned I was going to be a father. There was only breathlessness, like the wind had been knocked out of me, and a quiet, shaking kind of joy that tasted more like awe than triumph. We had talked about having children, sure. I had always wanted to be a father. A big family, even. I would've kept going if Veronica hadn't wisely set the limit at four. And truthfully, she was right. Four was, and is, more than enough. But the moment it moved from theory to reality, from "someday" to "this day," I was overwhelmed. Not by fear of them, but by the weight of me.

How could I raise anyone else when I was still trying to figure out who I was?

I wasn't afraid of holding a baby or changing diapers or the midnight feedings. I was afraid of what I couldn't hear. I was afraid of what I couldn't give. I was afraid my children would grow up resenting the parts of me I had spent a lifetime trying to accept. Would they hate my Deafness? Would they be embarrassed by my voice? Would they walk ahead of me in public, answering questions on my behalf? Would they one day look at me and feel that same gnawing disappointment I had felt in myself?

There were nights early on when I would rock a child back to sleep, their breath soft against my chest, and whisper prayers I wasn't even sure how to finish. Not polished prayers. Not bold, declarative ones. Just fragments: "Help me." "Guide me." "Let me be enough." I was exhausted, bone-deep, soul-worn exhausted, and not just from lack of sleep. I was carrying the guilt of feeling like I was already failing.

I couldn't hear them cry from the other room.

I couldn't enjoy their plays or concerts the way other parents did, leaning forward with pride, laughing at the right moments, clapping with the crowd. I smiled anyway, of course. I sat in the audience and tried to read the faces of those around me to know when something funny had happened. I applauded when others did. I filmed the performances and watched them back with captions later, alone, just so I could understand what everyone else had experienced in real time. I felt left out of my own children's joy, and that left a deeper ache than I expected.

The older I get, the more that ache shifts. It's not just about Deafness. It's about the world. The world they're walking into. A world that's loud and fast and often cruel. A world that labels kids before they know their own names. A world where boys are told not to cry, where girls are told they're not enough unless they shrink. A world where people still whisper cruel things about disability or difference or softness or faith. I'm not scared of who my children are. I'm scared of who the world might try to convince them to be.

But somewhere along the way, somewhere between diaper bags and science projects, between sleepless nights and early morning snuggles, something shifted.

My kids never asked me to be perfect. They just needed me to be there.

They didn't need me to hear every word. They needed me to listen with my heart. They didn't need me to fix every problem. They needed me to sit beside them in the mess. They didn't need me to become someone else. They needed me to be themselves with me.

And that's what fatherhood has become: not a performance, but a presence.

A sacred, steady, terrifying, tender presence.

Fatherhood didn't ask me to know everything. It asked me to stay. To keep showing up. To love without conditions and listen without sound. To trust that my presence, my flawed, stumbling, prayer-soaked presence, was enough to shape a life.

I've failed plenty of times. I've raised my voice when I should've asked a question. I've missed moments I can't get back. I've said the wrong thing, or nothing at all. But by grace, I've also held their hands when they were afraid. I've apologized when I was wrong. I've sat in hospital rooms and car rides and crowded gyms, praying under my breath, not for perfection, but for connection. That they would feel seen. That they would know they are loved.

And somehow, in the beautiful mystery of it all, they do.

What no one really talks about, what I didn't fully understand until I was in the middle of it, is how isolating fatherhood can be for someone who is Deaf. It's a holy calling, yes. A gift beyond words. But also a battlefield. And the enemy is not my children. It's the gap, the relentless, widening gap between me and the world they are growing up in.

Most parents worry about not being able to protect their kids. I worry about not being able to hear them in danger. I worry about missing their cries in the night, the subtle change in their breathing, the whispered fears behind their bedroom doors. I worry about what happens if they call out from another room and I don't answer. Not because I don't love them, but because I can't hear them. What does that silence teach them?

There have been moments, small, devastating ones, that most people would overlook. A lost tooth I didn't notice until the excitement had already faded. A joke at the dinner table that made everyone laugh before I caught on. A whispered "I love you" from the back seat that was swallowed by road noise and wind. I've missed things. Not from apathy, but from limitation. And those are the moments that haunt me.

My children live in two worlds. In one, they are just kids, full of energy, imagination, joy, and chaos. In the other, they carry the quiet burden of being my interpreters. They answer questions for strangers when they notice I didn't catch something. They repeat themselves more times than any child should have to. They've learned, far too young, how to navigate adult conversations in medical offices and school lobbies because the receptionist looks at me, then looks at them, and speaks past me anyway. I see it. I feel it. And it cuts deep.

My children never asked to be advocates, yet have learned to advocate for others.

My children didn't sign up to be teachers, yet with patience have taught others in simple, grace-filled ways.

My children have learned how to bridge the gap between me and the hearing world, but sometimes, I worry they're getting lost in the middle.

Sometimes I see it in their eyes, the hesitation, the weariness, the way they scan a room before deciding who to look at first: me, or the person who won't bother making sure I understand. I've watched them wrestle with questions I used to ask myself: Why doesn't the world try harder? Why is this our responsibility to fix? Why does it feel like we're always the ones doing the work of making others comfortable?

It is a sacred, aching thing to be both their father and their limitation.

There's guilt that simmers underneath the love. Not because I regret being Deaf, I don't. But because I know the world doesn't always honor Deafness the way it should. And so, my children inherit my burden not biologically, but culturally, emotionally. They didn't choose this. But they live in it. And I pray every day that it will make them more compassionate, not more bitter.

I pray they will see my Deafness not as a lack, but as a lens. That they will learn to listen with more than ears, to see with more than eyes. That they will grow into fierce, empathetic humans who don't pity me, but see me for who I am, flawed and faithful, broken and beloved.

My children, all children, while we are at it, are gifts, too. My children know how to pause. They know how to look someone in the eye. They've learned the art of presence, because they've grown up knowing how much it matters. They speak more with their hands and their faces than most adults do with their words. They know silence can be holy. That communication isn't just noise; it's intention.

But it's still hard.

Sometimes, they pull away, not because they don't love me, but because they're tired of having to work so hard to be understood. And I get that. I really do. And it breaks me.

Fatherhood is terrifying because I can't protect them from the world. But it's also terrifying because I can't protect them from me, from the shadow of my limits, from the cultural weight they didn't ask for. And yet, even in the tension, even in the fear, there's grace.

Because my kids don't ask me to be perfect. They ask me to stay.

And staying is the most radical, redemptive thing I can do.

Staying in the hard conversations. Staying at the soccer game even if I miss the goal. Staying in the recital audience, even when the music passes me by. Staying in the room when they cry, even if I can't hear the tears. Staying present when it would be easier to retreat into guilt or shame. Staying when the world says I'm not enough.

I may not always understand what they're saying.

But I will always listen.

I may not always get it right. But I will never walk away.

And if that's the only legacy I leave them, that love doesn't require sound, only presence, then I'll know I did something holy.

Wrestling with Calling: Deafness as Disruption and Doorway

Long before I ever stood behind a pulpit or taught in a classroom, I carried a quiet, persistent ache that there was something more for my life than just surviving. I couldn't articulate it, not in a world that measured success in sound and speed, but it stirred in me. A sense that my life was meant to count for something deeper. I didn't have the words for it yet. I just knew I wanted to matter, to contribute, to build something lasting. I wanted to make my family proud. I wanted to build a future. But the path in front of me didn't make space for all that I was.

I didn't fit the mold the world handed me.

I wanted ease, routine, predictability, a stable paycheck, a job I could clock in and out of without needing to explain myself at every turn. I wanted normalcy, not glamor, just something that didn't require fighting every day to be understood. But what I got instead were interruptions. Not the gentle, welcome kind, but the jarring kind. Divine interruptions that felt more like detours than directions. Human interruptions, misunderstandings, exclusions, side-glances, that chipped away at my confidence one unspoken word at a time.

I had learned early to read the room before the room ever read me.

I moved through life trying to anticipate everything, what I'd miss, what I'd need to interpret, how long I had before I made someone uncomfortable. I worked hard to keep up. I made jokes I didn't fully hear. I laughed at the right time, nodded when I was lost. Deafness, for much of my life, felt like a constant disqualifier. An ever-present barrier that separated me from the person I was trying to become.

I wanted to lead. I wanted to serve. But I didn't want to be seen as broken.

Deafness was the thing I kept trying to overcome. Not because I was ashamed of it, but because the world taught me to be. Every classroom, every job interview, every church foyer where someone waved and then gave up when I didn't respond fast enough, it all layered a subtle message: You're not equipped for this.

But then one day, something shifted.

It wasn't in a sanctuary or a classroom. It wasn't during a breakthrough moment. It was at practice. I was running drills, trying to prove myself, trying to make the cut, trying, always trying, to belong. And after practice, my coach pulled me aside. Not in a loud way. Not to correct me. Just to talk.

That coach was my father.

He didn't speak in riddles or sermons. He didn't need to. He just said, "You don't hear what's going on, but you feel everything. That's your edge."

At first, I didn't know how to take that. Was it pity? Encouragement? But then I looked in his eyes, and I knew. He saw something in me I hadn't yet permitted myself to believe: that my Deafness wasn't just an obstacle to overcome, it was an advantage.

A different way of moving, sensing, knowing. He had seen it all along. And in that simple sentence, he gave me permission to reimagine everything.

It was the first time I realized that Deafness might not be the thing that held me back.

It might be the thing that opened the door.

I started paying attention to moments that once made me feel disqualified: how I read a room through posture and pacing, how I felt people's emotions before they spoke, how my silence created space for others to speak truths they'd otherwise hide. I began to see the spiritual through-line in my own story, not as disjointed moments of loss, but as a rhythm of grace. A sermon I hadn't known I'd been living.

One night, I sat in church, in an unfamiliar congregation, a sermon that I couldn't fully follow. But the preacher's face burned with conviction, and even though I couldn't hear every word, something in the Spirit broke through. He preached about Moses and the burning bush. About how God didn't call Moses when he was polished and powerful, but when he was uncertain, hiding, and unqualified. That sermon hit different. Because for the first time, I saw myself not just as someone limping toward purpose, but someone called through the limp itself.

It was still a wrestle. I wasn't ready to say "Yes, Lord." I wasn't even ready to stand up and tell anyone I felt called. I was still sorting it out, still afraid, still unsure what shape my life would take. But the old narrative had been interrupted. The one that said Deafness was a wall.

Now it felt more like a window.

I wasn't saying "Yes" yet. But I had stopped saying "never."

I was beginning to whisper, through cracked faith and fragile hope, "Maybe."

And in that, maybe, the Spirit moved.

Spiritual Echoes: God's Voice in the Silence

When people say they "heard God's voice," I often nod politely. But inside, I wonder: Did they really hear it? Or did they just feel it like I do? Because for me, there was never a voice in the sky. No booming declaration. No burning bush with subtitles. There was silence. Not the passive kind, but the kind that breathes. The kind that presses in until you have no choice but to listen with your whole being. That's where God met me, not in sound, but in sensation. Not in volume, but in weight.

The Scriptures are full of people who didn't understand what they were hearing. That's the part they don't preach about enough. Moses didn't drop to his knees in immediate obedience. He stammered. He argued. He asked for someone else to go in his place. What I never caught until later, what matters to someone like me, is that even after God called him, Moses still didn't speak for himself. Aaron became his mouth. Even the called need an interpreter sometimes. I read that and wept. Because I've lived that. I've carried callings that didn't fit neatly inside my voice. I've stood on thresholds and wondered if anyone could hear the God who speaks in my silence.

Jacob wrestled with God in the dark, alone, unnamed, bruised. That story haunted me. Not because I saw myself as heroic, but because I knew what it was to fight all night and still not be sure who you're fighting. Deafness isn't just a physical condition. It becomes a lens, a battleground, a theology. I wasn't just wrestling with the world. I was wrestling with God. Why did

You make me this way? Why the silence? Why the misunderstanding? Why the missed cues, the repeated questions, the constant sense that I was a beat behind everyone else's rhythm?

And Samuel... That one cut the deepest. Because he had heard the voice three times before, he knew it was God. He wasn't resistant, just inexperienced. He was faithful, but unfamiliar with the language of calling. That's how it was for me. I didn't reject the idea that God had something to say. I just didn't believe He'd say it to me. And even if He did, how would I recognize it?

I was in the wilderness. Not in the romanticized, Lenten way. In the real wilderness, overworked, underpaid, newly married, newly exhausted, holding babies and bottles and shame in both arms. I was working night shifts where no one spoke to me, and I was too tired to care. I was serving people in silence, feeling overlooked not just by men, but by heaven itself. I prayed. But it felt like shouting into fog.

The world said: Find your voice.

God whispered: Find Me in the quiet.

And slowly, painfully, I did.

Deafness was no longer just the condition of my body, it became the condition of my calling. Not because it made me special. But because it taught me how to live in the gaps. To see what hearing people ignore. To feel what others cover with noise. To know when someone is faking a smile. To pick up on tension before it's spoken. To love with my whole body because communication is never just words.

That's when I started to realize: silence wasn't the enemy. Silence was sacred.

It wasn't a void. It was a voice.

God had been speaking all along, not in ways others expected, but in ways I had been uniquely designed to receive. Through weight. Through presence. Through patterns and pauses and unexpected grace.

I stopped looking for thunder.

I started paying attention to trembling.

I began to trust that Deafness wasn't a limitation, it was a revelation. A reorientation of how to live. A prism through which to see the Spirit in movement. A portal into God's slow and spacious language.

There is a kind of hearing that has nothing to do with ears.

And that's where I found my faith, not in clarity, but in attention. Not in volume, but in presence.

God did not break the silence for me.

God made the silence holy.

The Declaration: "I Am Here."

The declaration didn't happen in a sanctuary. There was no preacher beckoning me forward, no music swelling beneath raised hands. No altar lined with Kleenex boxes. No spotlight on repentance. It didn't happen during a revival or a men's conference or a mountain retreat. There were no witnesses, no photos, no social media status updates proclaiming spiritual transformation.

I don't remember the exact day. I couldn't tell you what the weather was like or where I had just come from. I don't remember which child I had just dropped off, or whether it was school or practice, or some event I half-understood because I missed something when it was spoken aloud. I couldn't give you a time or location. I only remember the feeling, the moment when I exhaled and realized I had been holding my breath for years.

I sat there with the engine off and the keys still in my hand. The kind of quiet that settles over you when the world is moving fast and you've finally stopped long enough to feel it. My body was still, but my soul was shaking. Everything in me felt worn thin. Not just from the long day, but from the longer journey of pretending. Pretending I was okay. Pretending I could do it all. Pretending that Deafness didn't make things harder. Pretending I didn't feel like I was failing in the small ways no one else could see.

That afternoon, I was not undone by a single crisis. I was undone by the accumulation of tiny moments. The missed jokes. The forced smiles. The polite nods when I hadn't really caught what was said. The helpless ache of sitting in an auditorium surrounded by proud parents, clapping at the right moments even though I didn't know what I was clapping for. The deep guilt of reading lips imperfectly and realizing too late that I had missed something important. The shame of watching my kids interpret for me. The weariness of trying to hold everything together when I was quietly unraveling inside.

My forehead dropped to the steering wheel, and I breathed deeply into the silence. The silence wasn't new. It had always been there. But that day, it pressed in on me differently. Heavier. Not just quiet, but cavernous. And yet, somehow sacred.

Then, without fanfare or eloquence, I whispered it: "I am here."

It wasn't a victory cry. It wasn't a sermon. It wasn't a line rehearsed in advance. It was a confession. A surrender. A desperate exhale that carried more truth than any prayer I had ever spoken. "I am here." I wasn't saying I had arrived. I wasn't declaring success. I was simply admitting that I wasn't running anymore.

I was no longer running from my Deafness. No longer running from the grief of missed moments. No longer running from the guilt that I wasn't enough as a father, as a husband, as a man. No longer hiding behind performance, or perfectionism, or the pressure to make everyone else comfortable while I quietly disappeared. "I am here" was the moment I chose to be fully present, to my life, my body, my limits, and the God who had never left me.

And something clicked.

Not like a bolt of lightning. More like a long-locked door inside me finally giving way. For as long as I could remember, I had believed in God. I had prayed. I had sung. I had stood when told to stand and bowed my head when told to pray. I had called myself a Christian. But this was different. That moment in the car was not belief. It was a transformation. It was when I crossed the threshold from Christian to Disciple.

I stopped asking God to bless the life I had built. I started asking how to lose it.

The next morning, I picked up my Bible with trembling hands. Not out of duty. Out of hunger. The Word felt alive in my chest, like something I couldn't consume fast enough. Every verse pressed deeper. Every chapter read me back. I wasn't reading for comfort. I was reading for fire. Because something had ignited in me, and I couldn't go back to casual belief.

I didn't just study, I served. Not for recognition. Not for approval. But because something in my spirit refused to stay still.

I couldn't explain it at the time, but I felt like I was being rewired from the inside out. Like the Word of God was reconfiguring my DNA. Like the silence I had once feared was now filled with the presence of God, shaping me.

Jeremiah said it best: "His word is in my heart like a fire, a fire shut up in my bones. I am weary of holding it in; indeed, I cannot." I read that and wept. Because that was it. That was the fire. Not a poetic metaphor. A consuming necessity. I wasn't preaching for applause. I was burning from within. It wasn't ambition, it was obedience.

"I am here" became my daily liturgy.

When my child whispered a question, I didn't catch it, and I had to ask them to repeat it. It was then that I stopped pretending. I looked them in the eye, placed my hand over my heart, and said, "I am here."

When Veronica was carrying burdens I couldn't fix, and there were no words left between us, I reached for her hand and held it longer. Not to explain. But to stay. I am here.

When someone at church looked at me and didn't know how to speak to me, I didn't shrink. I smiled with gentleness and waited for the Spirit to bridge what sound could not. I am here.

Even when God felt far, when prayers felt like they fell to the floor, when silence wrapped around me like fog, I stayed. And I knew that God was not asking me to produce miracles or memorize doctrine or win arguments. He was asking me to stay.

Because presence is a miracle.

I am Deaf. I am imperfect. I get tired. But I am not absent. I am here.

And God is, too.

Not because I found Him, but because I finally stopped hiding.

The Call Beneath the Noise

I didn't know where any of this would lead.

I still don't.

Back then, sitting in the silence of that car, whispering those three small words, I am here, I wasn't thinking about callings or pulpits or purpose. I wasn't dreaming of ministry or imagining a future where my Deafness could become a doorway instead of a wall. I was simply showing up to my own life. Not polished. Not confident. Just present.

And that presence didn't feel like the end of something.

It felt like the beginning.

Like standing before a closed closet door and realizing, after years of banging my fists on the wrong walls, that it was never locked. Just waiting. Waiting for me to reach out. Waiting for me to open it. And when I did, I didn't find clarity. I didn't find comfort. I didn't find a straight path. I found a wilderness. A mystery. A holy fire that refused to be contained.

And I stepped through.

Because once you've touched the edge of real presence, yours and God's, you can't go back to pretending.

For years, I had filled pulpits. I started preaching when I was thirteen years old, young, hungry, eager to say something meaningful. And I had. I had preached truth, preached Scripture, preached with all the sincerity I could muster. But it had always felt slightly outside of me. Like I was delivering something sacred that I hadn't yet fully absorbed. Like I was carrying the Word for others without letting it settle fully in my bones.

But now, the sermons were different.

They didn't come from my mind; they came from the fire. They came from the places in me that had been broken open and remade. They came from the tears I had never admitted, the silence I had learned to survive, the grace I had learned to receive. I wasn't preaching as performance anymore. I was preaching because if I didn't, I felt like I might explode from the truth rising in me.

Because God was no longer a concept to me.

He was a presence I had met in my pain.

And I had begun to listen. Not with my ears, but with my spirit. With my body. With my life.

I began to listen in the waiting rooms, where I sat with my children and had to ask them to speak up. I began to listen in the kitchen when Veronica's sigh meant more than her words. I began to listen in the quiet of the sanctuary, when the Spirit moved without sound but with undeniable weight. I began to hear the ache in people's posture. The longing between their sentences. The presence of God in their pauses.

Deafness hadn't shut me off from the voice of God.

It had made me fluent in another language entirely.

I came to realize that God wasn't calling me out of my Deafness, or my poverty, or my pain. He wasn't calling me to abandon the parts of my story I had long tried to escape. He was calling me through them. Through the silence. Through the missed moments. Through the aching questions. Through the decades of doubt and trying to blend in. He was calling me through.

That moment of surrender, I am here, wasn't a period. It was a threshold.

A passage.

The beginning of a life where I no longer measured my worth by how well I could perform in a world not built for me.

A life where faith wasn't something I wore, it was something I entered.

And I hadn't yet said yes to God, not fully.

But for the first time, I had stopped saying "no."

And maybe that's where it begins. Not in clarity. Not in eloquence. But in readiness.

I wasn't ready to say "yes."

But I was finally ready to open the door.

To stop standing in the hallway of borrowed belief, and step into a world where calling feels like hunger and obedience feels like home.

To stop echoing the words of others and begin speaking in the voice God had shaped within my silence.

To stop waiting for someone to affirm me and start walking with the One who had never left me.

This wasn't the end of the journey.

It was the beginning of a new one.

And all I knew, all I trusted, was that I was no longer alone.

I am here.

And so is God.

And together, we would walk through whatever came next.

CHAPTER 6

Life Between Silence and Sound

I grew up fluent in both silence and sound, but neither is completely welcome.

To be Deaf in a hearing world is not simply to live without sound. It is to dwell at the edge of belonging. A threshold is a strange and sacred place. It is not inside and not entirely outside. It is not quite the past and not fully the future. It is a liminal space, suspended in constant motion. For me, that threshold was where I lived. It was the invisible floor beneath every room I entered, a subtle reminder that I was both a part of things and somehow still apart.

There is a particular kind of loneliness that does not come from being alone but from being surrounded by people and still feeling profoundly unseen. I have sat in rooms filled with laughter, song, and prayer. I have shared tables with people I loved. And still, I often felt like I was watching life unfold through a pane of soundproof glass. Present, but not quite present. There, but not quite there.

Among hearing people, I learned to interpret myself constantly. I studied lips, memorized inflections, tracked context, and filled in gaps. I trained myself to smile at the right time, to nod when a nod was expected, to speak when silence would have drawn questions. I adjusted. I anticipated. I made others comfortable. When someone said, "You speak so well," they meant it as encouragement. What I heard, often without them realizing it, was that my value increased the closer I came to sounding like them.

Among Deaf peers, my experience was more layered. I could sign ASL fluently. I understood Deaf culture. I knew the stories, the jokes, the sacred silences. But when people learned that I had attended hearing schools or heard me speak or watched me talk on the phone, there were moments of hesitation. Trust took longer. Sometimes it did not come at all. I carried the smell of assimilation. I understood why. Still, it stung.

This is the tension of bicultural identity. It is not only about language. It is about survival. It is about carrying the weight of two worlds and being expected to do so without complaint. It is about being praised for how well you pass and questioned for why you do not belong.

To those who have never experienced this, imagine being asked to translate yourself every moment of every day. Not just your words, but your presence. Not just your ideas, but your very identity. You are not simply bilingual. You are bicultural, bi-coded, bi-everything. You are an interpreter, diplomat, chameleon, teacher, and gatekeeper. And all of it comes at a cost.

Translation is not neutral. It is labor. It is emotional, spiritual, and physical exertion. It means absorbing discomfort so that others can remain at ease. It means smiling through confusion, pretending understanding, softening your truth for the comfort of the room. It is a daily sacrifice offered quietly, unseen by most, known only to those who have lived it.

And yet, over time, the threshold began to change for me.

I once saw it as a place of dislocation, a constant ache, a wound that never fully closed. But over time, with the help of mentors, community, scripture, and sacred memory, I began to see it differently. The threshold was not a punishment. It was a revelation.

It was on the threshold that I learned to see with unusual clarity. I became sensitive to tone, gesture, stillness, and tension. I developed what some might call a sixth sense, though it is really just attentiveness. I could walk into a room and feel what others missed. I could see the crack in a voice, the flicker in an eye, the burden in a posture. I noticed silence not as emptiness but as fullness. Presence. Waiting.

For much of my early life, I believed I had to escape Deafness in order to fulfill my calling. I believed I needed to speak better, blend in more, and hide the fatigue. I thought holiness required assimilation. I thought leadership required accommodation. I was taught that to lead, I needed to perform a hearing.

And the world rewarded me for that performance. They gave me applause for sounding like them. They made space for me when I made myself smaller. But it was never wholeness. It was survival.

Only later did I begin to understand that Deafness was not the obstacle to my purpose. It was the doorway into it. It was the very lens through which I was called to see the world. My Deafness did not limit my ability to minister, to lead, to speak truth. It deepened it. It grounded it. It gave it weight.

I no longer view the threshold between silence and sound as something to be escaped. I see it now as sacred ground. It is the place where I learned to listen without ears and speak without words. It is the place where I discovered that presence is more than volume, and connection is more than clarity.

The threshold is not a hallway I must pass through in order to arrive. It is the place I have been called to stand. It is not a curse. It is a calling.

I live between silence and sound. And that in-between space, once a source of grief, has become for me the ground of grace.

Deafness Misunderstood: The Tyranny of Normalcy

Before exclusion takes shape in policy or practice, it is born in expectation.

At the heart of most social exclusion is a silent assumption that there is only one correct way to be human. One way to learn. One way to speak. One way to belong. Everything else is viewed as deviation. For Deaf people, this assumption comes with a particular name. That name is audism.

Audism is the belief that hearing and speaking are inherently superior to silence and sign. It is the assumption that the closer a person gets to sounding like a hearing person, the more successful they are. It is a system of thought, behavior, and structure that privileges those who hear while marginalizing those who do not. Sometimes it is loud, like a joke at a Deaf person's expense. Often it is quiet, like a conversation that continues while you are left behind.

Audism is not just ignorance. It is a framework. It operates in our schools, our churches, our healthcare systems, and our social spaces. It lives in classrooms where teachers give directions with their backs turned. It thrives in worship services that amplify microphones but offer no interpretation. It appears in family gatherings where no one learns even basic signs to include a Deaf relative at the dinner table.

Audism wears the mask of kindness. It hides in compliments, questions, and concern. People have told me for years, "You speak so well," as if that were the highest praise I could hope to receive. What they meant was that my Deafness was almost invisible. What I heard was that my worth increased the less I reminded them of it.

At church, I have been congratulated for preaching with my voice. At work, I have been praised for my ability to communicate clearly. These moments are intended as encouragement, but they are layered with something else. They affirm for how well I blend, not for how deeply I belong. They celebrate my ability to mimic hearing patterns rather than recognizing the full humanity of being Deaf.

People often ask questions like, "Have you thought about getting a cochlear implant?" or "Do you read lips well?" They ask as if they are helping, as if I am a puzzle they are trying to solve. After enough of these questions, I succumbed to pressure and got a cochlear implant in my left ear, which has resulted in a miserable experience with vertigo and migraines. Behind these questions is a longing to make me more like them. They are not curious about my life as it is. They are curious about how much of my difference can be made more familiar, more comfortable, more correct.

As a child, I learned that most people would not adapt to me. I had to adapt to them. Teachers rarely made eye contact. Coaches shouted across fields. Friends told stories without pausing to include me. I became the one who had to keep up. I did, to the best of my ability. I became a master interpreter of the world around me. I smiled when I missed things. I laughed when others laughed. I nodded when I wasn't sure. I learned to perform inclusion even when I did not feel included.

When I began to speak clearly and fluently, the praise grew louder. It was as if my voice, shaped by long hours of effort and exhaustion, was a trophy they could point to and say, "See, he made it." But I had not made it. I had simply learned how to make them more comfortable. I had learned how to disappear in plain sight. I cannot hear my own voice and rely heavily on my throat vibration and remembering the correct mouth and tongue shaping.

I was rewarded for blending in. I was punished, in quieter ways, for authenticity. The more I honored my Deafness, the more awkward others became. The more I signed, the more people assumed I was limited. The more I paused to understand, the more I was seen as slow. I could either perform the version of myself they wanted or risk losing the space they had made for me.

This is the emotional toll that many Deaf people carry. It is not the Deafness itself that causes pain. It is the constant pressure to soften, to translate, to reduce the fullness of who we are in order to be allowed into rooms we never designed. It is the knowledge that inclusion often comes with a condition—do not make us work too hard to include you.

For a long time, I did not realize the depth of what I was grieving. I was not grieving my hearing loss. I was grieving the loss of dignity that came every time I was told I needed to be more like someone else in order to matter. I was grieving the slow erasure of my identity at the hands of well-intentioned people who thought they were helpful.

The world celebrates Deaf people when we can inspire them, when we overcome obstacles, when we conform just enough to be palatable. But that celebration is fragile. It fades the moment we assert that we do not want to be changed. It disappears when we insist on being fully ourselves.

Our worth is not measured by how well we approximate hearing people. It is measured by how freely and fully we live in the truth of who we are. I am not Deaf because something went wrong. I am Deaf because this is who I am. My identity does not need correction. It needs recognition.

I no longer perform for acceptance. I no longer explain myself in order to be welcomed. I do not exist to comfort others with how "normal" I can seem. I am Deaf. I am whole. And I do not owe anyone an apology for being at peace with both.

The Gift of Deaf Culture

Deafness is not the absence of something essential. It is the presence of something holy. It is not a flaw to be corrected. It is a culture, a language, a way of living in the world that has its own integrity, its own depth, and its own sacredness.

Deaf culture is not just about shared experience. It is a civilization, complete with language, art, memory, and philosophy. It is shaped by the eyes rather than the ears, by movement rather than sound, by attention rather than noise. It is a culture where silence is never empty and where presence speaks louder than volume ever could.

I did not encounter Deaf culture for the first time in college. I had already lived it. I had attended a Deaf school. I had been immersed in environments where hands carried history and the air carried stories. I had learned from Deaf teachers, signed with Deaf friends, and felt the rhythm of a culture that moved through space rather than through airwaves. I knew the rules of visual attention. I knew how to feel the pulse of conversation in the room without a single word being spoken. I knew what it meant to belong without explanation.

Even with that grounding, the pull of the hearing world was constant. The expectation to speak, to blend, to minimize my difference never stopped. The world around me insisted that success meant distance from Deafness, not a deeper connection to it. And I spent years learning how to survive in spaces that had no interest in learning how to see me.

What changed in college was not my first encounter with Deafness. What changed was my willingness to stop apologizing for it. I did not discover something new. I returned to something ancient. I reclaimed what I had always known but had been taught to question. I stopped translating my identity to make others comfortable and began to receive my culture without shame. I still had much growing to do and did not fully understand or appreciate the community until years later.

In those years, I saw Deaf professors who signed with clarity and authority. I witnessed leadership conducted entirely in ASL, without any need for spoken translation. I participated in conversations where no one paused to explain the value of signing. I sat in worship spaces where the sermon was not amplified through speakers but delivered through the human body—hands raised not only in praise but in proclamation.

Worship in ASL is not a conversion of hearing forms. It is a theology of the body. Each sign carries intention. Each pause carries presence. It is not merely a visual substitute for a hymn. It is its own liturgy. The Holy Spirit does not need volume to move. The Spirit speaks through motion, through silence, through the living Word performed in flesh and space. The first time I saw someone sing a song in full freedom, I understood that sacredness did not depend on sound. It never had. Some of the most powerful poems and hymns I have ever witnessed were sung. With their whole body, spirit, face, and space immersed in the sense that made me hunger for more and want more when they had completed their articulation

In Deaf space, I did not have to explain who I was. No one asked how much I could hear. No one tried to test my speech. No one offered me unsolicited advice about cochlear implants or speech therapy. There was no sense of pity, no confusion about identity, no need to translate myself into something more acceptable. I was not a problem to solve. I was not an exception. I was simply a person.

That experience changed how I saw everything. It taught me that Deaf culture is not merely valuable. It is prophetic. Deaf culture is an extreme microcosm of the universe in religion, race, ethnicity, language, and ideology.

In Scripture, prophets are not defined by volume. They are defined by vision. They are not the loudest voices in the room. They are the clearest witnesses. They speak because they see what others overlook. Deaf people carry that same gift. We notice tension in posture, emotion in stillness, and story in silence. We are trained to read the world without relying on sound. We know what it means to listen without ears. We know how to respond to what is not said.

Deafness gives us that insight, not as compensation, but as a gift. It trains us to slow down. It teaches us to observe more deeply. It helps us hold space for things that are lost in the noise of modern life. Deaf culture does not shrink the world. It expands it.

Too often, the hearing world looks at Deaf people with pity. It assumes loss where there is richness. It sees limitations where there is legacy. It imagines that silence must be void, that signing must be second-best, that Deafness is an obstacle instead of a way of being.

But Deaf culture answers that with truth. It says clearly and without apology: do not call me hearing impaired. I am not missing anything. I am Deaf. And that is holy.

This holiness is not metaphorical. It is embodied. It is theological. It is cultural. It is born of community, language, survival, creativity, and joy. Deaf culture does not ask for validation. It offers vision.

To be Deaf is not to lack something fundamental. It is to live differently, to communicate differently, to know God, self, and neighbor in ways that many have never imagined. It is not merely a culture to preserve. It is a witness to carry. It is a light the world needs but too often refuses to see.

This is the gift of Deaf culture. It is not marginal. It is not broken. It is not behind. It is human. It is sacred. It is mine. And it is God's words, as a part of His creation, "it is good."

I will never apologize for calling it good.

The Double Bind: Bicultural Exhaustion

To live as a Deaf person in a hearing world is to walk a tightrope across cultures. It is not a simple matter of moving between two languages. It is a constant act of recalibration—of reshaping yourself based on what is expected in each setting, of holding your body and your voice in tension, of adjusting how you show up in the world depending on who is watching. And eventually, that tension begins to take its toll.

This is the quiet exhaustion that those of us who live in the space between cultures know well. It is not the exhaustion of labor or of hardship in the traditional sense. It is the exhaustion of performance. It is the daily work of assessing every environment and deciding which version of yourself you will be allowed to bring into the room. It is not a question of language proficiency or confidence. It is a question of perceived belonging—and how much of your truth can be shared before it makes someone else uncomfortable.

Among hearing people, I learned very early that my ability to speak made them feel more at ease. If I used my voice, they forgot I was Deaf. If I laughed at the right moments, nodded on cue, and responded quickly, they assumed I had caught everything. For a long time, I let them assume. Not because I wanted to be deceptive, but because correcting them was exhausting. I knew what would happen if I asked someone to slow down or repeat themselves. Faces would tense. Smiles would fade. Conversations would stall. The social cost was rarely worth it.

So, I learned how to pass. I spoke clearly, often too clearly, with a rehearsed fluency that came from years of practice. But speech for me was not easy. It was not casual. It was labor. Speaking well did not mean I was comfortable. It meant I had become good at suppressing discomfort. I had learned how to make others feel at ease by quietly carrying the burden myself.

The praise I received from hearing people was never about my wholeness. It was about my usefulness. They liked that I could make their world easier to navigate. I heard compliments like, "You don't seem Deaf," or "You speak so well," and though they were intended to affirm, I began to understand what they were really saying. They were saying, "You are valuable because you are less like them and more like us." I was being celebrated not for who I was, but for how well I could hide it.

That realization did not come easily. For a long time, I believed the praise. I believed that the more I appeared, the more successful I had become. Over time, I began to feel the strain in my body. I noticed the mental fatigue that came from lip-reading for hours at a time. I began to recognize the ache in my spirit from being understood only when I erased part of myself.

Then came the other side of the equation.

Among Deaf peers, the tension was different but just as real. I was never judged for having speech. But I was sometimes questioned about how much I relied on it. I remember moments in Deaf spaces when people assumed I was hearing. Sometimes they would ask directly, "Are you really Deaf?" Other times, it came through the slight hesitation before engaging, the skepticism in their eyes when I spoke instead of signing, or the way conversations would drift away if my signing rhythm didn't match theirs.

I understood why. In the Deaf community, speech has often been a tool of control, a marker of assimilation, a boundary line that separates those who had access to Deaf education and culture from those who were pushed into mainstream settings and told to survive. Many of us carry deep wounds from being forced to speak when we would have rather signed, from being praised for abandoning our language, from being told that ASL was a barrier rather than a birthright.

So, when someone saw me speaking with ease, it was not just about communication. It was about trust. Would I choose voice over sign in Deaf space? Would I center hearing comfort over Deaf connection? Would I represent the culture, or would I quietly slip into the hearing world and leave it behind?

The irony is that I felt the most tension not when I failed to meet expectations, but when I met both sets of them too well. I could speak fluently and sign fluently. Instead of that, giving me full belonging in both spaces, it sometimes left me feeling like I truly belonged to neither. In hearing spaces, I was too Deaf to be fully understood. In Deaf spaces, I was too hearing in behavior to be fully trusted. I was always adjusting, always negotiating, always proving.

This is the nature of the double bind. When you live in between, your presence is often mistaken for indecision. Your identity is questioned because it does not fit neatly into one box. You are asked to explain yourself in ways others are never asked to explain. You are rewarded for blending in but punished for doing so too well. You are constantly weighing how much of yourself you can bring to the table without losing access to the table itself.

Over time, this dual performance—this code-switching of the body, the voice, and the heart—creates a kind of fracture. You begin to wonder where the real you went. You begin to lose sight of your center. And the grief sets in.

The grief is not for being Deaf. It never was.

The grief is for all the ways the world convinced me that my Deafness needed to be apologized for. It is grief for the compliments that made me feel small. It is grief for the assumptions that came with my voice. It is grief for the fatigue of always being "on," always performing, always translating myself into something someone else could understand.

No one ever looked me in the eyes and told me to be ashamed. They didn't have to. The world taught me that shame would make me more acceptable. It would smooth my edges. It would help me survive. Shame taught me to speak when I wanted to use sign language—taught me to smile when I was exhausted. Taught me to say, "I'm fine," when I was anything but.

I am learning to name that grief now. And in naming it, I am learning to release it.

I do not have to prove my Deafness to anyone. I do not have to abandon my voice to belong to the Deaf community. I do not have to abandon my hands to be respected in the hearing world. I am Deaf. I am bicultural. I am bilingual. I am not an in-between. I am a both-and. I belong not because I perform well, but because I exist with integrity.

I do not grieve my identity. I grieve in the ways others tried to make me doubt it.

I am done shrinking. I am done apologizing. I am done contorting myself into something small enough to fit someone else's imagination.

I speak. I sign. I belong.

I am not tired of being Deaf. I am tired of being made to feel like I should be.

Jesus and the Silenced

For much of my life, people assumed that if I believed in God, I must also believe God wanted to fix me. The logic was subtle but pervasive. If Deafness was a limitation, then surely the loving thing for God to do was to remove it. If I had faith—true, strong, unwavering faith—then perhaps I would be healed. Not healed of grief or trauma or injustice, but of Deafness itself. This assumption often came from good intentions, but it revealed something deeper and more dangerous: a theology that cannot imagine wholeness outside the framework of hearing.

This is the theological tension many Deaf people feel but rarely name. Scripture has been used to justify the idea that Deafness is a problem God intends to solve, a curse to be lifted, a condition to be pitied. If we are not careful, we risk reading the Gospels not as invitations into belonging but as blueprints for erasure. The ministry of Jesus does not support that interpretation. When we read the healing stories closely, when we listen not with the ears of empire but with the eyes of the marginalized, a different pattern emerges. One rooted not in correction, but in restoration.

In Mark's Gospel, chapter 7, Jesus encounters a man who is Deaf and who also has a speech impediment. He does not immediately heal the man. First, he draws him away from the crowd. This detail is often overlooked, but it is essential. Jesus refuses to turn the man into a public display. He does not center the curiosity of the crowd. He removes the man from the noise, from the eyes, from the pressure. He refuses to perform. In a world where disabled people are often reduced to spectacles or charity cases, Jesus chooses privacy and dignity.

What happens next is profoundly embodied. Jesus touches the man's ears. He spits and touches his tongue. He does not shout a command. He does not require the man to speak first. He meets him where he is, with the language of the body, a mode of communication that mirrors the visual, tactile, and gestural world many Deaf people live in every day. Then Jesus looks to heaven and says, "Ephphatha," which means, "Be opened."

This moment has long been interpreted as a traditional healing. To stop there is to miss its depth. "Be opened" is not only about the man's ears or his speech. It is about access. It is about restored communion. The man is not healed in order to become more acceptable to the crowd. He is healed in a way that centers his humanity. Jesus does not reject his identity. He affirms it. The man is not required to assimilate. He is restored to the community. The miracle is not that the man becomes less Deaf—it is that the barriers between him and others are removed.

When viewed through this lens, Jesus is not just the fixer of broken bodies. He is also the restorer of isolated people. He is the one who tears down the walls that society builds around the disabled, the marginalized, the silenced. The healing is not just physical. It is relational. It is communal. It is theological.

This is consistent with the broader arc of Scripture. In Isaiah 35, the prophet offers a vision of justice, a holy reversal of everything that has been withheld. He writes, "Then the eyes of the blind shall be opened, and the ears of the Deaf unstopped." For generations, this passage has been read as a promise that disability will be erased in the coming Kingdom. But Isaiah's message is not about conformity. It is about liberation.

To say that the ears of the Deaf shall be unstopped is not to imply that Deafness itself is a curse. Rather, it is to proclaim that the systems and structures that silence, isolate, and oppress will be torn down. It is a vision of inclusion, of fullness, of justice. Deaf people will no longer be excluded from the temple, from the table, or from the conversation. What is unstopped is not just sound—it is dignity. It belongs. It is access to the holy.

This is where the heart of liberative theology begins. It begins with the belief that God is not standing apart from those who have been marginalized. God is standing with us. Not in condescension, not as a fixer, but as a co-sufferer and liberator. The God revealed in Jesus Christ is not neutral in the face of injustice. He is not indifferent to exclusion. He is the one who steps across boundaries, who violates purity codes, who heals on the Sabbath, who listens when others talk over, who sees when others pass by, who touches when others recoil.

Jesus does not merely restore function. He restores personhood.

That is the heart of the Gospel for Deaf people—not a promise of hearing, but a promise of being heard. Not a correction of identity, but a celebration of embodiment. Not a command to blend in, but a call to rise up.

I do not need to be cured to be whole. I do not need to be fixed to be faithful. I do not need to speak to be heard by God. My Deafness is not a mistake. It is not a detour on the way to divine purpose. It is a witness. It is a way of perceiving truth. It is a theology of attentiveness. It is a call to deeper presence.

When Jesus says, "Be opened," I believe he is still speaking—not to our bodies, but to the systems that silence us. To the churches that exclude us. To the theologies that pity us. To the imaginations that cannot conceive of holiness without sound.

He is speaking to the pulpit that assumes God's voice must always be loud. To the pews that never learned to sign. To the teachers who only face forward. To the ministers who pray for healing without ever asking what healing means.

"Be opened," he says.

Open your eyes to the prophets in your midst who speak with their hands. Open your ears to the wisdom carried in silence. Open your theology to the God who does not erase difference but dwells within it. Open your imagination to the possibility that the Spirit moves not despite Deafness, but through it.

This is the theological frame I now live in—not one of shame or repair, but one of reverence.

I do not worship a God who asks me to pretend. I worship a God who knows what it means to be silenced. I follow a Christ who entered the world not with fanfare but through flesh, who listened to the cries that others ignored, who spoke in ways only the humble could understand.

When Jesus said, "Be opened," he was not just talking to the Deaf. He was talking to the whole world.

Understanding All Margins

I remember the uneasy glances when I used my voice in Deaf spaces and the slow confusion when I signed in hearing ones. Over time, I realized those moments were not about me alone. They revealed something larger—something that was never truly about my ears. It was about a world that remains deeply uncomfortable with difference.

What was expected of me was not understanding, but adjustment. If I could translate myself into something easier to manage, then I would be more acceptable. But that pressure was never just mine to carry. It belonged to a broader system that constantly pushes people to conform—not out of love, but out of fear. It says, You may be welcome here, but only if you are willing to become a little less of who you are.

Once I began to recognize that pattern in my own life, I started seeing it everywhere. I saw it in the lives of Black colleagues who were praised for their professionalism only after changing how they spoke. I saw it in women who were told they were too strong to lead and too emotional to follow. I saw it in LGBTQIA+ siblings who were told to come as they are, but also to keep quiet about it. I saw it in people with mental illness who were encouraged to be honest, but only when their honesty did not disrupt someone else's comfort.

What connects all of these experiences? It is a deep and often unspoken expectation—one that stretches across race, ability, gender, and identity. This expectation is not limited to one group. It is a cultural habit. It is a theology of conditional love, a social contract in which authenticity must be traded for access. It rarely announces itself with hostility. Instead, it arrives in polite language, in carefully worded policies, in sermons that welcome everyone but never imagine everyone's full humanity in return.

Audism—the belief in the superiority of hearing and speech—was my doorway into understanding this deeper reality. What I experienced through the lens of Deafness turned out to be just one facet of a much larger system. Audism, like racism or sexism, or ableism, is not merely about individual bias. It is a structure that rewards closeness to a dominant norm and punishes any form of difference that challenges it.

This is why I say Deafness became a mirror. It allowed me to see how the world deals with difference, not just in my own life, but in the lives of so many others. It showed me how quickly we are taught to shrink, how often belonging is offered only to those who are willing to soften the parts of themselves that make others uncomfortable. It helped me understand how systems of exclusion disguise themselves as hospitality, how silence is confused with peace, and how performance is mistaken for participation.

Scripture tells us that all people are made in the image of God. That truth is not small. It is revolutionary. The divine image is not a single reflection, but a mosaic of identities, cultures, languages, and bodies. When we ask someone to erase their difference to be loved, we are not only doing harm to them. We are obscuring the image of God itself. That is not simply injustice. It is a theological error.

The creation account in Genesis does not say, "Let me make humanity in my image." It says, "Let us make humanity in our image." The language is plural. The image is relational. The fullness of God's likeness is found not in sameness, but in the sacred diversity of creation. To suppress that diversity is to build walls where God has built a table.

Jesus understood this. He did not require people to change before they were welcomed. He saw them, named them, healed them, and restored them without condition. When the woman touched the hem of his garment, he did not demand that she explain her worth. He turned to her and called her "Daughter." When Zacchaeus climbed down from the tree, Jesus did not ask him to fix his past before coming to dinner. He simply said, "I'm coming to your house today." His ministry was not about making people fit in. It was about bringing people home.

Deafness has helped me see the Gospel more clearly, not as a call to conformity, but as an invitation to communion. It has trained me to ask not only who is in the room, but who had to change themselves to be let in. It has made me sensitive to whose voices are missing, whose stories have not been told, and whose presence has been tolerated but never celebrated.

This clarity is not a burden. It is a gift. It is a prophetic responsibility.

Solidarity does not mean speaking for others. It means standing with them. It is not about charity or pity. It is about shared humanity. It is about equity. It is about understanding that if the system requires people to become smaller in order to be loved, then the system itself must be transformed.

Transformation begins with listening. Not the kind of listening that waits for its turn to speak, but the kind of listening that is willing to be changed. The kind that does not flinch when it encounters discomfort. The kind that honors silence, not because nothing is being said, but because something sacred is waiting to be heard.

This is why I ask, again and again: what if the problem is not that some people cannot hear—but that others refuse to listen?

This is not just a philosophical question. It is a pastoral one. It is a question for the Church, for the classroom, for the dinner table, for the pulpit. It is a question for every place where welcome is spoken aloud but never examined closely. And it is a question I carry with me into every space I enter.

Deafness has taught me to live in that question without rushing to answer it. It has taught me that God speaks through those the world overlooks. It has shown me that silence is not absence, but attention. It has reminded me that justice is not theoretical. It is relational. It begins when we stop demanding that others change in order to be seen.

I no longer carry the need to justify my identity. I carry the calling to witness—witness to the Gospel that breaks down every dividing wall, witness to the image of God in every body, and witness to the sacred truth that difference is not a problem to be solved. It is a revelation to be received.

When we begin to see that, we begin to listen not only with our ears, but with our lives. And in that listening, we finally begin to hear the sound of freedom.

Reclaiming Sacred Silence

For much of my life, people assumed that silence was a void—something empty, something missing, something broken. They imagined that because I am Deaf, I must live inside that void, distant from music, from connection, from God. They saw my world through the lens of their own fears about quiet. But their silence is not my silence.

The silence I know is not an absence. It is a presence. It does not come to erase meaning but to reveal it. It is not blank space—it is holy ground.

I love music. I always have. But I do not experience it the way most hearing people do. I feel it through vibration, through rhythm, through movement. I sense it in the floorboards of sanctuaries, in the pulse of a drum, in the breath between beats. I see it in the raised arms of worshippers, in the hands of a choir singing the words they cannot sing, in the body's response to a truth that cannot be explained. Music for me lives in flesh and feeling. It does not pass through my ears. It travels through my bones.

There are songs I have never heard in the traditional sense, yet I know them more intimately than some who can recite every lyric. I have watched worship in American Sign Language where the Spirit moved not through sound, but through story written in the air. I remember the first time I saw someone sing a hymn. Every motion was an offering. Every pause was a prayer. The silence in the room was not emptiness. It was reverence.

This kind of silence makes space for music to be felt, not just heard. In Deaf culture, silence and music are not opposites. They are partners. They both require presence. They both require attentiveness. They both rely on the body to carry what words cannot. What many people call silence is often just a deeper kind of listening.

That silence has shaped every part of my life. It has formed my ministry, not by limiting what I can say, but by teaching me when not to speak. It has trained me to see emotion in the face before it finds the voice. It has taught me that the holiest moments are often the quietest. I have stood at the edge of hospital beds where nothing needed to be said, and the silence wrapped around us like a sanctuary. I have sat in pews where no words were spoken, and yet God's presence was undeniable.

Silence like that cannot be forced. It cannot be manufactured. It must be received. It is a gift. And it is one I no longer resist.

There was a time when I thought my Deafness was something I needed to overcome in order to live out my calling. I thought my voice had to sound a certain way to be respected, that I had to prove my belonging in rooms built for others. But I no longer believe that. My Deafness is not a barrier. It is the doorway. It is not the absence of sound. It is the presence of a deeper sound. It is not the thing I had to rise above. It is the ground that taught me how to stand.

The threshold between silence and sound is no longer a place of confusion for me. It is where I pray. It is where I preach. It is where I live. It is where God meets me again and again—not in the noise, but in the quiet underneath it.

Scripture affirms this sacred quiet. When the prophet Elijah looked for God, he did not find God in the fire, or the earthquake, or the wind. God was not in the spectacle. God was in the stillness. The sound of sheer silence—that was where the voice of the Lord was found. Saint John of the Cross called this the dark night of the soul. Julian of Norwich wrote of a silence so filled with presence that it held the whole universe in the palm of a hazel nut. This is the company I keep. These are the echoes I trust.

Silence, for me, is not a retreat from the world. It is a return to the truth. It is the place where trauma softens, where grief breathes, where God waits. I no longer run from silence. I rest in it. I no longer fear it. I follow it.

I no longer see my Deafness as the thing I must explain to be understood. I see it as the lens through which I understand what others miss. I see it as the language through which God continues to speak. I see it as a sacred inheritance—not a flaw to fix, but a calling to carry.

I do not shrink from Deafness. I rise through it.

I do not perform for belonging. I belong by birthright.

I do not hear as others hear. But I hear what others forget to notice.

I do not live in the absence of sound. I live in the presence of attention.

I do not need to be cured. I am already whole.

I live on the threshold between silence and sound. And I know now—that threshold is holy.

I am Deaf, and I am whole.

I am Deaf, and I am called.

I am Deaf—and that does not limit my life.

Being Deaf illuminates my story.

CHAPTER 7

The Classroom of Inequality

The first time I sensed something wasn't fair, I didn't know how to describe it. I didn't know the words for it yet. I couldn't explain systemic racism or academic tracking, or educational neglect. I only knew that the room felt different. The difference wasn't just the desks or the walls. It was in the way we were seen.

This was my Self-contained classroom. A room designed for students like me, who didn't learn the way the school expected. I had speech delays and hearing loss. I was Deaf. I was labeled "learning disabled" and shuffled into a space they said would help. But even then, I knew there was more to the story. It was not until I was an adult that I was diagnosed with ADHD-Autism.

The students in that room were almost all Black or Brown. I was one of the only white kids. No one explained why that was. No one pointed it out. It was obvious. It didn't feel right. All the smart kids classes were predominantly white and well equipped, even in the same school.

The classrooms I found myself in were usually tucked in the back of the school. It wasn't decorated like the other rooms, and oftentimes resembled more of a closet than a room. The carpet was worn. The lights flickered and buzzed. The teachers seemed tired before the day even started. There were old workbooks stacked in cracked bins. Motivational posters were peeling off the walls. It didn't feel like a place built for success. It felt like a place where hope had been slowly drained out over time.

What struck me wasn't just the appearance of the room. It was how the students were treated inside it. The tone used with some of my classmates was sharp and cold. Some teachers would yell without hesitation. Instructions came with warnings instead of encouragement. When I messed up, they would crouch next to me and speak gently. When the Black boys in the room made the same mistake, they were shouted at and sent to the hallway.

One student I remember clearly was Rayvon. He was smart, quick on his feet, and full of potential. I knew this because we played football together, but the way the teachers treated him made it seem like he was dangerous. He would ask questions and get punished. He would react to unfair treatment and be labeled disrespectful. I could speak up and be heard. He could speak up and be silenced.

At the time, I didn't have the tools to name what I was seeing. I didn't know about school discipline data or the history of racial segregation in special education. I didn't know that Black students with disabilities were more likely to be suspended, expelled, or referred to law enforcement than anyone else. I didn't know how decisions made long before we were born had shaped which kids ended up in which classrooms.

I knew something wasn't right, even as a child.

This wasn't just about me and my struggles. It was about who was allowed to struggle and still be treated with care, and who was expected to behave like an adult before they even had a chance to be a child. It was about how people reacted when a white student didn't understand a lesson compared to when a Black student didn't. It was about who they believed could improve and who they believed was already a lost cause.

That classroom taught me more than any curriculum they handed out. It taught me how injustice can become invisible when it looks like routine. It taught me that some systems are not broken by accident. They are working the way they were designed. It taught me that even when I was struggling, I still had access to mercy that others didn't.

It also taught me to pay attention. Not just to what was said, but to what was allowed. Not just to what happened to me, but to what happened around me.

Years later, I would come to understand the deep history behind it all. The desegregation orders were never fully followed. The way special education was often used as a way to separate students by race without saying it out loud. The way poverty, disability, and race intersected created a pattern that too many people refused to see. I would learn that these patterns weren't unique to my school. They were common all over the country.

Even before I learned the history, I felt the weight of it.

I didn't grow up in a time when people talked openly about this. My parents didn't use words like "equity" at the dinner table. The church didn't preach sermons about racial justice. The schools didn't give us lessons on bias. But I knew that something was wrong because I lived in the middle of it.

I never forgot those rooms.

It was the first time I saw the cracks in the system up close. Not through statistics, but through faces. Not through lectures, but through silence. That silence stayed with me. It stayed with me when I sat in church pews where nobody mentioned injustice. It stayed with me when I watched some friends get pushed out of school while others got pulled along. It stayed with me when I began to ask myself what kind of man I wanted to become.

I was a white Deaf kid. I knew what it felt like to be misunderstood, to be seen as broken. But I also knew what it felt like to be protected by my skin color in ways my classmates were not. That truth is hard to carry. Nonetheless, it is necessary.

That classroom was not just a memory. It was a mirror. It showed me the cost of silence. And from that silence, something began to grow. A desire to listen more deeply. A refusal to look away. A call to name what I had once been afraid to see. This was where the work began.

The Brotherhood of Friendship

I didn't just grow up near Black and Brown friends. I grew up with them. On the same streets, in the same locker rooms, under the same relentless sun. We shared meals, jokes, music, bruises, and dreams. These weren't acquaintances. They were brothers. Not by blood, but by sweat, struggle, and sacred trust. They taught me how to fight and how to forgive. They showed me how to carry pain without breaking. They never said it aloud, but they lived like people who knew the world didn't offer second chances. And they loved me like someone worth keeping around anyway.

I was Deaf, white, and came from a working-poor family. I didn't fit in anywhere, but with them, I belonged. They didn't just make room for me. They made space for me to be myself. The more I look back, the more I understand how rare and holy that welcome was. In a world where Black boys are judged before they are seen, where suspicion meets them at every corner, welcoming a white friend is not just kindness. It is a risk.

We grew up inside broken systems. Public schools that talked about fairness but practiced something else entirely. We all saw it. We knew who got suspended faster. We knew who got followed in stores. We knew who got second chances and who didn't. We also learned how to survive it. And when the weight was too much, we turned to music.

Not just background noise. This music was the heartbeat of our lives. It gave rhythm to the rage, language to the sorrow, and breath to the hope we carried in silence.

N.W.A. wasn't just rebellious. They were prophets. Their songs didn't invent violence. They exposed it. When I first heard "F*** tha Police," I didn't understand. I had been raised to believe that if you followed the rules, you would be fine. My friends were raised to survive. They were taught how to speak softly when a badge was near. They were taught not to run, not to reach, not to resist. The song wasn't about hate. It was about truth. It was about telling the world what it means to be hunted for simply being who you are.

Then there was Tupac, a personal favorite. Although I cannot recite lyrics. He didn't just make music. He testified. He told the truth with fire in his voice and poetry in his pain. One moment, he was raging against injustice, and the next, he was whispering love to the mothers who held the family together. "Dear Mama" wasn't just a tribute. It was a prayer. "Changes" wasn't just a hit. It was a prophecy. Tupac gave us words for things we didn't yet know how to say. Through him, I began to understand that this music wasn't just entertainment. It was survival. It was sacred.

Black music wasn't limited to America. It reached across oceans and generations.

I remember the first time I heard Bob Marley in a way that changed me. We were in someone's backyard. The speaker was small, and the air smelled like charcoal and citronella. The song was "Redemption Song." I didn't know every word, but I felt its weight. "Emancipate yourselves from mental slavery. None but ourselves can free our minds." That line landed like a truth I had been waiting to hear my whole life. Marley wasn't singing for applause. He was singing to wake people up. His music came from people who had endured slavery, colonization, and exile. It didn't sound defeated. It sounded free.

What I didn't understand then, but see now, is that every genre they shared with me had been born out of struggle. Spirituals were maps to freedom. Blues was the sound of survival. Jazz was defiance in the key of improvisation. The Gospel was the sound of hope in the dark. Hip-hop was a raised fist and a raised voice when no one else was listening. None of it was accidental. It was intentional. It was powerful. It was an inherited strength turned into sound.

They shared it. Not as a trophy, but as a gift. They didn't let me just listen. They taught me to hear. They didn't ask me to explain myself. They asked me to show up. They didn't ask me to change who I was. They asked me to stop pretending I didn't see what they carried every single day.

Then came the night I can still feel in my bones.

We had just left a party. The music had been loud and bumping. The air is thick with laughter. Lionel, my best friend, offered to drive. We had met in my senior year. He was in college already. We connected over lifting weights and talking trash, the way guys do when they've both learned to smile through pain. He was strong, soft-spoken, steady, a giant of a man with an even bigger heart. The kind of person who made people feel safe just by being in the room.

The car was full. Six of us squeezed into the seats, still riding the high from the night. Kid Cudi played through the speakers. I was the only white guy in the car, though I hadn't even noticed. We were just people. Friends. Then the blue lights hit.

No siren. Just silence.

The car went still.

Lionel turned the volume down. His hands went to the steering wheel. He straightened his posture. No one moved. No one joked. No one reached for a phone.

The officer came to Lionel's window, flashlight first, eyes sharp. He looked right past me. Did not even address me. I was invisible. All his questions were for Lionel and the other friends in the car, coincidentally all black. Where were we coming from? Who owned the car? Did everyone have an ID?

Lionel answered clearly. Calm. Careful. The officer didn't say much. He didn't explain himself. He just looked, then walked back to his cruiser. When the lights disappeared, I let out a breath I didn't know I was holding. I turned to Lionel and said, "Man, you handled that like a pro." He didn't smile. He didn't speak for a moment.

Then he said, "I've been practicing since I was twelve."

That moment never left me.

I had never practiced how to stay alive during a traffic stop. I had never been told where to place my hands. I had never been warned about the danger of being misunderstood. I listened to the same songs, went to the same parties, and walked the same hallways. But I had never carried that fear.

Even when I was with them, I wasn't one of them. Even when I did not understand and even when I had not truly begun to unpack my own prejudices and biases, they still loved me.

They still let me in.

They never asked for my guilt. They asked for my honesty. They never demanded my shame. They demanded my witness. They shared their culture with me and then waited to see what I would do with the truth.

I could love the music. However, if I was going to love the people who made it, I had to carry the weight of what it meant. I had to stop pretending that being close to pain was the same as carrying it.

The brotherhood didn't change the color of my skin. But it changed the way I saw the world. It made me more human. It made me more accountable. It made me less willing to settle for silence.

I will carry that truth for the rest of my life.

Deafness and Whiteness: Double Layers

Growing up Deaf, I learned early what it felt like to be excluded. I remember sitting in classrooms where my body was present, but my presence was not. Teachers spoke too fast or turned their backs when writing on the board. Classmates laughed at jokes I didn't catch. School assemblies echoed with words I could not follow, while the lights buzzed and the crowd murmured. It was as though I lived in a world wrapped in glass, always seeing, never fully touching. And every time someone said, "Never mind," or waved off my confusion, I learned a little more about the architecture of silence. I was not just left out. I was left behind.

Even in the isolation of Deafness, I was not without privilege. Because I was also white.

That realization did not come quickly. In fact, for a long time, I did not realize it at all. I thought suffering was a shared experience. I thought the pain I carried made me closer to everyone who had ever been marginalized. I believed that because I knew what it felt like to be overlooked, I must understand what others were facing. But the truth is more complicated. Pain may be universal, but power is not.

In the very same classrooms where I was ignored, my Black classmates were punished. I struggled to keep up with verbal instructions. They did too. But when I asked for help, I was given a patient response or extra time. When they did, they were scolded for not paying attention. I was seen as a student with potential who just needed support. They were seen as distractions. I was the quiet, misunderstood kid. They were the loud, disrespectful ones. We had the same paperwork. The same IEPs. The same invisible battles. But the system did not see us the same.

It was not just the teachers. It was the way school security watched them more closely. The way adults spoke about them instead of to them. The way white classmates clutched their bags a little tighter when a Black boy walked behind them in the hallway, even if he was wearing the same school hoodie I was.

I began to realize that I was not just surviving injustice. I was also being protected by its boundaries.

That is not an easy thing to admit. Because I wanted to believe I was one of the good ones. I wanted to believe that my own pain gave me clarity. But my whiteness gave me something else. Access. Trust. Safety. A pass.

Even as I felt left out, I was still being let in.

Slowly, painfully, I had to face the truth that while my Deafness marginalized me in many ways, my whiteness insulated me from the full weight of oppression that my Black friends carried. I was navigating a world not built for me, but it still was not built against me.

That distinction matters.

I had to unlearn a lot. I had to look back at the moments I did not question. The moments I was treated kindly, while my friends were treated harshly. The times I believed a teacher's explanation about bad behavior without asking what really happened. The laughter I joined in when a joke was made about someone's neighborhood. The fear I never had to feel when I walked down the street in a hoodie.

I had to confront the fact that racism is not always loud. Sometimes it is polite. Sometimes it is subtle. Sometimes it is a raised eyebrow, a lowered voice, a missed opportunity, or a double standard. Sometimes it is just silence.

That silence lives in us. It lived in me.

My Deafness gave me access to silence in one way. But my whiteness gave me access to be heard in another. And I began to realize how deeply dangerous it is to confuse empathy with equivalence. Just because I had been silenced did not mean I understood what it was like to be feared. Just because I had been excluded did not mean I understood what it meant to be criminalized.

I began to notice how people leaned toward me in conversations, how they trusted my words. I started noticing the invisible currency of whiteness. How could I walk into a store without suspicion? How could I speak up in meetings and be affirmed? How could I make mistakes and still be offered grace? My friends did not get that. Not because they lacked discipline or intelligence or charisma. But because they were not white.

Even in the Deaf community, those layers played out. I learned about Black American Sign Language. It's powerful expressiveness. It's cultural rhythm. Its roots are in segregated Deaf schools where Black students were denied access to the education white Deaf students received. I learned how those divisions shaped not just language, but opportunity, access, and identity. I heard stories of Black Deaf friends who had to fight for interpreters, for jobs, for inclusion, in ways I never had to.

I began to understand that my identity sat at an intersection. Not of equal suffering, but of layered truth. I had felt left out. But I had also been let in. And in a world where whiteness often opens doors and Deafness often closes them. I had to reckon with the ways those forces collided inside me.

One moment in particular still echoes in my memory.

The full story lives earlier in this chapter. The late-night ride home. The party. The flashing blue lights. Lionel is in the driver's seat, calm and still. Me in the passenger seat, shielded without trying. The officer looked past me and straight at him. The moment passed, but the meaning never left.

That night taught me something my Deafness never could. What it means to be watched not for help, but for harm. What it means to be seen as dangerous before you say a word. What it means to survive a moment not because of anything you did right, but because of who you were sitting next to—and who you were not.

I had always known what it felt like to be silenced. But I was only beginning to understand what it meant to be listened to when others were not.

That realization broke something open in me.

I began to see how easy it is to mistake shared pain for shared experience. I began to see how dangerous it is to speak over stories I was only beginning to understand. I began to realize that my role was not to center myself, but to stand beside. To listen. To learn. To tell the truth. Not just about what had happened to me, but about what I had seen happen to others.

So I speak now not to equalize oppression, but to expose it. Not to claim sameness, but to claim responsibility.

I am Deaf. I am white. I live in that tension every day.

The only way I know to live in it faithfully is to stay awake to it. To stay honest about it. To say the names of those who are still being silenced. To name the systems that still treat Black children like criminals and white children like late bloomers. To stop making excuses for inequality and start telling the truth about how it works.

While not all oppression is equal, all oppression is real.

No matter how different our stories are, we are bound by one truth. Silence helps no one. Only truth sets us free.

The White Church and the Sin of Silence

I grew up in churches that taught the Bible as the highest authority. We memorized verses, studied the letters in red, held hands in prayer circles, and spoke earnestly about salvation. The altar was always open. The worship music stirred the soul. And for a long time, I believed that made us faithful. I believed it meant we were righteous. But the older I got, the more I noticed something missing. Something loud in its absence. Something we refused to name.

We did not talk about race.

Not in sermons. Not in Sunday school. Not in small groups or prayer meetings. Not when another Black child was killed on the news. Not when white nationalists marched through Charlottesville. Not when Black communities pleaded for justice after another police shooting. We might offer a moment of silence or a vague prayer for peace. But we did not name the sin. We did not name ourselves. We did not confess.

I began to understand that silence is not neutral. Silence is not safe. Silence is a decision.

Sunday became, for me, the most segregated day of the week. Not only in the color of the congregation, but in the kinds of truths we were willing to tell. The white churches I knew were filled with people who loved God and tried to live good lives. But when it came to race, we chose comfort over honesty. We avoided hard conversations not because of overt hatred, but because of spiritual cowardice. Because once you tell the truth about injustice, you become responsible for responding to it.

We preached love but refused to name pain. We sang about grace while staying silent about inequality. We talked about heaven while avoiding the hell that many of our Black brothers and sisters were living through on earth.

I remember sitting in a Bible study when someone quietly asked why the church had not spoken about the police shooting that had rocked the nation that week. The room froze. People shifted in their chairs. Eyes darted to the floor. The leader responded, "We are all God's children," and moved on. No lament. No listening. Just polite evasion.

The silence said more than words ever could.

As I grew more aware, I began to notice not only the absence of conversation but the disparity in resources. Predominantly white churches in our area had multi-million-dollar buildings, full-time staff, advanced sound systems, and robust youth ministries. Many of the Black churches I visited had one bi-vocational pastor serving three small congregations, no secretary, and an outdated furnace. Their choirs sang with fire. Their preaching thundered with power. But the financial support was threadbare. These churches were doing more ministry with less support, serving more needs with fewer resources.

This was not a coincidence. It was the result of generations of systemic inequality.

The Black Church in America was not created out of preference. It was born out of rejection. In the late 1700s, Richard Allen and Absalom Jones were pulled from their knees while praying in a Methodist church simply because they were Black. That moment gave birth to the African Methodist Episcopal Church. It was not a schism of style. It was a cry for dignity. A declaration that Black people deserved to worship in freedom, without being treated as second-class believers.

From its beginning, the Black Church became more than a sanctuary. It became a schoolhouse, a political meeting place, a counseling center, and a refuge. It was the first institution fully controlled by Black people in this country. It preserved culture. It fostered education. It provided food, shelter, and hope. And it did all this while being systemically excluded from the economic advantages extended to white churches.

Black pastors have long been underpaid, overworked, and under-resourced. They have been responsible not only for sermons, but for funerals, crisis response, food distribution, mentoring youth, fighting for justice, and comforting a grieving people. Still, denominational budgets continue to reward larger, wealthier white churches with discretionary funds and development grants. Meanwhile, Black churches struggle to keep the roof from leaking and the pastor from burning out.

Even in predominantly white denominations, Black clergy are routinely passed over for prominent appointments. They are asked to preach but not lead. They are praised from the stage but left out of the planning room. This is not just about income. It is about power. It is about access. It is about who is trusted to lead and who is told to wait.

Still, Black Christians show up.

They continue to serve in white-majority churches. They continue to preach, to sing, to mentor, to give. They keep showing up with faith that humbles me. They keep trusting God even when the people of God remain untrustworthy. They show up in places that do not honor their pain or their history. They pour themselves into churches where their concerns are minimized. They do it not because they are welcome, but because they are faithful.

That is a miracle.

It is also a mirror. Their faithfulness reveals the deep unfaithfulness of the white Church. Their persistence unmasks our fragility. Their strength exposes our avoidance. Their love for God puts to shame our unwillingness to confront the systems that distort His name.

As I watched and listened, I began to feel the weight of responsibility. I could no longer ignore the gap between what I preached and what the Church practiced. I could not talk about the body of Christ and stay silent while part of that body bled out from neglect. I could not claim to follow Jesus while refusing to name the suffering inflicted by the systems I had benefited from.

Structural sin is not just about individual bigotry. It is about the systems that good people uphold through inaction. It is about the budgets, the boardrooms, the bylaws, and the blind spots. It is about who gets hired and who gets tokenized. It is about whose stories are celebrated and whose suffering is ignored. It is about how we fund missions overseas while failing to fund equity at home.

If the Church is to be the Church, we must tell the truth.

We must say that the white Church helped build systems that continue to disadvantage Black churches. We must say that while white pastors are given sabbaticals, housing allowances, and multi-staff support, many Black pastors are struggling to stay healthy and paid. We must say that silence is not an oversight. It is a strategy. One that has protected white comfort at the cost of Black dignity.

This is not about guilt. This is about responsibility. The Church should be the first to confess, not the last. The Church should be a place of truth-telling, not truth-burying.

And so I write this not from a place of blame, but from a place of deep conviction. I love the Church. I believe in her potential. I believe in her people. But love without truth is just sentiment. And I cannot love the Church while hiding from her sins. I cannot serve the body while pretending the wounds do not exist.

Let us be the Church that confesses. Let us be the Church that listens. Let us be the Church that repents not just with words, but with budgets, with policies, and with power-sharing. Let us become the Church where Black leaders are honored, where Black congregations are supported, and where Black pain is met with holy response.

This is what resurrection looks like. Not just the raising of the individual soul, but the restoration of what has been broken. If we believe that the tomb is empty, then we must also believe that systems of death can be undone.

Let it begin with the Church.

Let it begin with us.

The Prophetic Call: From Comfort to Confession

Grief is the preface to unspoken guilt. A grief I could not quite name at first, but felt in my bones when I looked at the headlines, when I sat in rooms where Black and Brown voices were diminished, when I stood in pulpits that had never grieved the loss of a single Black body in the news. A grief that settled in when I realized that some of the most faithful Christians I knew were also the most silent about injustice. And that I had been one of them.

Then Scripture began to break me open.

Not the verses about blessings or personal salvation. Not the ones printed on greeting cards or graduation banners. It was the prophets who undid me—Isaiah, Amos, Micah. It was the words that most of my white faith upbringing had skimmed over, words that sounded too political, too uncomfortable, too angry. But once I let them speak, I couldn't unhear them.

Isaiah declared that God was tired of our songs, weary of our worship, disgusted by our sacrifices when they were disconnected from justice. He did not say to pray harder. He said to loose the chains of injustice, to feed the hungry, to bring the poor into our homes, to clothe the naked, to stop hiding from our own flesh. Micah stood on the witness stand of heaven and said that God was not impressed by burnt offerings or ten thousand rivers of oil.

What God wanted was justice, mercy, and humility. Not ritual. Not performance. Righteousness. Relationships. Repair.

The book of Amos, Amos lit a fire in me that I could not extinguish. He spoke to people who thought their prosperity was proof of God's favor, who confused religious ritual with divine approval. "I hate, I despise your feasts," God said through him. "Take away from me the noise of your songs." And then the cry that has echoed through every movement for justice since: "Let justice roll down like waters, and righteousness like an ever-flowing stream."

These were not poetic flourishes. They were indictments. They were divine demands. And they confronted me with the terrifying truth that God does not inhabit all worship. That some worship offends Him because it refuses to confront the sin in the room.

Jesus confirmed that truth in His own body. He did not simply go from village to village preaching personal salvation. He disrupted systems. He touched lepers, welcomed outcasts, challenged religious authorities, and drove exploiters from the temple. That act—the flipping of tables—is not just a symbolic flourish in the Gospel story. It was a political, spiritual, and economic disruption. The tables He overturned were not neutral furniture. They were instruments of exclusion. Set up in the Court of the Gentiles, they pushed out the very people the temple was meant to welcome. And Jesus, the Son of God, responded not with a sermon, but with a whip. Not with a smile, but with righteous fury.

That image haunted me. I realized I had spent most of my life keeping the temple neat. I had organized programs, written liturgies, raised funds, and tried to keep things running smoothly—

while people were being priced out of the courts of grace. While Black and Brown believers sat in pews that never acknowledged their pain. While wealth replaced welcome. While quiet replaced truth.

Then came the vision from Revelation. The one I had often quoted, often admired. Every tribe, every tongue, every nation gathered in worship before the throne. I had imagined it as unity. But now I saw that it was something deeper. It was liberation. Not a choir where everyone sings the same song in the same key, but a redeemed gathering where every story, every language, every culture, every scar is honored and healed. This is not assimilation. This is resurrection.

That vision broke me. And then it began to rebuild me.

As a white man—even one who had known the pain of exclusion because of my Deafness—I could not claim prophetic authority without first entering into prophetic repentance. Not the kind that weeps and wails for applause. The kind that costs something. The kind that re-sees the world and refuses to look away, no matter how uncomfortable and shattering. The kind that steps off the stage and into the street, not to lead, but to listen.

I had to confront the ways I had centered myself. I had to surrender my need to be the one with answers. I had to lay down the instinct to explain, to moderate, to soften the truth. And I had to stop asking to be seen as an ally and start asking myself where I had failed as a follower of Christ.

That is when I began to understand the call to repair.

Repair is not a concept. It is a command. Scripture is clear. In the law of Moses, if you stole something, you returned it with interest. If you caused harm, you made restitution. Zacchaeus understood this when Jesus came to his house. His salvation was not a private prayer. It was a public commitment to restore what he had taken. Fourfold. Because justice requires more than confession. It requires correction.

In the Black prophetic tradition, repair has always been about more than money. It is about memory. It is about voice. It is about the reordering of power. It means that white Christians must listen—truly listen—to the stories of those we have ignored. It means we must cede space—surrender the stage, the spotlight, the center of the conversation. It means we must use whatever privilege we have not to protect our comfort, but to protect others from the systems that comfort has built.

This is not theoretical. I have seen Black pastors dismissed, disrespected, and disempowered in rooms where I was treated with honor for doing less work. I have watched white churches raise half a million dollars for a building campaign but send leftover furniture to Black congregations who had already been doing more ministry with less. I have stood in denominational meetings where "diversity" was a checkbox but not a value, where Black leaders were asked to share their stories but not given the authority to shape decisions.

Still, Black Believers showed up. They show up with grace and grit. They show up with sermons and songs and faith that makes the ground tremble. They show up in spaces that have tried to erase them, and they lead with the kind of integrity that can only come from generations of surviving betrayal.

If I have any calling in this moment, it is not to explain them. It is to stand beside them. To follow their lead. To tell the truth about the systems I have benefited from. To give up the seats I was handed without earning. To spend my life making space for the justice I once avoided.

This prophetic call is not a phase. It is not a sermon series. It is the way of Jesus.

It is the sound of tables falling and voices rising. It is the sound of weeping mothers and roaring ancestors. It is the sound of the Gospel when it refuses to be domesticated.

It is not enough to be grieved. We must be changed.

Let justice roll. Not as a metaphor. Not as poetry. As a flood that washes away comfort and baptizes the Church into the power of repair.

Lessons from the Margins

There are things the margins teach you that the center cannot. These lessons are not offered in polished classrooms or credentialed lectures. They are passed down through presence. Through pain. Through friendship. They are taught in the quiet strength of those who have lived through more than most people will ever understand. My friends—mostly Black and Brown—were my first teachers in this kind of knowledge. They showed me a faith that breathes in sorrow and sings through struggle.

From them, I learned what resilience looks like when no one is watching. Not the kind celebrated in media campaigns or success stories, but the kind that gets up every morning under the weight of injustice and still offers kindness. I learned rhythm—the ability to live with depth and movement, to laugh even while lamenting, to worship with joy while carrying grief. I learned resistance—not in loud declarations, but in the quiet decision to stay. To show up in churches that often ignored their truth. To survive in schools and systems that tried to erase them. To remain faithful to a God whose people had so often failed them.

They showed me Jesus—not the domesticated figure I'd grown up with, but the real One. The One born under an empire. The One who knew poverty. The One who was hunted, betrayed, arrested without cause, and murdered by the state. The One who refused to stay silent when silence would have kept Him safe. They showed me the Jesus who walks with those who carry chains. Who bleeds with the broken. Who sees George Floyd not as a symbol, but as a son. Who knows Breonna Taylor not as a headline, but as His beloved. Who recognizes Trayvon Martin not as a threat, but as a teenager carrying Skittles and God's image.

In Scripture, when God sees, God acts. "God heard their groaning and remembered His covenant." God's memory moves mountains. God's remembrance parts seas. And God's justice does not wait for our comfort.

Once I began to see what had been right in front of me, I couldn't go back. I couldn't just preach the parts of the Gospel that made people feel good. The Gospel is not about maintaining comfort. It is about transformation. And I realized that I could no longer claim to follow Jesus while avoiding the very people He always moved toward.

I had to confront the false belief that being marginalized in one area somehow excuses you from examining your privilege in another. I am Deaf. I have known exclusion. But that does not give me a pass. It does not exempt me from acknowledging the power I still carry as a white man in America. And it certainly does not excuse me from confronting racism in myself or around me. Too often, people—especially white people—point to their own hardships to avoid responsibility. They say, "I grew up poor," or "I've suffered too," as if suffering automatically makes someone an ally.

Suffering does not make you just. Only justice does that. Pain does not excuse prejudice. Being wounded does not absolve you from wounding others. And no identity, no struggle, no story can justify ignoring or perpetuating racism.

Racism is sin. Not opinion. Not ignorance. Sin. And it must be named. Repentant of. And opposed.

As a preacher, that realization changed everything. I could no longer write sermons that floated above reality. Jesus did not stay in the clouds. He came down. He walked dusty roads. He flipped tables. He named hypocrisy. He stood with the poor and the oppressed and the forgotten. If I were going to preach His name, I would have to do the same.

As a parent, I had to change how I raised my children. I could not raise them to be colorblind. I had to raise them to be color-honoring. I had to teach them that Black lives matter not because of politics, but because of Genesis. Because every human being bears the image of God. I had to teach them that silence in the face of injustice is not faithfulness. It is betrayal.

As a pastor, I had to step back and listen more than I spoke. I had to ask whose voices were missing from the table. Whose stories were being skipped over? I had to make space—not as a favor, but as a faithful act of surrender. I had to stop being afraid of saying the wrong thing and start being afraid of saying nothing at all.

Still, my friends and colleagues, those formed by the Black Church and by the Black experience, continued to teach me. They showed up in rooms where they were overlooked. They led with strength when others looked for permission. They preached with power even when the people in front of them could not recognize their authority. They sang with the Spirit while the world tried to drown them out.

From them, I learned the Gospel is not neutral. It has never been. The Gospel is always good news for the oppressed and always a warning to those who protect their comfort at the expense of justice.

That Gospel—rooted in the margins, lived in resistance, drenched in resurrection—is the one I now give my life to. Not as an expert. But as a student. Not to be congratulated. But to be corrected. Not to be safe. But to be faithful.

This is what the margins taught me: that God is always moving toward the people we try to forget. And if we are going to follow Him, we must move in the same direction.

Let us not wait until the pain knocks on our own door. Let us listen now. Let us repent now. Let us act now. Because Jesus is already there. Waiting. Watching. Weeping. Calling us to remember. To repair. To rise. This time, let us not miss Him.

Becoming an Unfinished Ally

There was a time when I believed allyship was something a person could achieve. Like a degree earned through empathy. A reward given for good intentions. A final destination for those who had done their homework, posted their support, and spoken up in just the right ways. I treated it like a status—something I could arrive at and then carry proudly. But I have since come to see how wrong I was. Real allyship—authentic, holy, transformative—is not a title to claim. It is a posture to adopt. It is not a certificate of virtue. It is a long, slow walk into humility. And it never ends.

To be an ally in the way of Jesus is to give up the comfort of distance and step fully into the tension of another's pain. It is to sit in rooms where you are not the center and still choose to listen. It is to surrender the safety of your own story and let someone else's truth undo you. It is to resist the urge to fix, to explain, to perform—and instead learn the deeper discipline of quiet, persistent, sacrificial presence.

Allyship is not about being seen doing justice. It is about learning to see—truly see—who is missing, who is mourning, who is being silenced, and who has always been there, holding everything together without recognition or reward. And once you begin to see, once the veil of innocence is lifted, you cannot look away. Not if the Spirit of God is still working in you.

I used to think awareness was enough. But what good is awareness if it doesn't interrupt your decisions? What good is empathy if it never costs you anything? What good is love if it always protects your reputation but never challenges your comfort? What good is faith if it never demands more than the illusion of goodness?

I began to realize that many white Christians—myself included—had been trained to mistake politeness for love and comfort for peace. We wanted unity without confession. Reconciliation without repair. We could mourn the death of Jesus with drama and solemn hymns, but avoid naming the deaths of George Floyd or Breonna Taylor because we had convinced ourselves that justice was too political, too divisive, too soon.

The truth is this: the Gospel is never neutral. It is always good news for the oppressed, and it is always a warning to the comfortable. If our Gospel does not disturb unjust systems, then it is not the Gospel of Jesus Christ.

The Jesus I follow was not born into the heart of the empire. He was born on the margins of it. He came into flesh not in Rome or Babylon or Alexandria but in Israel—a small and often dismissed territory that, while central to the biblical narrative, has remained on the edges of global power, trade, and empire for much of recorded history. And that, I believe, is no accident. It is prophetic. It is holy. That the Savior of the world came through a people who were occupied, colonized, and constantly overlooked—that He chose to enter through the narrow gate of the oppressed—is the most profound declaration of solidarity the world has ever known.

Jesus did not come with applause. He came with rejection. He was not born into a palace, but a borrowed stable. His first breaths were taken under the shadow of empire. His first cries were heard not by kings, but by shepherds. From his first day to His last, He was marked not by status, but by suffering. And when He walked into the temple, He didn't congratulate the institution—He disrupted it. He flipped tables. He called out corruption. He exposed the systems that had turned worship into exclusion and holiness into hierarchy.

That is the Jesus I follow. And that means I cannot settle for a faith that only soothes me. I must seek a faith that stretches me, challenges me, breaks me, and rebuilds me in the image of the One who gave everything to set others free.

I've learned that I cannot claim to love justice and still be silent at the dinner table. I cannot preach love while allowing racism to live in my church pews, my curriculum choices, or my children's bedtime stories. I cannot raise my kids to be colorblind when God created color to be seen. I must raise them to be color-honoring. Color-celebrating. Color-protecting. Because if they do not learn to see color, they will never learn to see the wounds racism inflicts on the bodies and souls of those who do not look like them.

I cannot be a pastor who offers platitudes in the face of oppression. I cannot be a father who avoids hard conversations because they are uncomfortable. I cannot be a man who accepts privilege without asking how that privilege came to be and who it came at the expense of.

And I must say this, clearly: your pain does not excuse your prejudice. Your suffering, your trauma, your story—real and valid though they may be—do not free you from the need to examine how you may still be complicit in systems that crush others. My own Deafness does not erase my whiteness. My wounds do not cancel my responsibility. No amount of marginalization in one area absolves us from the sin of ignoring injustice in another.

Racism is not a misunderstanding. It is not a matter of opinion. It is not just "someone else's problem." It is sin. And sin must be named. Confessed. Repented. Dismantled.

This is why allyship cannot be performative. It must be persistent. It must move from hashtags to habits. It must move from intentions to interruption. It must show up not just when it's safe, but especially when it's not. Not just when people are watching, but especially when they aren't.

It means asking why your pastor has never preached about justice. It means noticing who gets hired, promoted, or welcomed—and who doesn't. It means staying in the conversation after the moment has passed. It means building tables that reflect the diversity of the kingdom, and yielding your seat when necessary. It means being willing to lose friends, influence, and comfort in order to follow Christ more faithfully.

Following Jesus into justice is not a detour. It is the road.

It is a road we walk as unfinished people.

Philippians says that "He who began a good work in you will be faithful to complete it." My hope is that I am still being shaped. Still being sanctified. Still being unraveled and re-formed. I do not speak as one who has arrived, but as one who has been awakened. And once awakened, I cannot go back to sleep.

So, I will keep walking. Not to prove anything. But because love compels me.

I am not perfect. But I am present.

I am not finished. But I am faithful.

I am not the answer. But I am no longer silent.

I am an unfinished ally.

Let justice roll. Not someday, but now. Not as a metaphor, but as a movement. Let it roll through our churches, our classrooms, our boardrooms, our homes, our hearts.

CHAPTER 8

The Call and the Cost:
A Mother's Witness

She did not arrive in ministry by accident or ambition. Long before anyone called her Reverend, my mother, Rebecca Collison, was the living heartbeat of the local church. She showed up early to turn on the lights, stayed late to stack folding chairs, and knew how to cook a funeral casserole without ever needing a recipe. She led Vacation Bible School with a dollar store wig and a Bible verse tucked into every craft. She taught Sunday school from a folding table and a handwritten lesson plan. She sang soprano in the choir, organized fundraisers for the youth group, and took phone calls from church members at all hours. She knew the hymnal well and the heartaches of half the congregation by name.

People sought her out. For prayer. For wisdom. For comfort. For clarity. And she gave herself away without hesitation. The church never had to ask. She was already there.

By the time she answered the call to the pastoral ministry, the foundation had already been laid. She had already ministered in living rooms, hospital rooms, church basements, and muddy parking lots after youth retreats. The official call was not the beginning. It was simply the next act of obedience.

I was a teenager when she began that next act. Old enough to understand what it meant, and young enough to believe that people might be better than they turned out to be. I watched her study late at night, surrounded by books and sermon notes, sometimes still wearing church clothes above her fluffy pink slippers. She had always been a student of Scripture, but now the stakes were different. She wasn't just seeking understanding. She was preparing to step into a pulpit that some believed did not belong to her.

The response was not silent. It was swift. Some whispered. Others walked away. Still others said it out loud, clear enough for the whole sanctuary to hear.

"We don't believe women should preach."

"I won't stay in a church led by a woman."

"She's a good person, but that doesn't make her a pastor."

"I can't take communion from her hands."

Some wrote letters to the district office. Others made phone calls. Some simply left without saying anything at all. They did not leave because of incompetence or scandal. They left because a woman had dared to answer the same call that had once come to Peter, to Paul, to every laborer who ever dropped their nets and said yes.

It wasn't a theological disagreement. It was fear wearing the language of faith. They were not resisting error. They were resisting her presence.

What made it all the more painful was that many of the people who objected were the same ones she had ministered to for years. They had eaten at her table. They had wept on her shoulder. They had watched her love the church with a fierceness that was maternal, holy, and entirely authentic. They had praised her gifts when she used them behind the scenes. But the moment she stepped forward and said, "Here I am, Lord. Send me," they began looking for the door.

I remember those Sundays. The pews felt thinner. The silence was more strained. The fellowship hall more cautious. My mother stood in the pulpit with grace that seemed carved from stone. She preached the Gospel as if her life depended on it, and maybe in some ways it did. Her sermons were not loud, but they were piercing. Her prayers were not dramatic, but they were drenched in truth. She poured herself out without reserve, and still, some turned away.

She never defended herself from the pulpit. She never used her position to retaliate. She simply kept showing up. She studied harder than anyone I had ever known. She wrote and rewrote sermons until every word felt like breath. She prepared for meetings as if the kingdom of God were on the line. She gave more of herself than was ever asked, because she knew the cost of being underestimated.

And I—her son—watched it all. I watched her put on her robe with trembling hands and a steady heart. I watched her lay hands on the grieving, even when her own heart was breaking. I watched her serve communion to people who doubted her authority and still bless them with the words, "This is the body of Christ, given for you."

Her call was never in question. Not from heaven. Not from me. But in the eyes of many in the church, it was always under suspicion. She could be faithful but not favored. Gifted, but not legitimate. Trusted in private but questioned in public. She could be the pastor in every way that mattered—except in their eyes.

Yet she never stopped.

She prayed. She preached. She persisted.

She showed me what strength looks like when it refuses to wear armor. She showed me what grace looks like when it chooses to stay present in the face of rejection. She showed me what a true pastor looks like, even when the church struggles to recognize one.

She was not just called. She was gifted. She was faithful. She was already bearing the fruit of ministry long before they allowed her to plant her feet behind the pulpit.

But in a church that still allowed gender to define grace, none of that was enough.

Familiar Pain: Watching from a Deaf Body

There are some wounds that require no translation. Wounds spoken in glances and silences, in clenched jaws and long exhales. Some pains are so deeply shared they need no introduction. That is what it felt like, watching my mother carry her calling through rooms where it was doubted from the moment she entered. At first, I witnessed it as a son. I felt the pride of seeing her preach, the ache of watching people turn away, the tension of learning too early that the Church can say "welcome" with its lips and "not you" with its posture.

And I began to realize that I recognized that ache.

Not just as her son, but as a Deaf man.

I knew what it felt like to walk into a room and be met with silence that was not reverence. I knew what it meant to be measured before I was known. People assumed incompetence before curiosity. If I signed instead of speaking, I was considered unprepared. If I spoke and stumbled, I was considered incapable. Even when I excelled, the praise came with surprise. "That was actually really good," they would say, as if my presence was the miracle and not the message.

I was not alone in that feeling. And neither was my mother.

Over time, I began to see that the pain she carried was not hers alone. It belonged to every woman I had served alongside in classrooms, churches, locker rooms, board meetings, and community centers. I saw the same weight in their shoulders and the same fire in their eyes.

I saw it in the teachers I worked with. Women who walked into multilingual classrooms and taught history with three languages humming in the air. Women who carried lesson plans home in tote bags and brought food for students who came to school hungry. Women who translated grief, managed chaos, listened with full attention, and still led professional development meetings with a stack of student data tucked under one arm. Yet I watched those same women be talked over by male colleagues, second-guessed by administrators, and handed more responsibility without more respect.

I saw it in the women I coached beside. They scouted talent, organized transportation, fundraised their own gear, and still taught athletes how to play their sport with skill and live with integrity. They commanded the sideline with wisdom and patience, earned the loyalty of their players, and kept stats and hearts at the same time. But I heard the way other coaches questioned their toughness. I saw the way parents whispered about their authority. I knew they had to prove what their male counterparts were simply assumed to be.

I saw it in the church. Again and again.

Women who preached the Gospel with clarity and courage were asked to wait for appointments. Women who led with conviction were told to soften their tone. Women who brought theological brilliance were told to keep it practical. Women who had already held broken congregations together with prayer and grit were passed over for roles they had already functioned in for years.

I could never know their pain, but I knew that road. I had walked it too.

I knew what it meant to be asked for your story but not your leadership. I knew what it meant to be welcomed for a testimony, but never invited to teach. I knew what it felt like to hear, "That was inspiring," and yet never be seen as someone worth following.

What we had in common was not simply marginalization. It was the ability to see how systems could praise you for surviving while denying you the right to lead.

The church often preached grace, but practiced hierarchy. It called us beloved while holding us back. It quoted Galatians but enforced its own unspoken rules about who could stand behind the table and who was expected to serve it.

My mother preached sermons with a fire that could split stone and soften it in the same breath. The teachers kept teaching, even when their voices cracked from overuse. The coaches kept coaching, even when their presence was questioned more than their results. And I kept speaking, even when every word felt like a climb.

We did not persist because we were unbothered. We persisted because we had heard the call of a God who did not confuse difference with deficiency.

That shared pain made us stronger. It deepened our compassion. It sharpened our voices. And it gave us a different kind of authority. The kind that cannot be appointed by people because it has already been affirmed by God.

Mutual Creation, Equal Calling

To reclaim the biblical narrative is to recover the vision of dignity and partnership that God spoke over humanity from the very beginning. Genesis is not just the beginning of time—it is the foundation of theology. And the story it tells is not one of hierarchy, but of mutual creation.

In Genesis 1:27, we read that "God created humankind in His image, in the image of God He created them; male and female He created them." The first declaration of human identity is a shared one. Both males and females are made in the divine image. Both are called to steward the earth. Both are blessed with sacred responsibility. This was not a chain of command. It was a co-mission.

When we look at Genesis 2, we often encounter a misunderstanding. God declares, "It is not good for the man to be alone," and creates a companion. The Hebrew term used here, *ezer kenegdo*, is often translated "helper," but this flattens its power. The word *ezer* is most often used in the Old Testament to describe God Himself as Israel's helper and deliverer. The second word, *kenegdo*, means "corresponding to," or "equal to." Together, this phrase does not describe an assistant, but a strong and equal partner—someone who stands face to face. Eve is no less than Adam. She is the other half of the whole.

What follows in Genesis 3 is not a divine endorsement of male rule, but a tragic result of sin. "Your desire will be for your husband, and he will rule over you," God says to the woman—not as a command, but as a consequence. This is not God's intention. It is the distortion of a good creation now cracked by disobedience. Yet much of church tradition-built theology is based on this fracture rather than on the original design. Instead of resisting the curse, we reinforced it.

Throughout Scripture, however, God continues to affirm the calling and leadership of women. In the Old Testament, Deborah serves as both judge and prophet—exercising civil, military, and spiritual authority over Israel. Huldah is the prophet who interprets the Book of the Law for King Josiah during a national crisis. Miriam leads Israel's worship after the crossing of the Red Sea. Ruth demonstrates covenant loyalty and becomes an ancestor of the Messiah. Esther risks her life to intercede for her people, becoming a model of courage and holy intervention.

This divine affirmation of women does not stop with the prophets. In the Gospels, Jesus consistently defies cultural norms to uplift and empower women. He speaks publicly with the Samaritan woman, a social and theological outsider, and entrusts her with the truth of His identity. She becomes the first evangelist in John's Gospel. He defends the woman caught in adultery, challenging the hypocrisy of her accusers and restoring her dignity. He praises the woman who anoints Him, saying her act of love and insight will be told wherever the Gospel is preached. Most profoundly, after His resurrection, Jesus appears first to Mary Magdalene. He calls her by name and commissions her to go and tell the others—making her the first preacher of the resurrection.

This is not a romantic detail. It is a theological announcement. In entrusting the Good News to a woman, Jesus rewrites every limitation the world tried to place on her. The resurrection begins not with Peter's preaching, but with Mary's witness.

The early Church, empowered by the Spirit, continues this pattern. On the day of Pentecost, Peter quotes the prophet Joel: "In the last days, God says, I will pour out my Spirit on all flesh. Your sons and your daughters will prophesy" (Acts 2:17). The

Spirit does not discriminate. The outpouring of power falls without prejudice. Women prophesy. Women lead. Women preach.

In his letters, the Apostle Paul often gets misquoted as restricting women. But we must read Scripture in its fullness, not in fragments. While Paul did write difficult passages—such as "let the women keep silent in the churches"—he also wrote expansively about women in leadership. In Romans 16, Paul names Phoebe as a deacon, Priscilla as a teacher of theology, and Junia as "outstanding among the apostles." These women were not assistants. They were co-laborers. They were leaders. They were trusted with doctrine, with pastoral care, and with the spread of the Gospel itself.

When Paul says in Galatians 3:28 that "there is neither Jew nor Greek, slave nor free, male nor female, for you are all one in Christ Jesus," he is not erasing difference. He is announcing that difference no longer determines worth, access, or authority in the body of Christ.

Theologically, this is a declaration of radical inclusion. Ecclesiology—that is, for the life of the Church—it is a call to reorder our assumptions. The Spirit does not assign gifts by gender. God's calling is not filtered through cultural expectations. Spiritual authority belongs to those whom God anoints, not to those whom institutions have historically privileged.

Yet, the modern Church often continues to tether leadership to maleness. Women are asked to support but not lead, to speak carefully, or not at all. I have watched women labor for the Gospel without recognition. I have listened to their exhaustion. I have seen them burn with the Word of God, only to be told to stay seated. Still, they preach—in their kitchens, in classrooms, in hospital rooms, and in sanctuaries that try to contain them.

I have seen this in my mother, who endured delay and dismissal but never stopped serving. I see it rising in my daughter, who carries a voice that will not be silenced. I have walked alongside women in ministry, women in business, women in the classroom, and women in the pulpit—each of them burning with gifts the Church cannot afford to ignore.

God created man and woman differently—but never hierarchically. Difference is not a ladder. It is a mirror. It reflects God's image more fully. Our callings are shaped by grace, not chromosomes. Our authority flows from the Spirit, not tradition. And the Gospel has never been guarded by gender. It has always been carried by grace.

To affirm the full calling of women is not to conform to secular culture. It is to return to the culture of the Kingdom—a kingdom where daughters prophesy, where women lead revivals, where Christ appears first to the ones others tried to erase.

Let us be clear: reclaiming this truth is not about power. It is about presence. It is about faithfulness to what Scripture has always shown and the Spirit still reveals.

When the Church listens to her daughters, she begins to heal.

When the daughters prophesy, the Church begins to breathe again.

When the body of Christ stands side by side—male and female, each fully called, fully gifted, fully free—the Gospel begins to rise in power.

How the Church Preaches Patriarchy (and Ableism Too)

If the injustice were always loud, we could confront it with ease. If it came with slurs or shouted doctrine, with slammed doors and open threats, we would know what to name. But the kind of injustice that most often takes root in the Church rarely wears a name tag. It slips in dressed as reverence. It speaks softly in the voice of tradition. It smiles from behind pulpits and board tables and votes cast in private meetings. It does not need to announce itself. It has been here for centuries.

Patriarchy in the Church is not new. It was not invented in our lifetime, nor in our mothers'. It reaches back through generations of men who interpreted Scripture through the lens of empire and passed their power down like a birthright. Though the early Church was filled with women who led, prophesied, taught, and funded the mission of the Gospel, by the time Christianity aligned with empire under Constantine, the leadership of women was systematically erased. What was once a grassroots movement of Spirit-filled disruption became an institution managed by those who looked alike, spoke alike, and governed alike. And in every era since, the pattern has repeated. When control is the goal, diversity becomes a threat. When power is guarded, those who lead differently are framed as problems to solve rather than prophets to follow.

The biblical record tells a more honest story than the traditions that followed it. The Gospel was first preached not by Peter or Paul, but by Mary Magdalene. It was a Samaritan woman—an outsider among outsiders—who carried the news of the Messiah to her village and led many to believe. Lydia led a house church. Junia was an apostle. Deborah judged a nation. Huldah interpreted Scripture for kings. Priscilla taught Apollos. And yet, generation after generation, churches have chosen to interpret Paul's isolated words to Timothy as the blueprint for silencing half the body of Christ.

Ableism, too, is not new. It exists in the way the Church has interpreted healing stories as erasure of identity rather than affirmation of dignity. When Jesus healed the blind, the deaf, and the lame, he never said their condition made them less worthy. He healed out of compassion, not requirement. The miracles were not prerequisites for their belonging. Yet somewhere along the way, the Church began to treat disability as something to be fixed before leadership could be entrusted. The body became a barrier. The difference became a disqualifier.

I have lived this truth. I have felt the sting of being asked to testify but not to lead. I have preached sermons that moved people to tears, only to be told afterward that my clarity was "surprising." I have walked into meetings where my ideas were met with silence, then repeated by others and suddenly considered profound. I have seen invitations rescinded when the logistics of Deaf access were deemed too complicated. I have been applauded from the pews but rarely welcomed behind the pulpit without condition.

I watched my mother experience the same rejection—different in form, but identical in substance. She was welcomed to teach children, to serve on committees, to sing and cook and clean, and organize. But when she responded to God's call to preach, the same hands that had received her casseroles could no longer receive her leadership. Her calling did not change. Their comfort did.

I have stood shoulder to shoulder with countless women who have borne the same burden. I have taught beside women whose brilliance could not be measured by test scores. I have served on ministry teams with women who carried churches through conflict, grief, and growth without recognition or fair compensation. I have watched them pray in labor rooms and gravesides, stand firm in the face of theological debate, and pour themselves out for communities that questioned their right to lead. These women are not tokens. They are theologians. They are teachers. They are torchbearers.

In modern churches, patriarchy often survives not through explicit policy but through silent patterns. Search committees say they want "the best candidate," but quietly hope for a man. Congregants praise the "soft skills" of women pastors while reserving the language of "authority" and "vision" for men. Women are told they're called, but not to senior leadership. They're asked to serve, but not to speak with power. Their gifts are celebrated, but their leadership is contained.

Ableism, too, takes quieter forms in the modern church. It lives in buildings without ramps or elevators. In worship services that depend entirely on sound. In leadership teams that don't provide interpreters or accessible materials. In mission trips that invite the Deaf to be evangelized but never empowered. In assumptions that those with disabilities are objects of ministry rather than agents of it.

The Church continues to preach inclusion while practicing exclusion. It builds entire ministries around the concept of welcome while preserving systems that favor one kind of body, one kind of voice, one kind of story.

This is not just a theological issue. It is a spiritual crisis. Because when the Church resists the voices of the marginalized, it resists the movement of the Holy Spirit. Pentecost did not come through one language or one voice. It came through the chaos of many tongues, through the fire that landed without bias, through the Spirit that filled all flesh.

The Church cannot claim to be Spirit-led and Spirit-filled while maintaining leadership tables that look nothing like the body of Christ. We cannot say we are followers of Jesus if we reject those he affirmed. We cannot preach the Gospel of liberation if our pulpits only echo the voices of the powerful.

There is no neutral position in a system built on exclusion. Silence protects the structure. Tradition defends it. Only repentance transforms it.

The prophets have already spoken. The daughters have already dreamed. The sons have already prophesied. The Spirit has already poured out on all flesh.

The question is not whether God is calling.

The question is whether we will listen and respond.

A Daughter, A Mirror, A Mandate

She stood on the pew beside me, no taller than my elbow, her fingers sticky with syrup from a church potluck and her eyes wide with wonder. The organ played its final chord, and before I could stop her, she spun—twirling in her Sunday dress down the center aisle as if it were her stage. Heads turned. Some smiled, some winced. But I saw something holy in her motion, something that made my breath catch.

My daughter danced in the sanctuary not out of irreverence, but out of joy. She didn't yet know there were places women had to fight to stand. She didn't yet know that pulpits were often protected like thrones. She didn't yet know how the Church, the very body meant to reflect the image of Christ, had for centuries distorted that image by deciding which bodies could represent God—and which ones could not.

Unfortunately, she would learn. And I felt it in my bones—the ache of time folding in on itself. I had seen this story before. I had watched my mother, Reverend Rebecca Collison, step into pulpits she was never meant to reach, carrying a Bible and a burden. I had seen her met not with gratitude, but with resistance. I had heard people whisper doubts before she ever spoke a word. And now, I saw my daughter dancing in the same space where my mother had bled quietly from invisible wounds. I saw her not just as a child, but as a mirror. As a sign. As a question, God was asking me in real time.

What will you leave for her?

History has not been kind to women with spiritual authority. The earliest church communities included women as apostles, prophets, teachers, and financiers of the Gospel. The New Testament does not erase them. It uplifts them. Mary Magdalene, the first to see the risen Christ, was sent to proclaim the resurrection to the apostles—making her the apostle to the apostles. Priscilla, along with her husband Aquila, instructed the learned Apollos in the way of God more accurately. Lydia hosted Paul and Silas and led a house church in her home. Junia was imprisoned for the Gospel and named an apostle by Paul himself.

As the Church aligned with the empire, women were pushed from leadership back into silence. By the time Christianity became the state religion under Constantine, ecclesiastical power was consolidated into male-only hierarchies. The memory of women's leadership was suppressed. Their stories were spiritualized, sanitized, or erased. And the legacy of that erasure lives on in modern sanctuaries where women still struggle for access to the pulpit, where young girls are still taught that leadership is a male calling, where female pastors are praised for their compassion but denied positions of authority.

As a father, that history lives in my throat when I watch my daughter scribble sermon notes beside me. It burns behind my eyes when I hear her pray bold prayers at bedtime. She doesn't know yet that many pulpits are still gatekept. She doesn't know that her questions might someday be met with suspicion. But I do. And so I speak.

I speak because silence would make me complicit. I speak because she is watching. She is listening to how I describe the church. She is paying attention to who I uplift, who I quote, who I invite into the room. And every time I say nothing about injustice, I am teaching her to expect it. Every time I avoid the subject, I am making her carry what I am unwilling to confront.

She deserves better than that.

She deserves a church that doesn't simply tolerate her gifts, but treasures them. A community that doesn't see her questions as disruptive, but as sacred. She deserves a theology that does not diminish her, a sanctuary that does not silence her, and a leadership structure that does not ask her to shrink in order to serve.

It's not only about her.

It's about the daughters in every pew who are watching, who are waiting to see if the Church will make room for them. It's about the girls who feel the fire of God in their bones but keep quiet because they have never seen a woman preach. It's about the young women who are told to marry pastors but never told that they might become one. It's about the teenagers who are told they can lead a youth group but not stand behind the pulpit on Sunday morning. It's about the ones who leave the Church not because they stopped loving God, but because they grew tired of defending the image of God in themselves.

It is about the fathers, the pastors, the teachers, the mentors—those of us entrusted with influence and called to create a different legacy. The Church has told a half-truth for too long. It has recited Paul's words about women being silent without teaching the cultural context of temple disorder in Corinth. It has upheld male-only eldership based on letters without considering the full testimony of Scripture. It has built hierarchies using selective verses while ignoring the witness of Mary, Deborah, Huldah, Priscilla, Phoebe, Junia, and the countless unnamed women through whom God has spoken life into the world.

If we are to be faithful, we must tell the whole story.

As a Deaf man, I understand what it means to be treated as an inspiration but not as a leader. I have felt the slow erosion of dignity when people celebrate your perseverance but never expect your voice to carry vision. I have lived the contradiction of being welcomed to share my testimony but excluded from the table where decisions are made. And I have seen women—especially Black women, Deaf women, poor women—navigate that same terrain with even more weight on their backs.

So I teach my daughter what my mother taught me. That calling is not a popularity contest. That obedience is costly. That the Kingdom of God is wider than the systems built to contain it. I teach her that the Holy Spirit cannot be domesticated. That her voice is a sacred vessel. That her questions are not problems to fix but prophecies to honor.

She does not need to ask for permission to lead. She needs to discern the call and walk in it with holy boldness.

And the Church? It needs to catch up.

If my daughter stands in a pulpit one day, I want her to stand without the ghosts of past rejection clouding her view. I want her to stand without having to first convince the people in the pews that God speaks through her, too. I want her to preach without shrinking, to lead without apology, and to shepherd with the fierce tenderness that has always lived in the women of my family.

I want her to know that when she speaks, she is not speaking alone.

She is speaking with the voice of generations who were told to stay quiet and chose instead to keep proclaiming anyway. She is speaking with the breath of Mary, who carried the Word. With the strength of Deborah, who judged a nation. With the clarity of Huldah, who interpreted sacred texts. With the memory of a grandmother who preached when others left. And with the love of a father who finally understood that silence in the face of injustice is not peace. It is betrayal.

I pray the Church listens, because the daughters are rising, the Spirit has already spoken.

From Comfort to Confession

The prophetic voice has never made its home in places of comfort. In the Bible, the prophets were not born in palaces or platforms of prestige. They were called from the wilderness, from vineyards, from prison cells, from lives marked by hardship and interruption. These were not polished leaders. They were reluctant mouthpieces for divine truth. People like Jeremiah, Amos, Elijah, and even John the Baptist did not volunteer for influence. They were summoned. And when they spoke, their words were rarely met with applause. More often, they were met with anger, rejection, or exile. This is because the prophetic word has always exposed what people would rather ignore. It does not cater to what is familiar. It calls us out of what is comfortable into what is right.

This same dynamic exists today. The modern Church, though full of faithful people and sincere intentions, has also become too aligned with comfort. We have grown attached to predictability, to inherited structures, to leadership that looks and sounds familiar. When someone comes along—especially someone from the margins—and speaks a truth that challenges the way things have always been done, the first response is often defensiveness rather than discernment. That defensiveness, more often than not, hides behind language like "order," "tradition," or "sound doctrine." But in reality, it is fear.

As a pastor, as a Deaf man, as the son of a woman who was called to ministry before the Church was ready to receive her, I have watched this happen in real time. I have watched communities turn away from prophets sent to them by God simply because they did not arrive in the packaging people expected. I have seen brilliant women passed over for pastoral leadership because of their gender. I have seen Deaf leaders asked to share their testimony but not trusted to preach the Gospel. I have seen churches claim they want diversity, but then fail to do the soul work of repentance that true diversity requires.

I have come to see clearly that until the Church confesses these patterns, we cannot be free.

Confession is not simply saying that we all fall short. That is too vague to carry the weight of transformation. Real confession names what has been done, who has been harmed, and what must change. Real confession says aloud what others have had to carry in silence. Real confession opens the doors we have kept shut and says, "We were wrong." It tells the truth even when it costs us. Especially when it costs us.

The truth is that the Church has a long history of excluding women from leadership, not because Scripture demands it, but because patriarchy has shaped how we read Scripture. From the early centuries of the Church, even after women served as apostles, prophets, house-church leaders, and financiers of the Gospel mission, ecclesiastical power shifted toward male-only hierarchies. The rise of the empire of Christianity under Constantine solidified that exclusion. The names of Junia, Priscilla, Phoebe, and Mary Magdalene were either erased or reinterpreted. Their witness was buried under centuries of church policy that protected male control and called it a spiritual order.

This exclusion also played out in the modern feminist movement. During the first wave of feminism in the nineteenth and early twentieth centuries, women like Elizabeth Cady Stanton and Lucretia Mott fought for the right to vote and for equal protection under the law. Stanton even wrote her own commentary on Scripture, challenging interpretations that subjugated women. However, the gains of the first wave of feminism were not shared equally. The movement largely excluded Black women, whose voices were seen as too radical or whose pain was inconvenient to white agendas.

Black women, however, never waited to be included. They led their own movements. Sojourner Truth, a formerly enslaved woman, stood before a crowd in 1851 and asked a question that still haunts the Church: "Ain't I a woman?" She had worked, birthed children, been beaten, and loved Jesus. Yet she was treated as something other than fully human by both white women and white men. Anna Julia Cooper, Ida B. Wells, Frances Ellen Watkins Harper—these were women of deep Christian faith who held the Church accountable even as they labored for its renewal.

During the Civil Rights Movement, Black women such as Ella Baker, Fannie Lou Hamer, and Pauli Murray carried the prophetic mantle again. These were not background figures. They were theologians, organizers, and preachers. They understood that freedom required more than laws. It required spiritual courage. It required telling the truth. Their witness laid the groundwork for womanist theology—a theological tradition that centers the lived experience of Black women, critiques both racism and sexism in the Church, and insists that God's justice must be embodied in every community.

Today, womanist theologians like Katie Cannon, Renita Weems, and Emilie Townes continue this legacy. Their work challenges the Church to see how deeply the exclusion of certain bodies from leadership is not a biblical mandate but a cultural inheritance. These women do not speak only for inclusion. They speak with a prophetic fire that insists the Gospel is not complete unless it liberates those on the underside of history.

We cannot claim to follow Jesus while ignoring these voices.

Jesus consistently elevated the voices of women, the disabled, the poor, and the marginalized. He did not just minister to them. He listened to them. He healed on the Sabbath, not to break the rules for fun, but to remind the religious leaders that compassion must always come before control. He spoke with women in public. He affirmed their witness. He welcomed children. He told the rich to sell their possessions. He spoke plainly to power and was crucified not for kindness but for disruption.

If the Church is to follow this Jesus, then we must confront the ways we have betrayed his example.

We must confess that we have prioritized comfort over truth. That we have celebrated survival while refusing to dismantle the systems that required it. That we have silenced prophetic voices from the margins because they made us uncomfortable. That we have preached inclusion while guarding the microphone.

We must repent.

Repentance is more than saying sorry. It is changing direction. It is rewriting bylaws, restructuring leadership, and reinterpreting Scripture through the full lens of justice. It is not enough to place one woman on a committee or to install a ramp at the back of the church. True repentance changes the questions we ask, the decisions we make, and the people we empower.

This is not a call to shame the Church. It is a call to save her.

The Church is still beloved. But beloved does not mean blameless. God is not asking us to feel bad. God is asking us to be brave. Brave enough to listen. Brave enough to tell the truth. Brave enough to rebuild.

I say this as someone who still believes in the Church. I believe in her because I have seen her at her best. I have seen her feed the hungry and clothe the stranger. I have seen her lift people from addiction and despair. I have seen her teach children and comfort the dying. I have seen her come alive in moments of mercy.

I believe she can be better. But only if she is willing to change.

The prophetic call will never be comfortable. It never has been. But it is the only way forward. It is not the voice of destruction. It is the voice of resurrection.

So let us confess. Let us repent. And let us be born again.

Lessons from the Margins

The Church has long claimed to be a community shaped by the stories of the faithful, but too often it forgets which stories it has silenced. It forgets the women.

Women have been the quiet architects of nearly every revival the Church has known. They have birthed movements from kitchen tables and prayer closets. They have taught the Word in basements and sanctuaries, baked communion bread and broken generational curses, written hymns in journals never published, and stewarded the Gospel through oppression, dismissal, and disregard. And yet the Church has often treated its wisdom as a side dish instead of the main course.

The Church has expected women to serve without voice, to lead without title, to labor without recognition. And when these women have spoken—when they have dared to preach, prophesy, or challenge the structures that confined them—they have been labeled difficult, divisive, unqualified, or "out of order." But they were not out of order. They were in line with the prophets. They were aligned with the Spirit.

Throughout Scripture, it is often women who see what others do not. Hagar, cast out into the wilderness, becomes the first person in Scripture to name God. She calls God El Roi—"the God who sees"—a name not given by patriarchs, but by a woman abandoned by them. Deborah led Israel as judge and prophet in a time when few men had the courage to act. Miriam stood beside Moses and Aaron, co-leading a people through liberation. The unnamed women who defied Pharaoh by hiding Hebrew babies—including the midwives Shiphrah and Puah—set the Exodus in motion before Moses ever raised his staff.

Mary of Nazareth bore not just the Son of God in her womb, but the weight of social scorn and theological misunderstanding. Her Magnificat in Luke 1 is not a lullaby. It is a revolution. It declares that God casts down the mighty and lifts up the lowly. Mary's voice is the theological overture to Christ's ministry—bold, radical, and rooted in justice.

At the tomb, when the men were hiding in fear, it was women who remained. And it was women whom Jesus trusted with the first proclamation of the resurrection. The Church was born on the tongues of women, yet centuries of tradition have tried to mute them.

Why?

Patriarchal systems—both in religious and secular spaces—have always known that women's voices are dangerous to the status quo. A woman who knows she is called by God cannot be controlled by men who are threatened by her. A woman who preaches the resurrection is harder to dismiss than a woman who only tends the nursery. And so, across centuries, churches built on the stories of Mary, Martha, Phoebe, Priscilla, and Junia began to forget them. Their names were omitted from lectionaries, their stories twisted or erased, their spiritual authority questioned or ignored.

The early Church remembered them differently. In Romans 16, Paul greets a long list of women who led alongside him—Phoebe the deacon, Junia the apostle (whose name some scribes tried to masculinize), and Priscilla, who with her husband Aquila instructed the scholar Apollos in the Gospel. These were not exceptions. They were leaders. And their leadership was not marginal to the mission—it was central.

History continued to press women to the edges. By the time Christianity was entangled with the empire in the fourth century, female leadership was increasingly forbidden, and their contributions were reframed as supportive rather than directive. And yet, women continued to lead. Saints like Macrina the Younger, who shaped her brothers Basil and Gregory of Nyssa into theological giants, and Catherine of Siena, who advised popes and shaped the mystical tradition of the Church, persisted. But institutional acknowledgment remained rare.

In the modern era, women led again. The first-wave feminists of the nineteenth century—including Elizabeth Cady Stanton and Lucretia Mott—were women of deep spiritual conviction. Stanton's Woman's Bible was a daring critique of the ways Scripture had been used to keep women submissive. Even that movement, as bold as it was, failed to make space for the voices of Black women.

Black women carved a path of their own. Sojourner Truth, in her 1851 speech, asked, "Ain't I a woman?" That question still reverberates through every pulpit that refuses a woman's leadership. Anna Julia Cooper declared, "Only the Black woman can say... when and where I enter, the whole race enters with me." These were not just speeches. They were sacred proclamations—sermons born of fire.

The Black Church, long a sanctuary of resistance, still struggled with patriarchy, not just among white men but black men as well. Yet women persisted. During the Civil Rights Movement, it was women like Ella Baker, Septima Clark, and Fannie Lou Hamer who organized, taught, strategized, and sustained the movement. They preached without pulpits, taught theology through practice, and embodied the Spirit's work.

Their legacy birthed womanist theology—a tradition of deep biblical scholarship rooted in the lived experiences of Black women. Womanist theologians like Katie Geneva Cannon, Delores Williams, Renita Weems, and Emilie Townes insisted that the experiences of women were not theological side notes. They were sacred texts. They invited the Church to re-read Scripture with fresh eyes—to see Hagar not just as a castaway, but as a survivor and a theologian. To hear Mary's Magnificat not as sentimental poetry, but as a declaration of God's revolution.

Still, in far too many churches today, women are only welcome to speak if they do not speak too boldly. To lead if they do not challenge the power structure. To preach if they wear the right dress and keep the right tone. Women are expected to minister with power but without authority. To serve without being seen.

I have witnessed this injustice personally. I saw it in my mother, who had been living her call long before the Church was willing to acknowledge it. I saw the doors that opened for less gifted men while she waited faithfully in the hallway. And yet, she never stopped loving the Church. She never stopped showing up. She taught, prayed, cooked, organized, and comforted. She carried the Gospel in her hands, even when the Church would not let her carry it in her voice.

Now I see that same strength rising in my daughter. She has no patience for small boxes. No fear of hard questions. No hesitation in speaking the truth. And I will not let her inherit the silence that was handed down to the women before her. I will not let her think that spiritual gifts are gendered or that her calling must be diminished to make someone else feel secure.

The truth is this: the Church has survived because of women. And if it is to be renewed, it must be renewed through their leadership, their vision, and their voices.

We must listen to the lessons they have already taught us— through tears, through endurance, through sermons preached in living rooms and hospital rooms, through songs sung at gravesides and victories shouted in sanctuaries where they were never fully welcomed. We must make room at the table. Not just for their presence, but for their power.

God has already called them.

The question is whether we will finally listen and stand with them.

Becoming an Unfinished Ally

There was a time when I believed that being respectful toward women in ministry was enough. I believed that if I encouraged their calling, applauded their sermons, and affirmed their gifts in private, I was somehow helping. I thought admiration was an action. I thought support was sacrifice. I now understand that I was wrong.

Admiration does not dismantle injustice. Quiet support behind closed doors does not correct generations of public exclusion. Silence, even when it feels polite, is not neutral. It is protective. And often, it protects the wrong things—systems of power that were never built with women in mind, traditions that have normalized inequality in the name of God, and hierarchies that reward proximity to control rather than faithfulness to Christ. I am learning that allyship is not a status one claims. It is a lifelong practice. It is a posture of humility, a rhythm of listening and yielding, a commitment to repentance that moves beyond apology into the hard, holy work of repair.

The Church has too often chosen the safety of tradition over the cost of truth. We have clung to inherited roles instead of inherited grace. We have built our theologies with bricks handed to us by culture rather than the cornerstone laid by Christ. We have told women they are essential, but not central. We have celebrated their strength while denying them space. We needed their gifts, but failed to bless their callings.

I have watched it unfold in real time. I saw it in my mother's story—her call was unmistakable, her gifts undeniable, her heart unmistakably shaped by God's Spirit. And yet, I witnessed the resistance she faced, not because her doctrine was flawed, but because her gender was seen as disqualifying. I remember the Sunday she was invited to preach in a new church. Before she even opened her mouth, several people stood and left the sanctuary. They walked out in protest, not because of what she said, but because of who she was. Still, she stood. She preached with power. And I, her son, saw the Gospel come alive in her voice that day. I will never forget the courage it took for her to speak in a room already trying to silence her.

Now I see that same fire rising in my daughter. She is bold and tender, perceptive and brave. She asks good questions and speaks truth with clarity. And I know—if things do not change—she will face the same dismissals. The same "not yets" and "not here." The same theology twisted into barriers. I cannot prevent every hardship she may encounter, but I will not hand her silence. I will not ask her to wait her turn in a kingdom that was never meant to be built in lines of succession. I will not let her think that God made her to be quiet when her very breath is a testimony.

I have also come to understand that Paul, whose letters have often been used to exclude women, did not stand against them. When read carefully and contextually, Paul's words affirm the leadership of women in the early Church. He commended Phoebe as a deacon, not as an assistant but as a leader in her own right. He celebrated Priscilla as a co-teacher of the Gospel, someone who helped shape the theology of Apollos. He recognized Junia as an apostle, imprisoned for the sake of Christ and outstanding among the early witnesses. These women were not marginal. They were essential. Paul did not silence them—he blessed them, thanked them, and trusted them with the message of Christ. The problem is not Paul's writing. The problem is how we have chosen to read it, and how we have refused to listen to the women who still live it.

To be an ally is not about centering myself. It is about stepping back and making space. It is about relinquishing the privileges I never had to ask for. It is about naming the pain that systems of exclusion have caused, not as unfortunate outcomes, but as spiritual violence. It is about asking who is missing from the table, and then moving aside so they can sit down and lead the meal. It is about recognizing that so many women have led without titles, shepherded without pay, mentored without acknowledgment, and held the Church together with little more than faith and grit—and that we have benefited from their labor without repenting for their lack of recognition.

The Gospel does not call us to protect comfort. It calls us to cruciform love. Jesus did not build fences. He built tables. He tore the curtain. He lifted up the lowly and sent the powerful away empty. When he rose from the dead, he did not appear first to Peter or John, but to Mary Magdalene. And he did not ask her to keep quiet. He told her to go and tell.

That is not just a beautiful moment. That is a commission. That is the Gospel.

I believe in the resurrection of the Church. I believe the Church can still be transformed. But it will not happen through clever strategies or polite compromises. It will happen through confession, repentance, and a re-centering of the voices we once refused to hear. It will happen when pulpits are opened and pay is equal. When theology includes women's bodies, stories, and wisdom. When allyship becomes a verb and not a badge.

So here is my commitment.

I will not stay silent when women are silenced.

I will not let theology be used to justify harm.

I will not ask my daughter to wait.

I will not forget my mother's tears.

I will not pretend that my learning is complete.

I will be an unfinished ally.

Still listening. Still yielding. Still learning what it means to be faithful to the Gospel, not just in word, but in structure, in action, and in love.

Because I believe the Church can be more than it has been.

I believe it can become the community it was always meant to be.

Not a gatekeeping institution, but a holy body—called, gifted, and alive with every voice God has given breath.

CHAPTER 9

Lies of the Mind

The moment wasn't dramatic. No one screamed. Nothing shattered. No ambulance arrived. It was quieter than that. And somehow, that made it worse.

I saw you. You were just sitting there in the front seat of your car. Parked outside the grocery store. You had walked inside, grabbed a cart, maybe made it a few aisles in, but then you left it. The cart stayed where it was, somewhere between the canned beans and the day-old bakery rack. You came back outside and got in your car, but you didn't start it. You didn't drive anywhere. You just sat.

The keys were still in your hand, your other hand resting in your lap. The sun was warm through the windshield. The plastic on the steering wheel had that worn, greasy shine from years of work and wear. You were staring straight ahead, but not really looking at anything. At one point, a man walked by and gave you a polite nod. You forced yourself to smile. He kept walking.

From the outside, nothing was wrong. That's what people don't understand. Falling apart doesn't always look like what they think. It doesn't always mean crying or yelling or collapsing. Sometimes it just means nothing. Blankness. Silence. Staring into a space you cannot name. Existing in a body, you suddenly feel disconnected from.

You were the one who had it all together. That's what people saw. That's what they said. You were strong. Reliable. Capable. A provider. A preacher. A teacher. A man of faith. A man who had survived what others didn't. A man who had pushed through poverty and loss, and hardship and still kept showing up.

But your mind was on fire.

There's no other way to describe it. The thoughts weren't just fast. They were crashing. Loud. Unrelenting. A storm you couldn't outrun. Panic. Dread. Numbness. Guilt. All of it mixed together, with no warning and no direction. Your body was still, but your heart was racing. Your breath was short. Your mouth was dry. You couldn't move. You couldn't speak. You couldn't even cry.

You had felt this before, in different ways. Enough times to have a list of diagnoses handed to you. PTSD. Autism. ADHD. Depression. Anxiety. The words came later in life, after years of confusion and questions, and exhaustion. They helped in some ways. Gave names to things you had carried since childhood. But they didn't fix anything. Not really.

The mind is more than a list of symptoms. It is not a machine with broken parts. It is a world. A mystery. A place of wonder and of pain. You believe in the power of psychology to some degree. You believe in therapy, in medicine, in the effort people are making to understand what cannot be seen. But you also know that no diagnosis can fully describe what it's like to live in your own skin. No label can capture what it means to survive when the world was never designed with you in mind.

Sometimes the worst part is trying to explain it. Trying to find words for a language your body already speaks fluently. The weariness of having to translate your pain into something others will take seriously. The way people tilt their heads and say, "Have you tried gratitude?" or "You just need to stay positive." As if you haven't already tried everything. As if you're not already doing your best just to breathe.

And still, underneath it all, that old voice returns. That familiar whisper. The one you learned early and never quite unlearned.

You're supposed to hold it together.

Especially as a man.

Especially as a leader.

Especially if you've already overcome so much.

Especially if people look up to you.

Especially if your faith is supposed to be strong.

There is this lie that once you make it out of the fire, you never get burned again. That once you overcome, you are immune to weakness. That if you stumble now, it means everything you've built will fall. That if you ask for help, it will prove what they've suspected all along—that you were never as strong as they thought.

So, you carry it.

You carry the weight with a straight back and a forced smile. You answer, "I'm good" when someone asks. You crack jokes. You get the job done. You post encouraging words online even though you haven't felt encouraged in weeks. You pray for others even though your own prayers feel empty.

But no one told you the truth.

No one told you that survival comes with splinters. That you can make it out alive and still feel broken inside. That grace does not always come in the form of healing, but often in the form of presence.

That was the day you almost broke.

In a strange way, it was also the day something holy happened. Not a rescue. Not a miracle. Just a presence. Just a stillness. A flicker of something sacred in the middle of your unraveling. Not a voice booming from heaven. Just a quiet knowing.

God was still with you.

He wasn't waiting for you to be okay. He wasn't expecting you to prove anything. He was already there. Sitting with you in the silence. Breathing beside you in the stillness. Not asking you to move. Just reminding you that you are not alone.

Sometimes, God does not come to fix you. Sometimes He comes to sit beside the pieces and call them beautiful.

Deafness, Mental Health, and the Silence Between

There is a kind of silence that hurts more than shouting ever could.

It is the silence that settles in when you walk into a room and realize the conversation never included you. It is the silence that wraps around your shoulders after you ask for help and are met with a nod, a pause, and then nothing. It is the silence that follows your honesty when you finally open your mouth to speak your truth, and the people who once said "reach out anytime" quietly disappear.

That silence, I've known all my life.

For Deaf people, that silence often begins with sound itself. The absence of it. Or rather, the absence of access to it. Not just the inability to hear, but the inability to be heard. When I was a child, the silence I lived with was not peaceful. It was not sacred. It was not chosen. It was heavy. It was isolating. It was survival.

Over the years, I've come to understand that silence like that does not only belong to the Deaf. I've come to see that the silence I carried lives in many others too. In veterans who jump at fireworks and smile through nightmares. In teenagers who laugh on social media but cry under blankets at night. Mothers are too afraid to admit their exhaustion and the despair of post-partum depression. In pastors who preach strength while privately wondering how much longer they can last. In teachers, in fathers, in students, in survivors. All of them are learning how to live with a storm no one sees.

Deafness gave shape to my silence. But I am not the only one who has carried it.

I grew up in a house where I could not fully communicate. That is the truth for most Deaf children in America. Over ninety percent are born to hearing parents, and the majority of those parents never become fluent in sign language. Which means that most Deaf children grow up unable to fully express their needs in the one place that should be safest. Home.

Language deprivation is not just about missing vocabulary. It is about a missing connection. Without a shared language, there is no shared reality. No secure attachment. No clear understanding of what it means to be loved when words don't reach all the way. I didn't have the words for my feelings. I didn't have the words for fear. For confusion. For sadness. For rage. And so they lived inside me without expression, without explanation. They built up like pressure behind glass.

That experience is unique in form, but not in spirit. There are children who speak the same language as their parents and still grow up feeling completely unheard. There are husbands and wives who live under the same roof but have no way to name the grief sitting between them. There are entire communities that have never been taught how to speak pain aloud. Who have only ever been taught to bury it beneath strength or silence.

In school, I was labeled. I was called disruptive. I was called defiant. I was told I needed to "try harder" or "be more respectful." No one asked me why I was acting out. No one stopped to consider that I didn't fully understand what was being said. No one imagined that my frustration was not rebellion, but desperation.

That is not just my story. It is the story of so many others. Black and Brown children in under-resourced schools are labeled as problems before they are understood as people. Neurodivergent students are disciplined for behavior that stems from overstimulation and confusion. Trauma survivors are written off as dramatic. Women with chronic anxiety are told to calm down. Men with depression are told to man up. Autistic adults are told to try harder to fit in. Veterans with PTSD are given citations before compassion.

There is a name for this. It is called diagnostic overshadowing. It means that when you have a visible identity or a known label, people stop seeing the whole you. Everything gets filtered through that one lens. For me, it was Deafness. For someone else, it might be race. For another, poverty. Or a disability. Or a past mistake. The result is the same. People stop asking questions. They stop listening. They start assuming.

I still remember the day the interpreter was pulled from my classroom without notice. Just gone. I asked the teacher what happened. She yelled at me. Told me I didn't need special treatment. I went home and sat on the floor of my bedroom and said nothing. I knew there was no point. No one was coming. No one was listening.

It would take years before a therapist handed me a list of diagnoses. PTSD. Autism. ADHD. Depression. Anxiety. I looked at the paper and saw words that fit in some places but felt hollow in others. The language was helpful, but incomplete. It gave shape to the ache, but not its origin. It offered a frame, but not the painting. Because the mind, especially when shaped by trauma and Deafness, and isolation, is not a simple thing to name. It is vast. It is holy. It is broken and still worthy of love.

The Church has not always known how to hold this truth. Too often, we have been told to pray harder, to fast, to rebuke, to declare victory. And I do believe in prayer. I do believe in the healing power of God. But sometimes what we need is not a miracle. Sometimes what we need is presence. Not someone to fix us. Someone to sit with us. Not a scripture to be quoted. A truth to be lived.

The Bible says we are fearfully and wonderfully made. That includes our nervous systems. That includes our sensory sensitivities. That includes our depression and our compulsions and our need to stim and rock and cry in private. That includes the scars we carry from childhoods that were never quiet. From bedrooms that were never safe. From churches that used theology as a shield instead of as a welcome.

Jesus knew silence, too. He wept alone in a garden. He cried out on the cross and heard no answer. He was misunderstood by those closest to him. He was labeled. Accused. Abandoned. He sat with the broken and did not rush them to joy. He listened first. He touched the untouchable. He healed without spectacle. He loved without condition.

That is the Jesus I met in the silence.

That is the Christ who stayed when I could not speak. That is the God who heard me before I had the language to pray.

So if you are reading this and you have lived in that kind of silence, I want you to know you are not alone.

If you are Deaf, you are not alone. If you are neurodivergent, you are not alone. If you have survived trauma and carry shame for how your brain responds, you are not alone. If you are tired of performing wellness for others while privately drowning, you are not alone.

If you have never lived this story, I pray you pause and listen. I pray you ask better questions. I pray you learn the language of the ones who sit quietly in the back row, who avoid eye contact, who flinch at sudden touch, who cannot sit through the sermon without pacing, who speak too loudly or not at all, who disappear for a few weeks and come back changed. These are not problems to fix. They are people to love.

Silence can be holy. But only when it is chosen. Silence can be healing. But only when it is shared.

The silence that destroys is the one we pretend not to hear.

The Myth of Invincibility

I grew up believing that strength was not just expected—it was required. It was the currency of survival, a shield I was taught to polish every morning before stepping out the door. In the churches, I knew, strength wasn't just rewarded—it was sanctified. It was held up as the sign of spiritual maturity, reinforced through memory verses and Sunday sermons, and passed down like an heirloom, even if it never quite fit.

We didn't always say it outright, but the message was clear: Be strong. Don't let them see you cry. Pray it away. Get over it. Smile. Keep going. Trust God and move on. These weren't tools for healing—they were expectations. Rules. Boundaries drawn tightly around pain, keeping it out of sight, and often, out of compassion.

As a Deaf man, I felt those expectations press even deeper into my skin. The cultural and religious demand for invincibility was compounded by my difference. I already knew I was being watched, scrutinized, and evaluated differently. I feared that if I ever broke down, they would blame my Deafness. That if I showed vulnerability, they would call it weakness. That if I asked for help, they would see it not as human, but as proof that I didn't belong in the room. I learned, slowly and without being told, that vulnerability was a luxury I couldn't afford.

So, I became what they needed me to be.

I was helpful. Funny. Reliable. Strong. I learned to translate my inner storms into palatable smiles. I adjusted my tone, my posture, my pace—reading rooms like maps I wasn't given, trying to walk without making noise. I turned pain into punchlines, fear into fuel, and exhaustion into excellence. I became fluent in the language of public composure, even when I couldn't fully hear the world around me.

Underneath the surface, I was coming undone.

There were panic attacks that struck like lightning in a blue sky, sudden and electrifying. There were days when my chest felt like a closed door I couldn't open. I would sit in silence, overwhelmed, unable to speak or sign what I was feeling. There were nights when my thoughts refused to slow down, racing in circles I couldn't escape. I experienced dissociation—moments where I watched myself nod and smile while my mind stood outside the room. And always, there was the fear: If I fall apart, will I ever be trusted again?

That silence wasn't just external. It was internal. It was mine.

Psychologists call this "emotional masking." It's the learned behavior of hiding pain behind socially acceptable expressions—laughter, productivity, sarcasm, and stoicism. It's especially common among men, leaders, and those in marginalized communities. It is a response to trauma, to expectation, to centuries of messaging that says survival means never letting your guard down. For Deaf individuals like me, emotional masking is magnified. The world already assumes we are difficult. We learn to be easy, even when we are breaking.

Studies confirm what many of us have lived. Men raised in conservative or religious cultures are less likely to seek help for depression, anxiety, or trauma. They are more likely to interpret emotional pain as spiritual failure. They are more likely to believe that admitting struggle would mean forfeiting trust. Deaf children, especially those born to hearing families, are frequently misdiagnosed, misunderstood, and overlooked—not because the pain isn't present, but because the systems around them are unequipped to hear it. Silence, in this case, is not a lack of sound—it's a failure of listening.

The Church has not been innocent in this.

We have glorified the image of the unshakable believer, the strong leader who presses on no matter what. We have elevated the one who declares their healing while ignoring the one still holding a wound. We have taken phrases like "God won't give you more than you can handle" and turned them into shields against empathy. We have quoted Scripture like medicine but failed to offer presence like Christ.

Yet Scripture tells a deeper story.

The Bible is not the story of invincible people. It is the story of broken people who were met by a faithful God. Elijah, the prophet who called fire from heaven, once sat under a broom tree and begged God to let him die. Job, righteous and upright, tore his robe and cursed the day of his birth. David, the man after God's own heart, wept until his bones ached and his vision blurred. Jeremiah wished he had never been born. Even Jesus, in the garden, fell to the ground, sweat like blood pouring from His brow, and cried out, "My soul is overwhelmed with sorrow to the point of death." And when He hung on the cross, He did not smile through it. He cried out in anguish, "My God, my God, why have you forsaken me?"

If these are the people of God, then surely, we do not need to pretend.

The Apostle Paul declared, "When I am weak, then I am strong." That is not a metaphor. That is theology. Paul's thorn in the flesh was not removed, and yet he was still used. God's power is not perfected in our performances—it is perfected in our vulnerability. Strength, in the kingdom of God, is not the absence of struggle. It is the presence of honesty.

John Wesley understood this. He never taught that holiness was a linear ascent. He wrote of "wilderness states," of spiritual dryness, of painful sanctification. He did not demand perfection. He invited surrender. Wesleyan theology, at its core, honors the ongoing work of grace—a grace that doesn't demand that we be strong, but walks with us when we are not.

In my ministry, I have sat with people who carried this myth of invincibility like a burden on their backs. I've met pastors afraid to tell their congregations they were in therapy, terrified they would lose their jobs. I've counseled leaders who smiled from the platform and wept in the parking lot. I've listened to veterans who serve on church security teams but haven't slept through the night in years. I've spoken with mothers whose postpartum depression was met with anointing oil and then silence. I've hugged young men who served faithfully in ministry but carried suicidal thoughts they dared not confess. And I have stood in the mirror, wearing my own mask, wondering if I was the only one faking it.

We have built churches where testimony is celebrated but confession is shamed. Where "deliverance" is expected, but grief is not given space to speak. Where healing is preached, but therapy is whispered about in secret. Where disability is tolerated only when it looks inspirational. Where leadership is reserved for those who never seem to struggle. Where tears are dried quickly, and joy is forced like a song sung off-key.

We can do better. We must do better.

We must build churches that tell the truth. That honors mental health as part of spiritual health. That affirms therapy as a tool God can use. That creates room for lament, for rest, for silence, for questions without quick answers. We must teach that Jesus does not only come in strength—He meets us in weakness. That the cross is not just a symbol of victory, but of vulnerability. That resurrection comes, but only after death is named and honored.

Strength is not pretending. It is showing up anyway. Strength is saying, "I need help," and trusting that you will not be abandoned. Strength is removing the mask. Not because you are no longer afraid, but because you are no longer willing to lie.

So, if you are carrying the myth of invincibility, I want you to hear this.

You do not have to perform. You do not have to hide. You do not have to be invincible to be worthy of love. You are not weak because you are tired. You are not broken because you cry. You are not less spiritual because you ask for help. You are not less called because you sit in a therapist's office. You are not less holy because you take medication. You are not alone.

You are not alone.

The God who knit you together is not disappointed by your need. He draws near to the brokenhearted. He weeps beside graves. He sits with the overwhelmed. And He does not flinch when you come undone.

Let this be the place where the myth breaks—and you do not.

Let this be the page where you are finally allowed to be human.

And let that be the beginning of healing. Not a detour. The way.

Trauma, Survival, and the Mind's Defense

Trauma does not always arrive with sirens. Sometimes it walks in quietly, barefoot and unnoticed, and takes up residence inside the body. It can enter through a single violent moment, or through the accumulation of ten thousand small wounds: not being believed, being mocked for your voice or your silence, being touched when you did not want to be, losing a home, being left out, being left behind. It lodges in the nervous system, in the breath, in the gut. It hides in memory, but it shapes everything.

Clinically, we now know that trauma changes the architecture of the brain. It does not just sit in memory like a file in a drawer. It rearranges the entire filing system, even the file retrieval mechanisms. The amygdala, the brain's fear center, becomes hyperactive. The hippocampus, which normally gives us linear memory and a sense of time, begins to lose clarity. The prefrontal cortex, where we reason and plan, and weigh consequences, begins to dim. The body becomes a warning system, even when there is no longer anything to fear. You begin to live with your shoulders tense, your breath shallow, your thoughts like stampedes.

I did not first learn this in a classroom. I learned it while gripping the steering wheel so tightly my knuckles turned white, unsure how I got there or what I was supposed to do next. I learned it in the tremor of my hands after a sudden laugh in a crowded room. I learned it during sleepless nights when my thoughts spiraled without mercy, and the air in my lungs felt too thin. When I did not want to die, but wanted to get off the roller coaster. I lived it before I ever had words to explain it.

Some of the trauma I carry is named in clinical language. Complex PTSD. Depression. Anxiety. ADHD. There is also the looming specter of CTE—chronic traumatic encephalopathy—a degenerative brain condition caused by repeated head trauma, often found in athletes, especially in those who played Football and Wrestled like I did. It cannot be confirmed until death, but I live with its fingerprints now. Unpredictable rage. Memory gaps. Language fatigue. Extreme light sensitivity. Sudden emotional shifts I cannot always explain. Football gave me strength, discipline, and purpose. But it also gave me a battered brain.

Then there are the other wounds.

I am a survivor of sexual assault. Writing that sentence still tightens my throat. The event itself left me shattered, but the silence afterward cut just as deep. I didn't know who I could tell. I didn't want to be pitied. I didn't want to be disbelieved. I didn't want to be seen as weak, or broken, or worse—used. The shame crawled over everything, covering my body and my voice. I buried it in years of busyness and ministry. But shame doesn't stay buried. It lives in your posture, in your pauses, in the questions you never ask. When I finally shared it, it was used as a means to dismiss me from opportunities.

Add to that the bullying I endured—because of my weight, my Deafness, my awkwardness. Add to that the times I was the bully, dishing out the very pain I had received, thinking power would protect me from more hurt. I remember the faces of those I made fun of, those I excluded, those I hurt out of my own hunger to belong. That, too, is its own kind of trauma: the memory of having hurt others while trying to protect yourself. There is no peace in being the one who survives if you become the reason someone else doesn't.

Still, not all trauma announces itself with violence. Sometimes it sounds like a parent or a family member whom you cherish walking away. Sometimes it feels like growing up in a home where no one speaks your language. Sometimes it is the confusion of needing help but having no words to ask for it. I grew up Deaf in a world that revolved around sound. I lived in houses where communication was effortful, incomplete, and sometimes impossible. Most Deaf children are born to hearing parents who never become fluent in sign language. Which is why for years, Deaf children, especially in impoverished cultures and regions, find their way into orphanages, foster care, or are simply abandoned in an institution. Imagine living for years where no one fully speaks your language. Where your questions are met with frustration. Where your silence is misread as disobedience. That is trauma, too. Not just linguistic, but relational, emotional, spiritual.

The brain learns to survive in these environments. But survival has a cost.

Survival rewires trust. It teaches you to scan every face for danger, to replay every conversation for signs you missed, to anticipate rejection before it arrives. It teaches you to people-please, to keep the peace even when it means betraying yourself. It teaches you to shut down emotionally, because feeling deeply is too dangerous. You learn to disassociate, to become a bystander in your own life. You smile through the storm, but you're not really there. Your body is. But your soul is curled in a corner, waiting for the world to be safe again.

Yet, I am not unique.

You may not share my Deafness, my diagnosis, my story—but I promise you, you share the room. The person beside you in church might be carrying flashbacks from the battlefield. The teen across from you in school may be recovering from abuse that still hasn't been believed. The man next to you in the staff meeting might cry in the shower every morning and still lead the team with excellence. The woman in your small group might be battling postpartum depression with a Bible in one hand and medication in the other. There are children in your Sunday School who flinch at raised voices and elderly saints who haven't told anyone how scared they are of the dark.

Trauma wears a thousand faces. Some wear suits. Some wear scrubs. Some lead choirs. Some lead communion. Some don't say anything at all.

Some trauma is not just individual. Some of it is inherited. Some of it is systemic. There is trauma passed down through generations of racism, colonialism, poverty, homophobia, incarceration, and religious abuse. There is trauma in being told your identity is a sin, your pain is a lack of faith, and your condition is your fault. There is trauma in being constantly asked to prove you belong.

God does not ask us to perform. He asks us to come.

Jesus did not rush to fix every person who came to Him. Sometimes He listened first. Sometimes He wept. Sometimes He stayed silent. The risen Christ still carried His scars. His wounds were not erased in resurrection—they were redeemed. That truth has carried me through seasons when I could barely carry myself. I do not worship a God who avoids suffering. I follow a Savior who enters it, stays with me in it, and speaks my name on the other side of it.

This book is not a formula. I am not giving you a cure. But I am bearing witness. Because I believe with all my being that empathy can be cultivated, that grace can be practiced, and that healing—real healing—begins not in the absence of pain, but in the presence of someone who chooses to stay.

If we, as the Church, the Body, the community, want to reflect the heart of Christ, we must become people who can sit with trauma without shrinking. We must stop judging the symptoms of survival. We must stop demanding smiles from the suffering. We must create spaces where vulnerability is not punished, where therapy is not taboo, where lament is not rushed, and where healing is not reduced to a checklist.

Some wounds will never fully disappear. But they do not define us. They are not our names. They are not our worth.

You are still made in the image of God. Even when your memory is fragmented. Even when your trust is fragile. Even when you shut down to survive. You are not a burden. You are a testimony.

I cannot tell you how your story will end. But I can promise this: you are not alone. You are not beyond grace.

Systemic Madness: Punishing Pain

What does a person in pain truly need?

They need safety before they need advice. They need presence before they need solutions. They need space to breathe, not more walls to crash into. They need to be seen, not as a disruption, but as someone worth staying with. And yet, too often, the response from our world is not compassion. It is criminalization. It is exclusion. It is silent. It is what I have come to call systemic madness.

This madness is not accidental. It is baked into how our institutions operate. We live in a society that tells people to get help, but then places that help behind locked doors, closed clinics, unaffordable specialists, and endless waitlists. We speak of personal responsibility, but do not acknowledge the system's refusal to take responsibility for the barriers it creates. For people dealing with mental illness, developmental disabilities, Deafness, neurodivergence, or the long reach of trauma, the expectation to function normally is like being told to run a marathon while your legs are bound and your lungs are half full.

In our public schools, children with Individualized Education Programs—known as IEPs—are legally guaranteed support for their differences. But in practice, these children are often treated as burdens. A child with ADHD is written up for being disruptive when his body simply cannot stay still. A Deaf child who struggles to follow spoken directions is labeled defiant. An autistic student who shuts down during a meltdown is accused of being manipulative or lazy. Teachers, undertrained and overwhelmed, are often doing the best they can. But the result is the same. The child is punished instead of supported. Their behavior is addressed, but their need is ignored.

When those children are Black or Brown, the consequences become even more severe. In school after school, a Black boy's frustration is read as aggression, a Latina student's silence as disobedience. Teachers may not intend to treat children differently, but the data is undeniable. Black students make up about fifteen percent of school enrollment, but nearly forty percent of suspensions. Black girls are suspended six times more often than white girls for similar behaviors. These are not differences in conduct. There are differences in perception. They are the long shadow of systemic racism, passed down and lived out in school discipline codes and office referrals.

This is the foundation of what researchers have long called the school-to-prison pipeline. The pipeline does not begin in high school. It begins in preschool, where children of color and children with disabilities are suspended at higher rates than their white and nondisabled peers. It continues in middle school, where students are removed from classrooms for expressing distress. It solidifies in adolescence, when police are called instead of counselors. These children are not seen as children. They are seen as threats.

When they become adults, the pattern continues. The systems do not lose track of them. They tighten their grip. Adults living with mental illness or cognitive disabilities are far more likely to be arrested, incarcerated, or institutionalized. Many are arrested for behaviors linked directly to their conditions—public outbursts, failure to comply with confusing instructions, inability to pay fines, or survival behaviors like loitering, trespassing, or self-medication. These are not crimes in a moral sense. They are symptoms of systems that have refused to care.

Once inside the justice system, people with mental health conditions receive little to no treatment. Instead, they are placed in overcrowded jails, often in solitary confinement, where their conditions worsen. According to the Bureau of Justice Statistics, nearly half of all people in jail or prison have a diagnosed mental illness. More than thirty percent have cognitive or developmental disabilities. These are staggering numbers. And behind every statistic is a story—a family torn apart, a future cut short, a person whose pain was interpreted as a threat.

Deaf individuals face additional layers of harm. In moments of crisis, Deaf people are often misinterpreted by police officers who do not know sign language. What looks like hand movements to communicate are mistaken for resistance or aggression. There have been cases where Deaf individuals were tackled, handcuffed, tased, and even killed for simply trying to be understood. Once incarcerated or institutionalized, they are frequently denied access to interpreters. They sit through hearings they cannot follow. They are medicated without explanation. They are isolated not only by concrete walls, but by the absence of language.

Faith communities have not always responded well, either. Mental health is often spiritualized in ways that deepen shame. People are told to pray harder, to rebuke fear, to cast out depression in Jesus' name. But depression is not a demon. It is an illness. Anxiety is not a failure of faith. It is a neurological response to prolonged threat. Trauma is not a lack of trust in God. It is the body's memory of what it survived.

When churches treat suffering as sin, they do not heal. They harm. I have seen people leave the church not because they stopped believing in God, but because they were told their suffering meant God had abandoned them. But that is not the God of Scripture. The God I know does not flee from suffering. He enters into it. Jesus crossed stormy waters to reach a man living among tombs. He listened to the cry of the bleeding woman. He paused in the crowd to restore the one everyone else had pushed aside. The heart of God beats most clearly in the places we try to avoid.

Still, it is not enough to tell hurting people that God sees them. We must ask whether the systems we have built reflect the heart of the One we follow.

Right now, our systems are failing. Mental health clinics are underfunded. Waitlists stretch for months. Counselors are burned out. Medicaid reimbursement rates are so low that many therapists stop accepting it altogether. Police departments receive surplus military equipment, but schools struggle to hire full-time social workers. Jails are now the largest mental health providers in many counties. This is not a broken system. It is a system doing what it was built to do—contain, control, and conceal pain rather than heal it.

There are better ways. Programs like CAHOOTS in Eugene, Oregon, have shown that when mental health professionals—not police—respond to nonviolent crises, outcomes improve dramatically. Restorative justice practices in schools reduce suspensions and increase graduation rates. Housing-first models, used in Finland and parts of Utah, have dramatically reduced chronic homelessness by giving people stable housing without requiring sobriety or compliance first. Churches are beginning to train their leaders in Mental Health First Aid, partner with local counselors, and create spaces where people are safe to speak their truth.

These are not theories. They are proven paths. The question is whether we are willing to walk them.

Policymakers can allocate funding for school-based mental health care. They can pass laws mandating interpreter access in all public services. They can expand Medicaid coverage for therapy and psychiatry. They can decriminalize survival. They can prioritize healing over punishment. Clergy can learn how to accompany the suffering with both spiritual and psychological wisdom. Educators can advocate for training and trauma-informed teaching. And we—all of us—can learn to stop judging what we do not understand.

We can stop punishing people for being in pain. Because that is what we are doing. We are arresting people whose grief has nowhere to go. We are suspending children who cannot make sense of their own emotions. We are locking up those who needed help long before they ever broke a law. We are doing it in the name of order, of safety, of stability. Real safety does not come from cages. It comes from compassion. Real order is not built through silence. It is built through understanding.

The prophet Isaiah spoke of a day when God's people would be called "repairers of broken walls, restorers of streets with dwellings." That is the calling. That is the work. Not to cast out the hurting. Not to control the vulnerable. But to rebuild what has been broken. To make the path level again. To become a society that treats suffering not as a sin, but as a summons.

Let us become that society. Let us become those people. Let us no longer say, "Get help," while making help unreachable. Let us no longer watch people fall and ask why they could not fly. Let us build ladders instead of trapdoors. Let us be repairers. Restorers. Healers. Witnesses. Because no one should be punished for being in pain. Any system that does so should be the first thing we tear down and rebuild with grace.

Lies the Mind Believes

There are some battles that do not leave visible scars. They do not announce themselves with casts or crutches or IV lines. Instead, they take place silently, relentlessly, in the confines of one's own mind. These battles are no less real for being unseen. They are no less brutal for being internal. And the ones who fight them are not weak or unstable. They are often among the strongest, most faithful, most courageous people you'll ever meet.

Mental illness, trauma, neurodivergence—they wear many names and faces. Sometimes they look like someone who laughs too loudly, always trying to lighten the mood. Sometimes they look like the quiet student in the back of the classroom who never makes eye contact. Sometimes they look like the preacher, the parent, the nurse, the athlete, the teacher. They look like people you know. People you admire. People you love.

They also look like me.

I've spent years fighting against lies that settled into my spirit like fog on a window. They never announced themselves as lies. They wore the face of logic, of humility, even of holiness. "You're too broken to be loved." That one came early. It was whispered after every rejection, every friend who drifted away, every relationship that couldn't hold the weight of unspoken things. "You'll never be understood." That one lingered, especially when I had to explain Deafness, trauma, or the exhaustion of masking my neurodivergence. "God only speaks to people who don't struggle." That one crept in from the pulpit, from devotional books, from casual prayers that suggested peace was a reward for obedience and clarity was a sign of closeness with God. And the most insidious of all: "If they knew your thoughts, they'd leave." That lie took root when the intrusive thoughts came—violent, shameful, irrational—and I didn't know what to do with them except hide.

If you've never experienced these kinds of thoughts, let me try to help you understand. They do not feel like choices. They are not born from selfishness or lack of discipline. They arrive like uninvited guests—loud, persistent, sometimes terrifying. You can know, rationally, that they are not true, and still feel powerless to stop them. You can be surrounded by people who love you and still feel profoundly alone. You can believe in God and still feel like you're sinking in darkness.

If you have experienced them—if your mind has ever turned against you—then you already know how much energy it takes just to keep going. To get out of bed. To eat. To answer a text. To sit in a room full of people and pretend you are fine when your thoughts are anything but. You know what it feels like to question your own worth, not just occasionally, but constantly. You know the shame of having a panic attack in a place where others expect you to be composed. You know the guilt of not being able to explain why today feels heavier than yesterday. And you know how exhausting it is to try and act normal when everything inside you feels like it's on fire.

These experiences may look different for each of us, but the ache of being misunderstood is something many of us share. That ache becomes deeper when we're told, either directly or by implication, that our pain is a weakness, that our struggle is a failure of faith, that we are broken in a way that disqualifies us from love or usefulness. These messages—spoken or unspoken, institutional or internal—create a kind of spiritual isolation that's difficult to describe. You begin to believe that you are a problem to be solved rather than a person to be loved.

Here's what I've come to believe, not because someone preached it to me, but because I have lived it and clung to it and found it to be true when nothing else made sense: struggling does not mean you are faithless. Wrestling with your own mind is not a failure. It is a form of sacred survival. It is evidence that you are still here. That you are still fighting. That you are still hoping, even if that hope is barely flickering.

Falling apart doesn't make you worthless. It makes you human.

Grace—real, relentless, undeserved grace—is not a reward for those who keep it together. Grace is the hand that reaches for you when you cannot hold on. It is the voice that calls your name when all you hear are lies. It is the truth that you are still worthy even in your lowest moment.

Sometimes grace sounds like a therapist saying, "You're not crazy." Sometimes it looks like a friend sitting with you in silence. Sometimes it arrives in the form of medication, or a diagnosis, or a name for what you've carried without words. Sometimes it is simply breath. The miracle of waking up and still choosing to stay.

I do not write these things as someone who has figured it all out. I write them as someone still in the trenches. Someone who has cried in the parking lot after preaching. Someone who has sat in the pew and wondered if I belonged there. Someone who has walked hallways pretending to be okay when my chest was tight and my thoughts were spiraling. I write as someone who has doubted God's nearness in my suffering and yet found, again and again, that God never moved.

I also write this to those who may not understand what it means to live with depression, anxiety, or neurodivergence. If you've never experienced the weight of mental illness, that is a gift. But please don't use that gift to judge those who do. Use it to offer compassion. Use it to hold space. Use it to ask better questions. The person beside you might look fine, but be barely holding on. You cannot always see the battle, but that doesn't mean it isn't raging. Sometimes the ones who seem the strongest are the ones fighting the hardest to stay alive.

So here is the truth we must speak louder than the lies:

You are not too broken to be loved. You are not alone in your struggle. Your mind may lie to you, but your identity is not up for debate. You are not a burden. You are not beyond grace. You are not disqualified from being a vessel of hope, of light, of purpose. And you are not the only one who has ever felt this way.

You are not just surviving. You are showing up. And that, in itself, is holy.

Faith in the Fire: Where God Met You

This is holy ground. Let no one rush past it. Let no theologian explain it away. Let no preacher polish it into something sterile or safe. Let it be known, with the weight of generations behind us and the trembling hope of the present before us: God does not wait for healing to begin before drawing near. He does not stay outside the storm and summons us to courage. He steps into the whirlwind, into the cracked open heart, into the unspoken chaos of the mind—and He stays.

The truth that has held me through the most tormented nights of mental and emotional anguish is not the promise that everything would be fixed, but the witness that I would never be forsaken. The presence of God is not reserved for the strong or the stable. It is not rationed out based on clarity or calm. It is found—most fiercely—in the furnace. Not only in the fire that rages around us, but in the fires that rage within us.

God met me in the hospital waiting room. He met me on the numb drive home after a panic attack. He met me in the breath that finally came after hours of invisible suffocation. He met me in a verse I almost forgot and in a friend's voice that came just in time. These were not dramatic miracles. They were flickers. And yet, they were everything. Not the parting of seas, but the steadying of my knees when I could not stand on my own.

Scripture does not sanitize the experience of mental anguish. David wrote psalms soaked in tears and asked, "Why are you cast down, O my soul?" (Psalm 42:5). Elijah, after calling fire from heaven, collapsed under a broom tree and begged God to let him die (1 Kings 19:4). Jeremiah cursed the day of his birth. Paul confessed despair that went "beyond our ability to endure" (2 Corinthians 1:8). And Jesus Himself—the sinless Son of God— sweat blood in the garden and screamed forsakenness from the cross. These are not moments of failure. These are revelations of divine solidarity. They testify that anguish is not foreign to God. It is sacred terrain.

Isaiah's prophecy did not say the Messiah would come laughing and victorious. He said He would be "a man of sorrows, acquainted with grief" (Isaiah 53:3). The Hebrew word for grief here is not symbolic—it refers to deep, bodily suffering. Jesus did not simply come to teach or to heal. He came to suffer with us. In theological terms, this is not just compassion—it is Incarnation.

The Word became flesh and dwelt among us (John 1:14). And the Word did not come invincible. He came vulnerable. Not immune to sorrow but immersed in it.

When the Apostle Paul writes that the Holy Spirit intercedes with groanings too deep for words (Romans 8:26), he is not speaking poetically. He reveals a truth every person with a broken mind or weary spirit already knows: there are moments when words will not come. And in those moments, the Spirit does not wait for our clarity. The Spirit becomes our prayer. Our silence is not a void to be feared. It is a sacred chamber where the Spirit prays in a language that even we do not understand.

This is what Henri Nouwen called "wounded healing." It is what John Wesley understood when he taught that grace is not justifying—it is sanctifying. It does not only forgive—it reshapes. But sanctification is not always clean or clear. Sometimes it is done in hospital rooms, in midnight cries, in moments where all that remains is the breath of God whispering that we are still held.

In my own life, the wilderness of mental anguish has not been a place of abandonment. It has become a tabernacle. Not because the suffering was good—but because God refused to let it be wasted. There is something holy about the place where God stays, even when others leave. Where He does not flinch from our pain or demand we fix it before we are worthy of His presence. The wilderness of the mind is not uninhabitable to God. It is often where He dwells most tenderly.

We must say this: to struggle mentally is not to be exiled from faith. It is often plunged deeper into it. Deeper than dogma. Deeper than Sunday platitudes. Into a kind of faith that bleeds, that groans, that questions without losing grip on hope. To be mentally ill or neurodivergent or broken in spirit is not to be disqualified. It is to be human. And to be human, fully and vulnerably, is the very place God chose to meet us.

This is not an idea reserved for elite theologians. This is what we must teach our teenagers, our elders, our pastors, our parents. We must stop preaching that mental health is a sign of spiritual strength. It is not. It is a condition of the body and mind, influenced by trauma, genetics, chemistry, oppression, and suffering. If the Church dares to preach the whole Gospel, it must proclaim with equal force: Christ did not die for the healed. He died from the hemorrhaging. He rose, still bearing wounds. He breathes peace into locked rooms of fear.

The call to the Church, then, is not to fix people. It is to sit with them. To silence the noise and become witnesses to pain. To declare that healing is not a prerequisite for belonging. To say what Jesus said to the man on the mat—"Take heart, your sins are forgiven"—*before* the man ever stood up (Matthew 9:2). To say what God said to Hagar in the wilderness: "I see you" (Genesis 16:13). To say what the Spirit says in every groan: "You are not alone."

This is not cheap comfort. It is a costly presence. It is the theology of fire. God with us, not beyond us. God in us, not after us. God for us, not because we deserve it, but because that is who He is.

So I declare, not as one who has arrived, but as one still walking through shadowed valleys: God did not wait for me to be okay to be present. He met me in the wilderness of my mind. He stayed until I could breathe again. He did not demand performance. He offered presence. And when I thought the fire would consume me, He stepped into it and called it holy ground.

This is not just my story. It is the Gospel.

And the Gospel does not flinch from pain.

The Gospel speaks of resurrection from within it.

Reimagining the Church's Role

The Church must reimagine its posture toward mental health not as a problem to be fixed but as a sacred landscape where compassion is incarnated. The way we treat those who suffer—whether from depression, PTSD, neurodivergence, dementia, or emotional injuries carried since childhood—reveals our deepest theology, no matter what our doctrines say. To follow Christ is not to stand above brokenness but to kneel in its dust and say, "You are still beloved here."

Yet for far too long, our churches have modeled an economy of performance over presence. We ask for praise before pain. We make room on the platform for those who appear strong, while those who are unraveling sit alone in the pews or stop coming at all. We have baptized silence, mistaking stoicism for strength, and cast healing only in terms of visible recovery. But healing, as Scripture teaches, is not always immediate, public, or complete. Sometimes it is slow, private, and ongoing. Sometimes healing is simply surviving another day with faith intact.

We must no longer demand that people demonstrate their wellness before granting them a seat at the table. The Church cannot be a stage for the "strong" if it will not also be a sanctuary for the vulnerable. It must become a place where grief is not rushed, where breakdown is not shamed, and where neurodivergence and emotional complexity are not treated as spiritual failures. This reimagining begins with acknowledging that trauma and mental illness are not sins to be confessed but wounds to be carried, often with great dignity and faith.

The pastoral and prophetic heart of the Church must be especially tender toward those whose struggles began in childhood—those who were born into neurodivergence, developmental delay, or early adversity. Too many children have been labeled "behavior problems" rather than understood as survivors of invisible storms. Too many elders have been discarded as "confused" or "difficult" when, in reality, they are carrying the compounded weight of grief, cognitive decline, or depression that surfaces after a lifetime of deferred pain. The Church must not only welcome these souls—it must learn their language.

It is not enough to say, "Come as you are." We must also mean, "Stay as you are, and let us walk with you as you become." Churches should invest in trained trauma chaplains, mental health first aid teams, and spiritual caregivers who understand that brain chemistry and spiritual formation are not enemies but companions. Our sanctuaries must have space for stimming hands, for wandering minds, for silence that is holy, and for tears that do not need to be explained. Neurodivergence should not merely be tolerated but honored as part of the Imago Dei—the image of God.

Likewise, the burdens carried by clergy, missionaries, and church leaders must no longer be hidden behind forced smiles or sanitized testimonies. The expectation that ministers be emotionally invincible has produced generations of leaders who crumble behind closed doors. When pastors are punished for burnout, depression, or breakdown, we do not just lose their ministry—we violate the Gospel itself. A healthy church is not one where leaders never bleed; it is one where leaders can bleed and be bandaged in the same place.

True transformation begins when pastors themselves confess their limitations, when church members with schizophrenia or bipolar disorder are not whispered about but embraced, when aging saints with dementia are not excluded from communion but included in every circle of care. In doing so, the Church bears witness to a Christ who not only walked among the well but who dined with the anguished, wept with the overwhelmed, and restored the outcast with a touch.

The calling now is urgent. We must become a people whose default is not suspicion but sanctuary. We must raise our children in spaces where mental health is not taboo but a shared language of trust and care. We must build communities where trauma survivors can breathe, where ministers can cry without fear of losing their collar, and where the aging can forget our names but never be forgotten themselves.

If the Church is to be the Body of Christ, it must have a nervous system. It must *feel*. And in feeling, it must respond—not with platitudes but with presence. Not with fixes but with fellowship. Not with pressure to be healed, but with the promise: you are not alone. You have never been. And you never will be.

The Mind Isn't the Enemy—Isolation Is

You are still learning to live with your own mind. Still unpacking it. Still naming what hurts and what heals. There are days when your thoughts feel like thorns and nights when silence feels like betrayal. But God is not afraid of the terrain you're still mapping. He doesn't require you to be at peace before drawing near.

This much, you've come to know: You are not a diagnosis. You are not the sum total of your lowest seasons. You are not disqualified by the noise inside your head or the fog that sometimes surrounds your name. You are a disciple. A whole, holy person whose value is not reduced by the fracture lines of anxiety, depression, OCD, bipolar disorder, schizophrenia, memory loss, or emotional disorientation. Your mind is not your enemy. Your isolation is.

The lie is that to be faithful, you have to be fine. That to be welcome, you must be well. But this is not the Gospel. The Gospel is that Christ, who sweated blood in Gethsemane, who cried out in agony on the cross, who bore the full weight of human sorrow, does not retreat from the wounded. He draws closer. The incarnation is proof that God chooses to dwell not in sanitized minds but in real ones—aching, overwhelmed, complicated, still becoming.

In every generation, the Church has too often stood at a distance from those whose minds do not align with the dominant rhythms. We've offered platitudes instead of presence. We've baptized perfectionism, shamed those who speak of therapy or medication, and treated emotional struggle as a theological problem instead of a human one. We've neglected those born with mental differences, avoided those marked by trauma, and forgotten those whose minds unravel with age. We've prayed for their "return to normal" rather than welcoming them into the beloved community as they are. This must change.

The Church must be more than a refuge for the well-adjusted. It must become a sanctuary for the unraveling. A place where pastors are not punished for burnout. Where missionaries are not discarded after breakdowns. Where laypersons are not silenced by shame. Where children with developmental disorders are not "disruptions" but revelations of God's creativity. Where elders battling dementia are not burdens but bearers of sacred memory.

Where survivors of abuse are not asked to smile through their healing, but are held as they weep through it.

Faith is not proven by having no scars. It is witnessed in those who keep showing up with them.

So to the one reading this who has wrestled with suicidal thoughts, who has wondered if your presence is more of a problem than a gift, who has been told to "pray harder" or "just be strong," hear me now: Your story is not over. Your pain is not too much for God. Your diagnosis does not nullify your discipleship. You are loved—entirely, intentionally, eternally.

And to the Church: let us be a people who don't flinch at brokenness. Let us be the ones who sit in the dark, who build ramps into our pulpits and softness into our language. Let us tell our stories—the hard ones, the unfinished ones—so that others may find the courage to tell theirs. Let us be stewards of sanctuary, not just in architecture but in attitude.

Because the lie was that we had to be okay to be faithful.

The truth is, we found God in the unraveling, and He stayed.

CHAPTER 10

Weights We Carry

He walked out of the courtroom like he was pushing through deep mud. Every step looked like it cost him something he didn't have left to give. His head was down, not out of shame but because lifting it would have meant meeting the eyes of a world that had already made up its mind about him.

I didn't know him well. We had met once, months earlier, at a local outreach cookout behind the church. He had stood near the edge of the parking lot with his arms crossed and his shoulders hunched like someone who had learned long ago not to expect kindness to last. He hadn't said much. Just nodded when someone offered him a plate of food. That was it. But I never forgot his eyes. They were the kind of eyes that looked older than the body they belonged to. Eyes that had seen too much too young and not enough good in the right places.

On the day of his sentencing, his mother waited at the bottom of the courthouse steps. She stood still, arms stiff at her sides, her eyes already red but dry. When he came through the doors, she took one step forward, barely even a movement, and a deputy raised his hand and told her she couldn't approach. She didn't argue. She just folded her fingers into her palms and nodded like someone who had spent years practicing how to obey rules she didn't believe in.

He never looked at her. Maybe he couldn't. Maybe he knew that if he did, the fragile shell of composure he was holding together would crack wide open in front of everyone.

And I, standing across the street waiting for my order at a restaurant, had my hands in my coat pockets and felt paralyzed, the sickening weight of helplessness settling in my stomach. I wanted to shout that this wasn't the end of his story. I wanted to tell her she wasn't alone. But I didn't say anything. I just watched. Because sometimes silence is not absence. Sometimes it is reverence for a pain too deep to fix with words.

People use the word burden like it's symbolic. But I have seen men and women walk through life with pain that physically shapes them. I've seen backs hunched not from age but from years of disappointment. I've seen eyes that flinch at every sudden sound because home never meant safety. I've seen the tremble in the hands of women digging through purses at recovery meetings, not looking for a cigarette or a mint, but for something that would give them just one more reason not to give up.

I've seen teenagers fold their arms across their chests during worship services, not because they are rebellious, but because they are afraid of being seen. I've heard kids speak too loudly in class and then apologize without even being corrected, because they have learned that their voices are too much. I have watched people carry pain like luggage no one ever offered to help them unpack.

And I have carried it too.

I carry it in my throat every time I speak in a room where I am the only Deaf person, where every sentence takes effort and every conversation feels like a test I did not study for. I carry it in my bones when I pretend not to mind being misunderstood, when I smile through exhaustion because it is easier than asking people to slow down. I carry it in the memories of classrooms where I was invisible and churches where I was prayed for but never truly welcomed.

Not all weight is visible. Some people carry court records. Others carry childhood trauma. Some wear the label of addict. Others carry wounds from marriages that look picture-perfect on Facebook but feel like war behind closed doors. Some have bruises on their skin. Others have bruises on their souls.

We carry shame. We carry rejection. We carry fear. And we are taught to carry it alone.

I need you to hear me. Grace does not ask for credentials. Grace does not demand an explanation. Grace does not need your trauma to be tidy. Grace does not wait for you to be clean or put together. It simply kneels beside you and says, "You were never meant to carry this alone."

There is no holiness in suffering for the sake of appearing strong. There is no prize for hiding your pain until it eats you alive. There is only this one truth that keeps me breathing on the hard days.

Grace does not require the weight to be justified. It just invites you to set it down.

And if the Church has forgotten that, then it is not the Gospel we are preaching. It is something else entirely.

Because the real Gospel does not ask, "How did you end up here?" It asks, "Can I walk with you the rest of the way?"

And that, my friend, is the kind of grace that can save a life.

Defining 'Margins' Beyond Stereotypes

If you had asked me as a child what it meant to be on the margins, I wouldn't have had the language to explain it. I knew what it felt like with every part of my body. It felt like sitting in a classroom while the teacher continued talking after turning to face the board, leaving me to guess what had been said. It felt like smiling when everyone else laughed, even though I hadn't heard the joke. It felt like learning to fake comprehension just so I wouldn't be called slow. It felt like being seen as an inconvenience instead of a child with a soul.

Marginalization doesn't always sound like slurs. It sounds like silence. It sounds like decisions were made without you. It sounds like a sigh before someone has to repeat themselves. It sounds like a compliment wrapped around a warning: "You're doing fine... for someone like you."

The margins aren't confined to the walls of the church. They extend through the hallways of public schools and the waiting rooms of doctors' offices. They are found in grocery store glances and PTA meetings and staff lounges and courtrooms and city buses, and family gatherings. The margins run through every layer of life. They aren't empty places. They are overflowing. But even in the crowd, there is a quiet kind of isolation that burrows into your spirit. The pain of the margins is not only exclusion. It is the exhaustion of always having to move.

People on the margins live like nomads. We travel between spaces, from classroom to classroom, from neighborhood to neighborhood, from job to job, from denomination to denomination, always adjusting, always translating, always wondering when the grace will run out. We learn how to shrink ourselves to fit into places that were never built to hold us. We pitch tents in communities that never invite us to lay a foundation. We adapt. We perform. We manage our presence like it were a problem to be solved. But we never truly rest. We never truly belong. We learn to carry our identity like luggage; we are not allowed to unpack.

I have stood in those spaces. I have ministered to people whose pain has no name and whose trauma has never been acknowledged. I have sat across from a young man who aged out of foster care with nothing but a grocery bag and a folded letter from a caseworker. He came to our church on a Wednesday night and asked if we had a men's Bible study. He didn't need doctrine. He needed a place to sit without being asked to leave. He didn't say much that night. Just nodded. But he came back. Week after week. And when someone finally asked if he would close in prayer, he wept—not because he didn't know how, but because no one had ever invited him to speak aloud in a room that wasn't judging him.

I have seen students labeled before they have the chance to speak. Black and brown boys are suspended for behavior that others are corrected for. Girls who are told to smile more but speak less. Children who are punished for surviving in systems that never made space for their grief. I have seen immigrants navigating life in a second language, translating for their parents, absorbing their teachers' impatience, and still managing to excel, only to be told they are lucky to be here. I have sat beside LGBTQAI+ youth who memorize escape routes in churches and schools alike, not because they are rebellious, but because they are afraid. Afraid of being outed. Afraid of being disowned. Afraid of being erased.

I have prayed with men who served their time and came home only to find the locks had changed. Employers won't look past their record. Landlords won't return their calls. Churches say they believe in redemption, but they never let them near leadership, near children, near the pulpit, near the table. They hear the word "grace" like a rumor, never like an invitation.

There are people whose entire lives have been spent moving from one level of tolerance to another. Tolerated in the classroom but not encouraged. Tolerated at the dinner table but not fully welcomed. Tolerated at the altar but never seen as equal. The ache of the margin is that you are always adjusting yourself to fit someone else's comfort. You are never simply received. You are translated. Modified. Managed.

It is not just what people say. It is what they withhold. The withheld embrace. The invitation that never comes. The leadership role goes to someone more "safe." The eye contact that never lingers. The silence when cruelty enters the room. The conversations that move on without you. Over time, you begin to believe that your existence is too heavy, too complicated, too much.

This is not a call to agree on everything. This is not a plea for doctrinal surrender or moral ambiguity. This is a call to stop withholding love. It is a plea for compassion that doesn't have to be earned. Because if your love requires sameness, it is not love. If your grace only applies to people who look like you, talk like you, worship like you, or vote like you, then it is not grace. If your welcome ends where your comfort begins, then it is not the gospel you are practicing. It is self-preservation.

The gospel was never meant to be an audition. It was always a welcome home.

So open your doors wider. Let your tables grow longer. Ask someone's name before you judge their story. And if you are standing in the margins yourself—if you are reading this while carrying the weight of being too different, too broken, too loud, too silent, too invisible—know this. You are not alone. You are not forgotten. You are not unworthy. You were never meant to wander forever. Grace has been walking toward you this whole time.

And this, right here, might be the first place you are finally allowed to set your bags down.

When Survival Is the Only Choice

People love the idea of free will. It's a phrase that gets tossed around in courtrooms, in pulpits, and in political debates. He made his choices. She knew better. They chose that life. It's a comfortable narrative because it puts distance between the speaker and the struggle. It allows people to believe that pain is always the result of personal failure. But what if there was no better option? What if the road was broken before they ever took their first step?

Some people are born into survival. Not because they sinned, not because they strayed, but because the ground beneath them was already cracked. I've sat across from a man who took his first drink at eight years old. Not because he wanted to rebel, but because his father came home from the factory angry and drunk, and the boy figured out that if he passed out first, the fists might not fly. That boy didn't choose addiction. He chose safety. And safety, when found in a bottle, becomes a cage that follows you into adulthood.

Addiction is rarely about thrill. It is more often about pain management. About filling the space left behind by grief, loss, or trauma. I've looked into the eyes of young men with gang tattoos—not because they loved violence, but because their only sense of belonging came from a group that saw them when no one else did. Sometimes the worst decisions are born from the best human needs: the need for connection, for protection, for being seen.

I've heard the truth in places where people had nothing left to prove. In prison visiting rooms, in halfway houses, in shelters, in recovery circles held in church basements that smelled of coffee and old folding chairs. I've heard confessions that shook me to the core, not because of the sin, but because of the sorrow. Not because of how far someone had fallen, but because no one had ever been there to catch them.

I remember a young woman who aged out of foster care and came to our church with her possessions in two plastic grocery bags. She asked if she could sit in the sanctuary while the sun was still up. She wasn't looking for a handout. She just needed to feel something holy for a few hours. Somewhere quiet. Somewhere where no one would touch her, yell at her, or ask her to leave. That evening, I realized that holiness isn't always wrapped in hymns and liturgy. Sometimes it's found in the stillness of a room where someone is finally allowed to breathe.

I remember a teenage boy at a youth event who quietly asked to speak with me during snack time. He stood off to the side, gripping the hem of his hoodie like it was the only thing holding him together. "Pastor Rick," he said, "if I tell my parents I'm gay, I won't have a home to go back to. I already packed a bag." His voice didn't tremble. His eyes didn't plead. He wasn't looking for permission or theology. He was looking for someone to hold space with him. For someone who would not flinch. For someone who would not disappear.

And I want to say something very clearly. Standing with him in that moment did not mean I surrendered my own convictions. It did not mean I had to condone everything about his journey or redefine my beliefs in order to offer compassion. What it meant was this: I refused to weaponize my faith against his humanity. I did not need to resolve every theological tension in order to be a human being in that moment. I did not need to agree in order to be kind. I did not need to compromise truth to reflect grace.

Jesus stood with sinners without sinning. He dined with tax collectors without defrauding anyone. He defended the woman caught in adultery without pretending adultery was good. But he loved her before he corrected her. He protected her before he preached to her. And when he did speak, it was with tenderness and clarity, not accusation.

Standing with someone in their pain does not mean you agree with every choice they've made. It means you refuse to abandon them in the middle of their story. It means you recognize that the image of God in them is not erased by their struggle. It means you choose to believe that grace is stronger than your fear of being misunderstood.

I've met more saints in jail cells than in pews. Not because jail is holier, but because it is more honest. It strips away performance. There are no illusions of control. Just people, raw and repentant, trying to make sense of their lives. In those rooms, I've heard prayers that shook me. I've seen faith flicker like a candle in a hurricane—and somehow still stay lit.

Incarceration is not just about personal failure. It is often about systemic collapse. About poverty that corners someone into stealing. About trauma that taught them to fight before being hurt. About schools that gave up. About mental illness, untreated, violence normalized, and neighborhoods forgotten by the very systems that were meant to protect them.

And addiction—again—is not a character flaw. It is a soul-level cry. An attempt to soothe what has never been comforted. To fill what has always been empty.

Even sexuality and gender identity, which the Church too often discusses with fear or disgust, do not emerge in rebellion. They awaken quietly. In loneliness. In dorm rooms. In whispered confessions. In years of hiding. Whether or not we understand or agree, we are not excused from love.

We ask people to rise above. But how do you rise when no one ever taught you how to stand? How do you move forward when every step is haunted by rejection?

Survival isn't a rebellion. It is resilience. And many of the people we judge have spent their whole lives surviving in ways we cannot begin to understand. To survive is not to thrive, but it is still sacred. Because it means they are still here. Still trying.

True grace—does not require full agreement to be extended. It does not wait for someone to clean themselves up. It does not demand understanding before it offers presence. It simply says, "Even here. Even now. You matter."

You can disagree with someone's choices and still honor their humanity. You can hold conviction and still walk with compassion. You can believe in holiness and still offer a seat at your table. Jesus did all of this. And if we follow him, so must we.

I would rather sit in a jail cell with someone desperate for grace than in a sanctuary full of people who have forgotten they need it. Grace does not come to prove a point. It comes to restore a soul.

Shame as a Cage

Shame does not begin with a mistake. It begins with a message. A whisper that says, "You are the mistake." It doesn't point to what you did; it attaches itself to who you are. And once that message takes root, it burrows into the bones, making even breath feel like a burden. Shame doesn't shout. It seeps. It cloaks itself in politeness, in performance, in silence. And before long, it turns vibrant people into shadows of themselves—still present, but afraid to speak, afraid to take up space.

I felt it young. Not just as a Deaf child in a hearing world, but as a human child in a world built for performance, speed, perfection, and assimilation. I learned to perform belonging. I learned to smile when others laughed, even when I hadn't caught the joke. To nod when someone explained something, even if I'd missed it the first or second time. I learned to speak clearly, not because it felt natural, but because it made other people comfortable. I learned that being "easy to manage" was the fastest path to inclusion. And that kind of lesson sinks deep. I began to believe that hiding was holy. That invisibility was maturity. That silence was a virtue.

The first time someone laid hands on me and prayed for God to "fix my Deafness," I was thirteen. I remember standing there, eyes wide open, more confused than comforted. I didn't know how to say that their theology felt like a knife. I didn't know how to name the feeling that maybe God didn't love me just as I was. I walked away from that altar wondering if healing was the only way to be accepted—and that kind of doubt grows roots fast and deep.

Shame doesn't always come from enemies. It comes from family. From friends. From the church. From teachers and mentors and Sunday school rooms. From glances that linger too long. From smiles that don't reach the eyes. From well-meaning phrases that miss the soul completely. "It's all part of God's plan." "Just have more faith." "Maybe you should pray harder." "Don't talk about that here." "Keep that between you and God." What they don't say is often louder than what they do.

I've seen shame in the woman whose miscarriage was spiritualized and brushed aside. In the man drowning in alcohol, who was told to "get right with God" but never asked why he was in pain. In the queer teenager who heard nothing but silence when they tried to ask where they fit in the Gospel story. In the father who lost his job and cried alone in his truck while his church smiled through another sermon on "God's provision."

I've seen it in the single mother told to step down from church leadership. In the Black woman labeled "angry" for speaking truth. In the immigrant parent attending school meetings conducted in English with no translation and no patience. A disabled student was told they were too disruptive. The man released from prison, welcomed with applause one Sunday and avoided the next.

Shame doesn't always attack. Sometimes it just clears its throat when you speak too long. Sometimes it smiles and changes the subject. Sometimes it says nothing at all—and that silence can be the most painful language of all.

Much shame has been packaged in religious wrapping, and many of us confuse it with conviction. But they are not the same. Conviction is the voice of the Holy Spirit calling us back into alignment with our sacredness. Shame is the voice of fear telling us that sacredness never lived in us to begin with. Conviction lifts the head. Shame bows it. Conviction says, "Come home." Shame says, "You never had a home here to begin with."

Even in Eden, it wasn't guilt that made Adam and Eve hide. It was a shame. It was the impulse to cover up, to run, to disappear. But God didn't storm through the garden demanding perfection. He came walking. Gentle. Asking, "Where are you?" That is the question shame fears most—because it calls us out of hiding and into love.

I know where I've been. I've been the boy in the back of the classroom pretending to understand. The teenager is masking pain with politeness. The young man was wondering if my voice was too broken to preach the Word of God. The pastor was trying to lead while silently asking if anyone else could hear my stuttered prayers and still believe I belonged at the table.

I have sat across from others whose shame runs deeper than mine. A woman told she had to forgive abuse before she could even name it. A man who carries his son's overdose like a secret tombstone in his chest. A gay teen who still prays every night but whispers, "God, I'm sorry I exist." A disabled young woman was told she would never be used by God because she could not walk on her own.

They didn't lose their faith. They lost their welcome.

That is what shame does. It cages the soul. It makes vulnerability a liability. It teaches people to manage their joy, minimize their truth, and measure their presence. It turns sanctuaries into stages. Worship into performance. Prayer into hiding. Psalm 32 says, "When I kept silent, my bones wasted away." That's not a metaphor. That's a diagnosis. I have felt it—bone-deep. I have seen it in others.

Jesus did not ignore shame. He entered it. Hebrews 12 tells us that he endured the cross, scorning its shame. He was stripped, mocked, beaten, and crucified—not just in pain but in public humiliation. And yet when he rose, he didn't hide his wounds. He offered them. He showed Thomas the holes. He served Peter breakfast. He found the disciples behind locked doors—not to condemn, but to say, "Peace be with you."

He does not erase shame by ignoring it. He erases it by entering the locked rooms where it hides.

So if your story includes shame—if someone told you that you were too emotional, too broken, too late, too much—hear me: That voice was not from God.

You were never too slow.

Never too loud.

Never too messy.

Never too complicated.

Never too far gone.

You were never supposed to disappear.

You were made in the image of a God who walks into shame and still says, "You are mine."

You don't have to earn your return.

You just have to come home.

That raises the question for so many of us:

Where is home for those who have been rejected?

Where is home for the person cast out of their church because of who they are or who they love?

For the child who aged out of foster care and never heard the word "welcome"?

For the man whose prison record clings to him like a scarlet letter?

For the woman who told the truth and was exiled by those who claimed to protect her?

For the Deaf teenager who was told, through sighs and side-eyes, that they were too much work?

For the grieving, the addicted, the doubting, the different, the excluded, the unseen?

Where is home when the door was closed behind you?

The painful truth is that for many, there is no physical home yet. No sanctuary without conditions. No pew that doesn't flinch. No table without fine print.

But home begins where shame ends.

Home is not just a place. It is a posture. It is found wherever someone looks you in the eye and says, "I believe you."

Where no one tries to fix your soul before feeding your hunger.

Where your silence isn't punished and your voice isn't policed.

Where grace is not a script. It is a presence.

Where someone stays—even when the questions are heavy and the answers are slow.

Home is the voice of Jesus still calling from the shoreline: "Come. Eat. You belong here." It may not be a building. It may not be your family. It may not be the church of your childhood. But it is real. The Church—when it remembers its first love—can become that home again.

For now, home is wherever grace is carried like bread, not like a sword. Wherever people make room for the entire story. Wherever shame ends and presence begins.

If you haven't found that place yet, if the doors keep closing and the table keeps shrinking—then maybe you're called to help build it. Shame told you that you would always be wandering. But grace has been walking beside you the whole time— waiting, watching, whispering. You can stop running now. You can come home.

From Comfort to Confession

There is a memory the Church has tried to forget.

It is not the forgetting of a verse or a creed, but of its place. It's posture. Its purpose.

The Church was born in the shadows of empire. It was baptized not in golden fonts but in back rooms, in catacombs, in jail cells still damp from blood. Its founders were not seminarian elites—they were fishermen, tax collectors, insurgents, tentmakers, formerly possessed women, men who ran from battle, and one who couldn't stop doubting. The early Church gathered under threat of arrest and death. They whispered hymns in the dark while Roman guards passed outside the door. They broke bread with trembling hands. Their tables held former zealots beside centurions, widows beside wealthy landowners. They didn't just teach grace—they needed it to survive.

But we've grown comfortable. Too comfortable. Somewhere along the way, many churches traded wilderness for stage lights, confession for branding, and the call to "come and die" for a call to "come and volunteer once a month if it fits your schedule." The language of the cross still hangs on our walls, but the weight of it rarely lands on our shoulders.

And nowhere is that amnesia more obvious than in how we talk about—or don't talk about—the incarcerated and the addicted.

Today's prison system is our modern leper colony. Not a place of healing or restoration, but of permanent social exile. The bars may unlock, but the exile continues. A person returns home, if they're lucky enough to still have one, only to find that home has changed—if it ever existed at all. The job applications ask about felony convictions. The landlords ask about criminal history. The voter registration is denied. The pastor asks if they've really repented. The usher smiles politely but doesn't make eye contact. Every step forward comes with a silent reminder that their record is still louder than their voice.

And this isn't new. Not really.

The ancient world used public shaming as punishment. Roman crucifixion was not merely about execution—it was about humiliation. Naked bodies hung as warnings. Names scratched from records. Citizens rendered "non-persons." Jesus didn't just die—he was erased. So when we forget those imprisoned, we forget Jesus.

In Scripture, prison is not where the villains live. It's where the prophets are sent. Joseph is falsely accused and forgotten in Pharaoh's dungeon. Jeremiah is thrown into a muddy pit for telling the truth. Daniel is tossed to lions for refusing to bow to the empire. Paul writes half the New Testament in chains. John receives Revelation while exiled. Peter is in and out of jail like a revolving door. And Jesus—Jesus is arrested, mocked, spat on, tortured, and executed in the most public, humiliating, imperial way possible.

What more do we need to remember where the Gospel lives?

We've built a world where prison is synonymous with failure. Where criminal records are seen as moral judgments. Where punishment is not only physical—it is spiritual. The person is no longer seen as a child of God but as a threat, a liability, a cautionary tale.

We have to name it: this exile is not equally distributed. In the United States, incarceration has never been about justice alone— it has been about control. After the Civil War, the Thirteenth

Amendment abolished slavery "except as punishment for a crime," and that exception became a loophole large enough to rebuild an entire economy. The Black Codes were passed to criminalize unemployment, vagrancy, and loitering—things that applied disproportionately to freed slaves. Convict leasing replaced plantation labor. Prisons swelled with Black bodies re-enslaved under another name.

Jim Crow laws built on that foundation. Segregation, redlining, lynching, underfunded schools, over-policed neighborhoods, and generational poverty. Then came the War on Drugs in the 1980s, when Black and Brown men were sentenced to decades in prison for crack cocaine while white users of powdered cocaine received slaps on the wrist. Three-strikes laws. Mandatory minimums. Private prisons. Policing quotas. Bail systems that punish the poor. These weren't accidents. They were strategic.

The Church—especially the white evangelical church—was silent. Or worse, supportive. Instead of dismantling the systems of empire, many churches blessed them. Instead of confessing complicity, they hosted "blue lives matter" prayer breakfasts. Instead of building bridges of reentry, they built fences around their sanctuaries.

Scripture never blesses that kind of silence.

Isaiah cried, "Woe to those who make unjust laws." Amos thundered, "Let justice roll down like waters." Jesus himself said, "I was in prison, and you visited me." Not metaphorically. Literally.

The prophetic call has always been clear: go to the margins. Stand with the condemned. Break bread with the forgotten. Tell the truth even when it costs you everything.

The same is true of addiction. In our pulpits, we preach resurrection. But in our board meetings, we hesitate to let the recovering addict lead a small group. We welcome the testimony, but only if it ends neatly. We love the redemption arc—but we fear the relapse. We claim to serve a God of second chances, but we treat relapse like betrayal instead of part of the journey.

Addiction is not a moral defect. It is a wound. A scar that never got a chance to scab. It is grief with no grave, trauma with no counselor, loneliness with no relief. People don't wake up one day and decide to destroy their lives. They reach for what numbs the ache. And when the Church avoids that ache, people learn to keep their pain elsewhere.

Recovery is holy ground. Messy, slow, sacred. It does not move in straight lines. It does not guarantee success on a timeline that suits us. It is not a one-time altar call. It is a lifetime of returning.

Instead of walking that road with people, the Church has too often created barricades. "What if he starts using again?" "What if she shares too much in the group?" "What if it's too risky to let them serve?"

What if Jesus had asked that about Peter?

Peter who denied him. Peter who panicked. Peter who got it wrong again and again. Jesus didn't fire Peter. He fed him breakfast. And then said, "Feed my sheep."

Jesus did not call perfect people. He called willing ones. Wounded ones. One's still learning how to love and fail and love again.

So what does a prophetic Church look like?

It looks like a table with no head seat. A sanctuary with no dress code. People who know the smell of a halfway house and the ache of an ankle monitor. A leadership team that includes the formerly incarcerated, the recovering addict, the trauma survivor, the single mother, and the non-traditional family. A theology that does not flinch from blood and dirt and relapse and redemption.

It looks like a confession.

We confess that we have made comfort our idol. That we have confused security with salvation. That we have preferred applause to repentance. That we have walked past prison doors and halfway houses and recovery meetings without once wondering what Christ looks like in those places.

It is time to confess. And after confession comes a call.

We are called not to gatekeep grace but to carry it. Not to control redemption but to participate in it. Not to fear the mess, but to remember that resurrection always begins in a grave.

So may we become prophets again. May we remember our story. Maay we return to the margins where Jesus has always waited—arms open, scars showing, table set.

I Don't Have to Agree to Love You

I have said things I cannot unsay.

I have spoken words that still echo in the back chambers of my mind—words spoken from pulpits, parking lots, prayer circles, and youth events. Words I wish I could scrub from the memories of those who heard them. Words I said with conviction but not with Christ.

I have said I hated homosexuals. I have said, "That's not how God made you," to a transgender friend whose full story I never even asked to hear. I remember telling them (not knowing they had not yet come out) "They chose it" or "They just want attention. I have flinched at pronouns, rolled my eyes at rainbow flags, stayed silent when laughter turned cruel, and nodded along when someone cloaked condemnation in a Bible verse. I have used the Gospel as a mirror to judge others instead of a window through which to see my own soul. And I have done all of this in Jesus' name.

There are nights I still dream about it with horror—the faces, the pain I saw and ignored, the chances I had to love but chose to correct instead. In those dreams, I am not standing beside Christ. I am standing among the crowd, stone in one hand and a lit torch in the other, quoting Scripture as justification while someone else bleeds in the dust.

So let me say this plainly, with no apology for its clarity: I was wrong. I did harm. And I do not write this section to earn back trust or to present myself as an expert on LGBTQAI+ experiences, Racism, Sexism, and other prejudices. I write it because silence, once broken, must give way to witness.

I am not writing to affirm or to reject identity. I am writing to reject cruelty. I am writing to refuse the temptation to tie love to agreement. I am writing because too many LGBTQAI+ people have been driven to despair and even death by those who claimed to be acting in God's name—and I will not participate in that any longer.

I do not need to have all the answers. I am not the judge. My theology is one facet of a God of infinite depth. And I will not use that theology as a wall to keep others out of reach of grace.

To every queer, gay, lesbian, transgender, intersex, nonbinary, questioning, and differently-identified person who has ever wondered if they were safe in the presence of Christians: you deserve to breathe. You deserve to live. You deserve to be loved.

Without needing my theological alignment to receive my Christlike compassion.

We have so often confused uniformity with unity, forgetting that Jesus built his closest community out of contradiction. Zealots and tax collectors, deniers and doubters, women with oil and men with swords, the ones who wept at his feet and the ones who betrayed him with a kiss. Jesus never once demanded agreement before offering love. In fact, love often came first—and changed people in ways that doctrine alone never could.

I disagree with people I love every day. I disagree with my children, my spouse, my colleagues, and my dearest friends. Still, I show up. Still, I listen. Still, I eat with them, cry with them, forgive them, and ask to be forgiven in return. Why is it that we can hold disagreement in almost every other relationship, but when it comes to gender and sexuality, suddenly our capacity for compassion collapses?

If the Church cannot learn to love without control, then it has no right to preach grace. If love must be earned, it is not love. If grace has limits, it is not the Gospel. If we only welcome people who make us comfortable, then we are not followers of Christ— we are gatekeepers of our own illusions.

I think often about the people I pushed away—not just the ones I hurt outright, but those I failed to pursue. The friend who came out and never returned my calls. The teenager who sat quietly in the youth group, terrified someone would ask about their pronouns. The person who sat on the back pew week after week, hoping someone would see beyond the surface and simply say, "I'm glad you're here."

I wonder where they are now. I wonder what they believe about God. I wonder if they survived the silence.

Jesus tells a story about a shepherd who leaves the ninety-nine to find the one. I used to think that meant we should go after the lost to bring them back into the fold. But now I wonder if sometimes we are the ninety-nine—so convinced we're already safe that we forget we've left someone behind. So certain we're in the center of God's will that we don't realize we've become the ones needing rescue.

The Gospel calls us to go. Not to correct. Not to coerce. But to go. To sit beside. To weep with. To listen. To stay.

I'm not asking anyone to abandon their conscience. I'm not demanding doctrinal compromise. I'm simply asking: can we love with the same wild, unearned, relentless love that Jesus poured out for us—while we were still sinners, while we were still questioning, while we were still enemies of grace?

The only reason I'm still standing here drawing breath and writing this book is that someone loved me before I was ready. Someone prayed for me while I was still a bigot. Someone welcomed me into grace while I was still ignorant and loud and sure of myself in all the wrong ways.

If God could do that for me, then who am I to say where grace ends?

I may not know what to do with every verse. I may not have the language right. I may not fully understand every nuance of identity. But I know what love looks like. It looks like Jesus kneeling in the dirt beside the ones everyone else is trying to stone.

A Deaf Pastor's Heart for the Silenced

I have always known what it means to enter a room already behind.

I don't mean behind on grades or skills, though I've had my share of struggles there, too. I mean behind in access. Behind in assumptions. Behind in belonging. As a Deaf child in a world built for sound, I learned from a very young age that the world doesn't slow down for people like me. Teachers didn't pause to make sure I was following. Coaches gave instructions while walking away. Friends forgot I couldn't hear the warning they were shouting or the joke they were telling. I was present, but unseen. There, but not fully known.

It wasn't always malicious. Most of the time, it was ignorance dressed up as efficiency. But that doesn't make the silence any less suffocating. When the world keeps moving and you're left nodding your head like you understood—even when you didn't—you begin to believe the lie that silence is safer than asking for help.

By the time I reached adulthood, I had mastered the art of invisibility. I could smile at the right time. I could play along. I could fake comprehension. But I could not shake the ache of feeling like a burden. That ache followed me into classrooms, locker rooms, sanctuaries, and social gatherings. It whispered, "Don't speak unless you're sure. Don't raise your hand unless you're right. Don't ask them to repeat it—they're already annoyed."

Yet, somehow, in the thick of that silence—God called me.

Not just once. Not just to one lane or one audience. God called me in the fullness of my being—to pastor people, to teach students, and to coach young athletes. To lead not from perfection, but from proximity. From experience. From the quiet corners the world so often forgets.

As a pastor, I carry this silence with me into the pulpit. I do not stand to perform. I stand to offer sanctuary to those who've been told they don't belong. My sermons do not flow from a place of confidence—they flow from the deep well of survival. Every word I speak costs me something, not just because of my Deafness, but because I know what it means to preach from a place the world tried to leave behind. When I speak of grace, I mean the kind that holds you up when you are exhausted from trying to be heard. When I speak of belonging, I mean the kind that doesn't ask you to audition. I don't preach to impress—I preach so that nobody else has to wonder if the Gospel is for them.

As a teacher, I enter every classroom with the memory of being overlooked. I teach with my eyes wide open, scanning the room not just for participation, but for pain. I pay attention to the kid whose head is down, not out of disrespect, but because they didn't sleep last night. I see the student who doesn't speak because English is their third language. I recognize the ones masking their learning struggles behind jokes or silence. I notice the ones who flinch when asked to read aloud. I teach the curriculum, yes—but more than that, I teach dignity. I teach presence. I teach grace. I teach that every student has worth, even when the system labels them "behind."

As a coach, I carry a different kind of authority—one built not on power, but on memory. I remember what it was like to give everything I had at practice and still be benched because I didn't fit the mold. I remember being strong enough to play, smart enough to lead, but overlooked because I wasn't the loudest, the fastest, or the most polished. So now, I coach for the ones who don't get the spotlight. I coach for the kid who shows up to every workout with something to prove—to themselves more than anyone else. I coach for the quiet leaders, the grinders, the overlooked. I coach because I know that sometimes a practice field is the only place a kid feels like they matter.

These three callings—pastor, teacher, coach—they aren't separate identities. They are braided together in my bones. They flow from the same place. They arise from the same fire. And they point to the same truth: the silenced are sacred.

I do not carry these roles as badges of honor. I carry them as a sacred trust. I carry them because I have been the kid in the back of the room, the player on the bench, the congregant too ashamed to go to the altar. I carry them because I know what it feels like to be prayed for, but not with. To be talked about in pity but not included in purpose. To be seen as a problem to solve instead of a person to empower.

So, when I teach, I teach in a way that says, "You are not broken."
When I coach, I coach in a way that says, "You are not forgotten."
When I preach, I preach in a way that says, "You are not too late."

I know what shame sounds like. I know what erasure feels like. And I also know what grace can do when it walks into a classroom, a locker room, or a sanctuary and says, "You still have a seat at the table."

That's why I show up.

That's why I stay.

That's why I keep speaking, even when it's hard.

Because if I can be a voice for the ones still finding theirs, then none of the silence was wasted.

So, if you've ever been silenced—by disability, by fear, by trauma, by failure—know this:

You do not have to earn your welcome.

You do not have to speak perfectly to be heard.

You do not have to win to be worthy.

You are not invisible to God.

And you are not alone.

This is the heart of a Deaf pastor.

This is the heart of a classroom teacher.

This is the heart of a field-tested coach.

And above all, this is the heart of grace—

A grace that stays in the middle.

What the Church Must Become

The Church must become something different, something deeper, braver, and more faithful than what much of it has settled for. Not because the Gospel has changed, but because too many churches have forgotten its center. Too many sanctuaries have become sanctuaries in name only. Too many altars have been turned into platforms. Too many pews have been filled with people performing righteousness instead of being met with grace. We are not called to keep the hurting outside the door. We are called to throw the doors wide open and meet them on the road.

For years now, I've watched people approach the Church with their hearts in their hands, only to be greeted with suspicion. I've seen fear in the eyes of young adults wondering if they can bring their full story to the table. I've seen recovering addicts sit in the back row, flinching at the word "holy" as if it could never include them. I've seen formerly incarcerated men volunteer to sweep the floor but never be asked about their gifts. I've seen LGBTQAI+ teens crying in their cars after being told they're welcome to attend but not to serve. I've watched single moms shrink into pews, ashamed to ask for help again. I've seen immigrants sit through entire services without understanding a single word, still hoping someone might notice they exist.

I've had enough of that kind of Church.

If we are going to call ourselves the Body of Christ, then we must stop judging people based on how they look, what they've done, where they're from, who they love, or how they vote. Jesus didn't come to elevate those who fit into tidy religious categories. He came to call the ones who had been cast out. The tax collectors, the prostitutes, the lepers, the possessed. The ones whose bodies were bleeding and whose souls were weary. He called them by name, not by label. And He brought them close— not to fix them first, but to show them they were already loved.

The Church cannot keep using holiness as an excuse to be heartless.

We must become a people who create space for honesty—not just polished testimony, but messy, unresolved, in-process truth. We must become the kind of church where someone can walk in carrying a relapse, a doubt, a criminal record, a divorce, a secret— and not be stared at but embraced. Not lectured but loved. Because if the Church is only a place for the perfect, then it is no longer a reflection of Christ.

Truth still matters. It always will. But truth must be spoken in love, or it ceases to be truth. Scripture says that Jesus came full of grace and truth—not half of each, but the fullness of both. And that balance is what the Church has lost. We have swung between extremes—either so soft we're silent about injustice, or so harsh we drive people away with our so-called clarity. But truth without love is a sword. And love without truth is a shadow. We are called to carry both, gently and boldly, like Christ did.

This must lead us into transformation—not just of hearts, but of structures, ministries, and cultures. We need more than slogans. We need change.

We must become recovery-friendly churches. This means not just tolerating the presence of people in recovery but actively creating environments that honor their stories. It means opening our buildings during the week for twelve-step groups, family recovery meetings, and sober living check-ins. It means training our lay leaders to listen without judgment. It means inviting recovering individuals into leadership—not someday, but now— because their stories carry a theology of survival that the Church desperately needs to hear.

We must invest in second-chance ministries—not just sermon illustrations about forgiveness, but systems that reflect it. Churches should partner with local businesses to advocate for second-chance hiring. We should host job fairs that don't require a clean record to participate. We should support returning citizens with rides to interviews, mentors who won't give up, and congregations that don't flinch when a man walks in with ankle monitors or prison tattoos. We should be the place where the story doesn't end with conviction but with a calling.

We must also become churches where LGBTQAI+ individuals are invited to belong—even when theological tensions remain unresolved. This doesn't require the entire Church to have the same perspective on identity. It requires the Church to have the same commitment to dignity. It means treating every person as a beloved child of God. It means refusing to use theology as a weapon. It means showing up to pride events not to protest, but to protect. It means being the one place in town where queer youth know they can sit in silence or speak in tears, and no one will ask them to change in order to stay. This kind of love doesn't abandon Scripture. It fulfills it.

We must train and support pastors differently. Not just in doctrine or homiletics, but in trauma, grief, conflict, and restoration. Too many pastors know how to teach a text but don't know how to sit with pain. We need shepherds who can tell when someone's shaking hands are not disrespect—but PTSD. We need leaders who understand anxiety, depression, and bipolar disorder, not as weaknesses, but as realities within the Body of Christ. We need preachers who don't just speak from the stage, but who can kneel at a bedside, who can wait with someone at a clinic, who can say, "You are not a burden. You are not too broken. And you don't have to walk alone."

The Church is not dying because culture is changing. The Church is dying where courage is absent.

And now is the time for courage.

The courage to speak truth when it's hard.

The courage to make space when it's costly.

The courage to become what Christ actually modeled: a place for the outcast, the broken, the misfit, the doubter, the addict, the queer kid, the felon, the foster child, the foreigner, the fatherless, the fearful.

If our churches are not safe for them, then they are not safe for any of us.

I do not want to lead a church that is impressive.

I want to lead a church that is faithful.

I want to walk into sanctuaries that reek of coffee and recovery meetings.

I want to hear weeping at the altar again—not because people feel ashamed, but because they feel safe.

I want to see Sunday morning greeters who know what it means to have been hated and found holy anyway.

I want to look around and see people who are still healing— and still showing up.

That's what the Church must become.

Not a museum of purity.

Not a theater of control.

But a field hospital.

A table of welcome.

A family of unfinished people.

A body whose scars match those of Christ.

The Weight Shared Is the Weight Redeemed

Everyone carries something. That is not just a poetic metaphor. It is a theological fact, a pastoral reality, a human truth as old as Eden. We carry the weight of memory—of words spoken too harshly or too late, of choices we wish we could take back, of people we buried and still dream about, of prayers we whispered that never seemed to echo back. We carry the weight of systems— of zip codes that predicted our outcomes before we could spell them, of classrooms that never noticed our silence, of courtrooms that made their judgments long before hearing our story. We carry the weight of expectations we inherited from generations before us and those we invented ourselves, each one heavier than the last. We carry the weight of performance, perfectionism, and pretending. Some of us carry these burdens openly, sagging beneath the visible strain of survival. Others carry them quietly, smiling on cue while bleeding inside. But whether we admit it or not, we all carry something.

These weights do not ask for our permission. They arrive uninvited—sometimes as traumas passed down like heirlooms, sometimes as secrets locked away behind the careful choreography of daily life, sometimes as habits that started with pain and ended with chains. And yet the deepest tragedy is not merely that we carry burdens. The deeper tragedy is that we have been convinced we must carry them alone. We have been conditioned to believe that asking for help is weakness, that silence is strength, and that vulnerability is best saved for therapists or late-night tears. And somewhere along the way, the Church—this body that was called to be the living extension of Christ's compassion—lost its ability to lift burdens because it became too focused on appearances. We made sanctuaries into stages, pews into platforms, altars into auditions. We stopped asking what people were carrying and started judging how they carried it.

This is not the Church Jesus gave His life to build. He did not die and rise again so that the wounded could be asked to behave before they belonged. He did not stretch out His arms so that we could shrink the Gospel to fit our comfort zones. He came not to admire the light-footed and well-adjusted, but to restore the broken and burdened. Grace, as the cross reminds us, was never meant to be a trophy awarded to the disciplined. It was—and still is—a lifeline thrown to the drowning. It is the bread handed to the famished before they even know they're hungry. It is the healing given to the outcast before they even confess their wounds.

So, I wonder—what if the Church became the place where people actually laid down their weights instead of being crushed beneath them? What if we stopped asking, "What did you do to deserve that?" and started asking, "How can I help carry it?" What if the goal of our ministries was not perfection, but presence? What if holiness were defined not by behavior modification, but by our capacity to love, to stay, to listen? What if the altar became a place where people wept without shame, where no one rushed to fix, explain, or theologize away the pain, but simply sat beside it, held it, and bore it together?

This would require the Church to become fluent in a different language, the language of solidarity, not superiority. We would have to retrain ourselves to hear pain without instinctively offering platitudes. We would have to learn how to speak truth only when it has first been soaked in love. We would have to create rooms where someone's presence is not contingent on theological alignment, social decorum, or personal cleanliness. And we would have to believe, truly believe, that grace does not require prerequisites. That it shows up before we're ready. That it begins not after the burden is named, but in the very moment it is noticed.

The weight shared is the weight redeemed. That is not just poetic theology. That is the Gospel. Because Jesus Himself bore the full weight of sin, sorrow, and shame—not to shame us further, but to liberate us from believing we had to carry it alone. He did not ask us to prove ourselves before offering peace. He did not demand theological clarity before washing feet. He carried the cross up a hill so that every burden carried by every person across every generation could be answered—not with blame, but with belonging. Grace does not erase the weight, but it refuses to let it crush us in isolation. Grace steps under the yoke beside us and whispers, "I'm not going anywhere."

When we become a Church that walks that closely, that stays that tenderly, that listens that long, then we will no longer need to convince people of God's love—they will feel it before we say a word. Then we will no longer struggle to attract the next generation; they will come not for the production, but for the presence. They will come because someone stayed with them when they were unraveling. They will come because the Gospel was not just preached—it was practiced. They will come because someone carried their weight until they could walk again.

This is the Church I still believe in.

The Church that throws off performance and puts on compassion.

The Church that kneels before the cross not to defend it, but to live it.

The Church that stops performing for God and starts participating in grace.

The Church that trades its judgment for gentleness and its fear for faith.

The Church that will not let anyone sit alone in the dark.

The Church that becomes a home—not a hotel.

A refuge—not a recital.

A family—not a filter.

This is the Church where prodigals run home and orphans find family.

This is the Church where silence breaks and songs return.

This is the Church where grace walks in, sits down, and stays.

This is the Church that will rise.

That is the Church we must become.

By God's mercy, we still can.

CHAPTER 11

Running From the Call

I was thirteen when "the call" came.

It happened in a church with no stained glass, no organ, no vaulted ceilings to echo our prayers—just fresh paint and folding chairs, a hand-me-down sound system, and people who believed Jesus could show up anywhere, even in a building that used to smell like rental shoes and vending machine grease. Our sanctuary was a new church plant, stitched into the bones of an old bowling alley, the lanes beneath our feet buried under carpet that still carried the shape of strikes and spares. It was holy ground, not because of what it had been, but because of who we were becoming inside it.

Most Sundays, I stood near the stage signing songs with the praise team—Casting Crowns, Chris Tomlin, maybe MercyMe—songs we sang with all the conviction our teenage lungs could muster. We weren't polished, but we meant every note. I didn't always stay through the whole service once I finished signing songs in ASL with the Praise Team. Sometimes I slipped into Sunday School or snuck out into the parking lot to laugh too loud with my friends during the services I was not "on". That morning, I stayed for the service to just be filled; I do not remember the reason. It could have been required by my parents, or my shenanigan partners may not have been there. What I do remember is that everything changed.

As we shifted from one song to the next, the room fell into a strange stillness. The vibration of the speakers faded. The shuffling of feet stopped. It wasn't the absence of sound—it was the arrival of presence.

As a Deaf person with residual hearing (Profound-Severe Deafness), I've lived most of my life between sound and silence, always navigating the flickering threshold between what the world can hear and what I can feel. My audiologist once explained it like an AM radio station that you could never tune it to absolute clarity. However, this silence was different. It didn't isolate me. It surrounded me. It settled deep into my bones, deeper than music, deeper than words. Not a scary, ominous silence, but a peace like a weighted blanket and the cool side of a pillow.

In that stillness, without a single sound, I heard it.

A voice—not with my ears, but with my soul. A knowing that filled the room with invisible light and made everything inside me go still.

You are called.

There were no fireworks. No audible words. Regardless, I knew. I knew in the same way you know when someone's eyes are already on you across a room. I knew in the way you know you are standing on sacred ground, even if your shoes are worn and muddy.

I was being called to ministry—not in some distant, someday future, but now. Called to lead God's people. To proclaim grace as more than a doctrine—as a lifeline. To shepherd, to teach, to serve. To the ordained Ministry and the international intertwining of need, gifts, and equity.

In that moment, I felt honored. Excited, even. As if heaven had placed something in my hands. I stood taller, breathed deeper. I thought: Maybe this is what it feels like to be chosen.

Then Monday came. And with it, all the reasons why this couldn't possibly be true.

I remembered who I wasn't. I wasn't whole. I wasn't holy. I wasn't consistent or clean or even particularly liked. I was the Deaf kid who spoke too loudly, who stumbled over his own voice and got laughed at for it. I was the one who prayed in the dark and cussed in the locker room. The one who said things I shouldn't, did things I regretted, and carried a deep ache for something I couldn't name.

How could someone like me lead?

How could a teenager still trying to survive high school help anyone find healing?

How could I speak for God when I could barely speak for myself?

So I ran.

Not in open rebellion. But with quiet resolve.

Not because I didn't love God. But because I didn't believe He could really want me.

I poured myself into good things—coaching, teaching, volunteering in youth ministry, doing everything that looked like ministry without ever truly surrendering to it. I told myself that partial obedience was good enough. That I could serve from the sidelines, teach from behind the scenes, love people without ever stepping fully into the light of calling.

Still, the call followed me.

It echoed in unexpected places—in the back row of someone else's revival service, in the silence before I stepped on the field, on a car ride down the backroads with my thoughts, in the middle of worship sets I was only supposed to observe. Every time I tried to forget it, it reappeared like breath on glass, reminding me that God hadn't forgotten me.

I tried to answer it a few times. I stood before an ordination committee once, believing—naively, maybe—that they would see in me what I had finally begun to see in myself. Instead, I left that room more wounded than I'd ever been, misread and misunderstood, carrying a shame I didn't know how to name. Another time, I accepted a ministry position that seemed like the start of something—but I was not ready. I had no roots, no rhythm, no true preparation. I carried passion like it was enough to build a ministry, and when it wasn't, I burned out under the weight of my own good intentions.

Years passed like this. Ministry in motion, but never settled.

I drifted—physically, spiritually, emotionally. I served in towns where I didn't stay long.

I poured out pieces of myself in volunteer roles, substitute pulpits, and back-row prayers.

All the while, I kept hearing that voice.

Calling.

Still.

Again.

It wasn't until I was twenty-six—older, quieter, more tired than I expected to be at that age—that something finally shifted. Not in the world. In me. I stopped waiting for the perfect timing. I stopped begging God for a cleaner past. I gave up on earning my worth and finally gave God my yes.

Not the kind of yes that comes with conditions. Not a trial run.

A full-bodied, trembling, exhausted, honest, yes.

Then came the wilderness.

Not punishment. Not exile. Preparation.

Years of ministry that nobody noticed. Years of learning how to pray when no one else showed up. Years of preaching to small rooms and visiting shut-ins and wrestling with Scripture not to perform, but to survive. Years of being black listed by the very people I considered family and mentors. Years of trying too hard to "make it". Years of God stripping away every illusion I had about what it meant to lead.

In that wilderness, something deeper took root.

I stopped performing.

I started becoming.

I became a pastor—not because I was finally good enough, but because I was finally grounded.

I became a preacher—not because I had found the perfect words, but because I had nothing left to hide.

I became a shepherd—not because I was unscarred, but because I had learned how to walk with a limp.

That church, the one birthed in the old bowling alley, never failed me. It shaped me as a teenager. It held space for me. It offered me a place to grow before I even knew what growing would cost. They believed in grace before I did. They believed in me when I couldn't yet believe in myself.

The call never left.

It lingered—through disappointment, through missteps, through committee rooms and tear-stained journals and whispered prayers in the dark. It never relied on my credentials or my consistency. It stayed because God had placed it there, and He is far more faithful than I ever was.

I used to think I had to be healed to help others. That I had to be whole to lead. That I needed to speak perfectly to proclaim the Gospel.

I've learned that God does not wait for our perfection. He waits for our permission.

He doesn't call the polished—He calls the willing.

He doesn't need the spotless—He uses the surrendered.

The call I carry is not evidence of my strength. It is proof of His persistence.

God never stopped calling.

Not when I stumbled.

Not when I hesitated.

Not even when I tried to silence Him with my own shame.

He kept calling because He knew I would stop asking if I was good enough and start trusting that He already is.

A Pastor's Son Who Saw Too Much

I did not grow up naive about ministry.

I grew up watching it up close—its glory, its weight, its wounds. I watched what it did to people I loved, and I learned early that saying yes to God didn't always lead to peace, applause, or security. Sometimes it led straight into the fire.

My mother was called. Of that, there was never any doubt. Her faith wasn't something she wore on Sundays. It was the air she breathed, the ground she stood on, and the language she used when words failed. She prayed with authority and served with humility. Her preaching wasn't flashy, but it was anointed—born from Scripture soaked in lived experience, from midnight tears and quiet acts of compassion most people never saw. God had gripped her heart long before the church gave her permission to preach, and even when permission was finally granted, the resistance didn't end.

She said yes to the call, but the Church didn't always say yes to her.

From the moment she stepped into leadership, I saw how people responded. Some were supportive, and they were her Aarons and Hurs. But others in the churches where she was sent often met her with doubt. With subtle dismissals and questions coated in politeness but heavy with condescension. I watched her pour herself out in hospital visits, Bible studies, crisis counseling, and funerals—only to come home from church meetings bruised by critique disguised as "constructive feedback," her authority questioned by men who had never walked in her shoes or carried half her spiritual weight.

It wasn't just about being a woman. It was about being a clergywoman.

It was about the way the Church often reveres the idea of calling but resists the reality of it when it shows up wearing the wrong skin, the wrong gender, the wrong style of voice.

She wasn't alone in this. The disrespect I witnessed didn't discriminate. I saw it affect clergy of all backgrounds—Black pastors, white pastors, Hispanic and Asian clergy, men and women alike. Those who served with the deepest faith often bore the deepest wounds.

I watched people praise my mother's sermons on Sunday, then criticize her decisions in the parking lot afterward. I saw her get thanked for her leadership in public while being undermined in private. And I learned that in far too many churches, pastoral authority was not given—it was constantly negotiated, contested, or revoked, especially for those who didn't fit the mold.

Then there was my paternal grandfather—a man of quiet strength and unwavering conviction. He, too, was a pastor, and though he served with grace and honor, he often found himself left out of key decisions or overlooked for leadership roles, not because he lacked ability, but because he refused to compromise the truth. He spoke with clarity when silence would have been safer. He valued integrity more than influence. He chose the harder road, and because of that, he walked much of it alone. He didn't chase titles. He embodied them. The Church, in many ways, was not ready for someone who refused to play politics with the pulpit.

From them both, I learned this: the call to ministry is sacred—but the work of ministry is often heartbreaking.

I grew up watching how easily clergy could be dismissed, how often their gifts went unseen, how rarely their burdens were acknowledged. I sat in the back of sanctuaries and listened to whispered criticisms. I rode home in cars that carried the weight of words no one else heard. I saw my mother lead with power and be ignored. I saw my grandfather stand with truth and be isolated.

These weren't isolated incidents; they were patterns. And they taught me early that ministry does not guarantee respect. In fact, it often invites scrutiny. It asks you to give more than you have, to love people who may never love you back, to serve even when you're empty, and to keep smiling while quietly bleeding.

So I made a quiet decision. Not in rebellion, but in resolve.

That would not be my life.

I didn't want that weight on my shoulders.

I didn't want my wife to carry that pain.

I didn't want my future children to grow up wondering why the Church hurt the people who served it most.

I didn't want to spend my life explaining why people who claimed to love Jesus could treat His servants with such cruelty.

If obedience meant walking into a furnace, then I prayed God would find someone with flameproof skin. I had seen the burn marks. I had smelled the smoke. I had lived with the cost.

And I wasn't sure I had the courage—or the foolishness—to pay that price myself.

Later, I would come to realize that this tension is as old as the call itself.

Moses didn't want to go back to Egypt. He argued with God. He gave excuses. He claimed he wasn't eloquent enough, strong enough, worthy enough. And God didn't disagree with him. God simply promised to go with him.

Jeremiah resisted, too. He wept. He raged. He told God that the call had ruined his life. "Your word," he said, "is like a fire shut up in my bones. I am weary of holding it in; indeed, I cannot." And still, no matter how much it hurt, he could not stay silent.

Even Jesus—the Son of God Himself—was rejected by His own people. He returned to His hometown only to hear, "Isn't this the carpenter's son?" They were offended by Him. And though He healed, taught, and loved without condition, many still walked away when the teaching became hard.

The Scriptures are not shy about the cost of obedience. They never pretend that saying yes to God will make your life easier. In fact, they show us again and again that saying yes is often what draws the fire.

When I was a teenager—fifteen, seventeen, even twenty-two—I wasn't thinking about holy fire. I was thinking about survival. I wasn't looking for a refining flame. I was trying to avoid the pain I had already seen play out in the lives of people I loved.

I told myself I was being wise.

That I was counting the cost.

That maybe God could use me in quieter ways.

And for a time, I lived in that tension—faithful enough to be nearby, but not surrendered enough to step in. The call never left me, but I left it unanswered, like a letter on the table I didn't have the courage to open.

What I didn't yet understand was that the fire wasn't there to destroy me. It was there to burn away everything that couldn't walk with me into the next chapter. It was not the fire of punishment. It was the fire of preparation.

But back then, all I could see were the ashes.

And I wanted no part of them.

No Lightning Bolts—Just a Job to Do

There was no lightning bolt. No angelic voice parting the clouds. No altar shaking beneath my feet. But don't confuse that for reluctance. I sought the pulpit like a man searches for water in the desert—thirsty, desperate, determined. From Delaware's rural chapels to storefront sanctuaries in D.C., from revival tents in

North Carolina to quiet Methodist churches tucked into the hollers of West Virginia, I carried my Bible and my conviction wherever a door opened. Maryland, Pennsylvania, New Jersey—no pulpit too small, no crowd too disinterested. I preached when invited and sometimes when I wasn't. I learned the feel of each sanctuary, the pulse of every people. Not every sermon soared. Not every congregation stood to clap. But I never once climbed those steps or stood behind those pulpits with anything less than my full heart, soul, and body. I preached with all I had, even when all I had was brokenness and breath.

The call didn't stop at the pulpit.

A year after I began preaching, I stepped into a classroom. Not with the fire of prophecy, but with the ache of necessity. I had mouths to feed and bills that didn't care whether I felt inspired. Teaching wasn't a mountaintop revelation—it was a hallway decision. A weary "yes" to a system I didn't fully believe in, but couldn't ignore. I had always suspected I'd be good at teaching. I just never wanted to do it under fluorescent lights and rigid bells and the heavy drag of institutional dysfunction. I love the students, make no mistake. I love their rawness, their rebellion, their questions. But I've never loved the system that cages them—or me—into roles that don't fit.

I came to teaching because it was a job, but stayed because it became a ministry. Not a ministry of sermons and altar calls, but of glances and gestures, of patience when everything in me wanted to scream. I came reluctantly, but I began to see something sacred in the chaos. Maybe, I thought, if I could show up as myself—as a Deaf teacher, as a pastor who knew pain, as a coach who believed in second chances—maybe that would teach more than the textbook could.

I didn't take the teaching job to fulfill a dream. I took it because there was a need. And because something deeper than logic whispered that this—this imperfect place full of broken desks and loud hallways—was the best place for me to serve.

Coaching was easier to explain. Football shaped me. The discipline, the teamwork, the way the field becomes a mirror for a boy's soul, it raised me. I wanted to give that back. I wanted to watch young boys become young men, not just by winning games but by learning to take a hit, get up, and hit back with integrity. I wanted to be the kind of coach who didn't just teach a playbook but taught life—through sweat, through silence, through showing up again and again.

Even then, I didn't always feel like I was doing something holy. Teaching, coaching, pastoring—they felt like three separate tracks until they didn't. Until I realized that God wasn't calling me to a single role, but to a life. A life where the sacred was hidden in the ordinary, where ministry wasn't confined to Sundays but spilled over into Mondays, where the Word became flesh not just in sermons but in lesson plans, whistle blows, and cafeteria conversations.

I used to think a calling would come with clarity. That if God wanted me to teach, He'd part the sky. That if God wanted me to coach, He'd place a trophy in my hand. But what I've learned is that God often works in convergence, not fireworks. I didn't choose the pulpit over the classroom. I didn't choose the field over the altar. I said yes, one obedient inch at a time, until suddenly the pulpit, the classroom, and the field became one unbroken altar of service.

Biblically, I think of Moses—not in the palace, not at the burning bush—but in the slow march through the desert, staff in hand, leading people who often didn't want to be led. I think of Ruth, who simply stayed faithful, gleaning in the fields, unaware that her small yes would carry the lineage of kings. I think of Paul, stitching tents by hand, still preaching with fire between the stitches.

There were no lightning bolts for me. Just one obedient "yes" after another. Just a Deaf man with a call in his bones and a job to do. Through it all, I've discovered this: the sacred isn't waiting on the mountaintop. It's already here—in the chalk dust, in the whistle's echo, in the trembling voice that still says, "Yes, Lord," even when the answer costs everything.

So I show up. Not because I always want to, but because God called me, and because the students need me, and because grace has a strange way of showing up where you least expect it.

A Deaf Man Called to Preach

It is one of the older ironies of my life—that I, a Deaf man, was called to preach. In a world that measures ability in terms of clarity and correctness, fluency and force, I was given a call that depended not on the sharpness of my hearing or the polish of my voice, but on the presence of a fire I could not extinguish.

God gave me a Word and told me to speak. Not after healing me. Not after making me sound more like everyone else. Just as I was—Deaf, different, uncertain. The world counted decibels, but God counted surrender. The world waited for polish; God looked for presence.

From the beginning, I poured every part of myself into preaching—not because it came easy, but because it came holy. I didn't stumble into the pulpit. I sought it out, especially when my own conference family pushed me out and I botched my opportunity as a Lay Speaker. In the five-year gap that I was essentially blacklisted, I preached wherever they would let me— in cinderblock sanctuaries, country churches, storefront fellowships, big city pulpits, and youth camps held under tents that flapped in the wind like the old tabernacles. I took invitations in Delaware and Maryland, Pennsylvania and West Virginia, Washington D.C., North Carolina, and New Jersey—wherever I could learn to grow sharper, more anchored, more emptied out so God could fill me in. Not every sermon landed. Not every word came out clean. I never once held back. I gave everything I had— heart, soul, body, mind—to each word I spoke. Every ounce.

Nevertheless, reaching has never been easy. Not for me.

What most people don't see is the amount of work it takes— not just spiritually or intellectually, but physically—to get the words off the page and into the air. My writing comes from the gut, from a sacred stillness. But speaking? That's a fight every time. I rehearse my sermons over and over, not to memorize them but to make sure my mouth can keep up with my mind. I practice phrases so that I don't trip over them when I'm tired. I try to slow my breathing, control my pitch, and check my articulation. All while praying that people hear the message, not just the mechanics. My biggest fear as a pastor is that my teaching or preaching may cause another to stumble in their faith. A big reason why I invite people to conversation, questions, and discourse. Deaf or not, no person should take their faith at the word of another plainly, but rather test reliability, validity, and soundness.

I stand in front of the mirror or pace in empty sanctuaries mouthing the lines again and again, because I know how quickly people tune out a voice that stammers. I know how they tilt their heads or blink with confusion when the clarity slips. I know how even a slight slur or broken cadence can distract from what I'm trying to say. I know the risk that some people will walk away not with the Word, but with a critique, even condemnation.

Underneath it all, there's a creeping doubt.

I worry—deep down—that my students, my players, my congregants, might be getting less than they deserve. That my voice, no matter how prayer-soaked and fire-breathed, might somehow deprive them of what another preacher, another teacher, another coach could offer. I worry that my limitations don't just cost me—they cost them.

I worry that I'm too hard to understand. That I ask too much patience. That they nod out of kindness, not comprehension.

And yet—God keeps calling.

God keeps whispering: You are not the source. You are the vessel.

Preaching does not erase my Deafness. It magnifies the grace that works through it. It reminds me that healing isn't always a miracle. Sometimes the miracle is in the holding—the way the Spirit cradles a trembling voice until it steadies. The way God takes a hesitant tongue and uses it to split stone hearts. The way grace does not demand perfection to become powerful.

When I preach, my voice does not become flawless. It becomes free.

I do not preach out of strength. I preach out of surrender. I preach out of the deep place that knows what it means to be overlooked. I preach because I have felt the silence. I have lived it. I have been judged by it. I have survived it.

If God can use me—a Deaf man who still stutters, still practices, still doubts—to speak light into darkness, then maybe someone else will believe that their voice matters too.

So no, I am not always confident. Nonetheless, I am called, and when I preach, something holy happens. My voice stops trembling. My stuttering lessens. Not because I am healed, but because I am held.

The Process Is the Fire

Many people told me the process would be longer and more arduous than I could imagine. After that first SPRC meeting—when they voted unanimously to recommend me for ministry—I walked out with my chest high, proclaiming with the certainty of a man standing on air: "I'm ready. I know what's coming." I even remember standing in my Mother's Parsonage with my mother and a family friend who was a long-time ordained elder. They both told me repeatedly, "You must be patient, this is a long road, even if things do go smoothly." Needless to say, things were neither smooth nor predictable.

I was so wrong.

What followed was not a road, but a wilderness. A drawn-out, grinding, emotionally raw process that broke open parts of me I didn't know existed. It wasn't just the paperwork or the interviews, the psychological evaluations or theological essays. It was the slow bleed of hope when emails went unanswered. The awkward silences after passionate sermons. The feeling that your life had already testified, but nobody heard it.

All the while, I was still living in Section 8 housing, dragging garbage bags full of laundry through parking lots, past cracked sidewalks and broken streetlights. There were seasons when we slept in borrowed bedrooms—my wife, our four children under the age of eight, and whatever little stability we could carry in our arms. Welfare was not an add-on; it was the system that sustained us. Food stamps. Medicaid. WIC. Purchase of Care. Veronica navigated it all with precision—because she had to. Because she'd learned the language of survival growing up. She turned shame into stewardship, government forms into holy tools, chaos into something resembling rhythm.

We took whatever work we could find. I stocked shelves. Cleaned. Preached when pastors were on vacation or leave. Took on gigs that barely paid for gas. All while both of us were in school full-time—chasing a future we couldn't yet touch, trusting God like a vine reaching for light through concrete.

I thought that walking into ministry would feel like a resurrection. The truth is that resurrection doesn't come without death first. For a long time, it felt like my struggles were the very grounds of my rejection. I wasn't just poor. I was too poor. Not just overweight. Unacceptably so. Not just Deaf. But Deaf in a way they didn't quite know what to do with.

There were moments I feared my calling would be buried beneath other people's discomfort with my story.

I remember holding a rejection letter from a critical committee that didn't just say "no," but rather said "not for the next 10 years." With no clear path forward. I stood there, reading it again and again, as if enough repetition could unlock a different outcome. My entire family had bought in, sacrificing endlessly.

And after the sting wore off, I folded it, slipped it into the front cover of my Bible, and made a promise: I would not let this break me. I would outgrow this moment. I would not remain bitter. I would become undeniable. This experience gave me a deep distrust for people in leadership, even people I had known for years. This experience cost me thousands and potentially may not be able to complete my seminary education in part because of the thousands more I needed to spend and lose to navigate the loss of this opportunity I foolishly believed with all but guaranteed.

The way I got through it is the way my experiences built me. No one is coming to do it for you or save you, so you need to get to work. I've always needed benchmarks to chase down. That's the football in me. The fire that says—if the line's been drawn, then drive through it. Hard. Repeatedly. Until the line becomes a scar in the dirt behind you.

Among the numerous recommendations used to justify my blacklisting from the ministry was my physical weight at my heaviest, which I had reached 560 pounds. By the time of the meeting, I had gotten down to 400lbs. Still, it was not enough. You don't get there all at once. You get there meal by skipping meals, cutting corners for the kids' sake, surviving off dollar menus, pretending it's not eating you alive. It wasn't just about food. It was grief, fatigue, shame, all of it. It was swallowing every part of myself that didn't fit the mold. I was losing track of when I last felt whole.

I fought back. I changed what I ate, how I moved, and how I prayed. I fought like I had something to prove—not to the world, but to the version of myself that almost gave up. I dropped to 180 pounds. And though I eventually stabilized at 250, I carry it now with strength. With pride. With a story.

I still carry that letter, not as a wound but as a witness. Not to failure, but to fire.

Here's what no one tells you when you're entering ministry: the process is not just about preparing your resume. It's about preparing your soul. It's not about perfecting your image. It's about surrendering your identity. It's not about proving you're worthy. It's about learning, over and over again, that God is able to do immeasurably more than we can think or imagine. The value in the experience forced me to gain skills and attributes I had not possessed before, but the way it was done and the way I was cut off and ignored could have gone a much darker path had it not been for mentors, family, and friends who sat with me in the wilderness.

There were other fires, too—fires that didn't come in official envelopes but in whispers and misunderstandings. I made mistakes in my first appointment. I said too much, or said it too sharply. I tried to fix what I didn't yet understand. I learned the hard way that passion without patience can wound people. That vision without collaboration can feel like tyranny.

I learned how to grow. How to lead without steamrolling. How to build systems, not just sermons. How to work with people instead of simply working for them. Over time, with grace and effort, we built trust. The church and I began to feel less like a forced pairing and more like a community trying to become something beautiful together.

I developed skills I didn't know I needed—budgeting, conflict mediation, administration, and the subtle, sacred art of simply being present when words won't do. And through it all, God kept teaching me: the call doesn't rest on your perfection. It rests on your willingness to stay in the fire.

In the fire, things melt—but they also forge. In the fire, old idols fall—but new clarity rises. I used to think fire was a punishment. Now I know it's the process. The process is where God meets us—not as judges—but as Refiner.

The Voice That Stayed

I have heard people talk about their calling as though it were a trumpet blast from heaven, a blinding light on the road, or a sudden and unmistakable moment of clarity. That was never my experience. For me, the call of God came not as a roar, but as a whisper I couldn't shake. It came quietly, persistently, and over time—an ember that refused to go out. Even when I tried to silence it with excuses, with fear, with unworthiness, it kept flickering in the dark corners of my soul.

I remember long nights when I would kneel at the edge of my bed or sit silently on the floor, staring at nothing while trying to sort through the chaos in my heart. I was exhausted from work, from parenting, from school, from the weight of trying to lead when I still felt so unfinished. There were moments I felt invisible and deeply ashamed, wondering how God could use someone like me—someone who had been overlooked, rejected, passed over. Yet that whisper never left me. Not once.

It was not a voice that told me to be successful. It did not command accolades or promise me comfort. It simply said, "Be faithful." And somehow, that was enough. That small voice carried more weight than any sermon I had ever heard. It did not compete with the noise of the world. It simply waited for me to be still enough to hear it. In the same way God met Elijah in the cave, not in the wind, nor in the earthquake or fire, but in the still small voice, God met me in the hush between doubts and the silence between heartbreaks. There, in that sacred quiet, I heard Him.

There were seasons I felt spiritually dry—where I preached messages to others that I was desperate to believe for myself. In those seasons, Scripture became both mirror and balm. The Psalms gave language to my grief and confusion. The Gospels revealed a Jesus who knelt, touched, wept, walked slowly, and never recoiled from the mess of humanity. The prophets reminded me that God has always called reluctant, unqualified people to bear sacred words to a world that didn't want to hear them. I found myself in Moses' stutter, in Jeremiah's youth, in Isaiah's unclean lips, in Mary's trembling yes. I found courage not because I was capable, but because they weren't either—and God still used them.

The study of Scripture was not academic for me. It was survival. It was breath. When I had no words to pray, I returned to the ones God had already spoken. I underlined passages until the paper tore, wrote notes in margins with shaking hands, and wrestled with verses that refused to let me go. Scripture did not answer every question, but it reoriented my soul toward hope.

I was blessed beyond measure by people who helped me listen more closely to that voice. A dear mentor—an old colleague of my mother's—sat with me through hours of phone calls, emails, and text messages. When I couldn't find the words to explain what I was feeling, he helped me name the ache and walk toward it instead of away. He believed in me when I didn't believe in myself, and gently reminded me that faithfulness often looks like continuing to show up.

I also found strength in a fellow Deaf clergy friend who had grown up alongside me. We met as preteens—two preacher's kids whose paths would later diverge and then find unexpected harmony again. At the time we met, his father was already a pastor. My mother was still teaching, only beginning to wrestle with her own call to ministry. Years later, we would both wear robes and serve the same gospel, albeit in different ways. He had made better decisions than I had in many areas of life, yet he never held that over me. Instead, we shared the same ache of being Deaf in a Church that didn't always know what to do with us. We processed similar rejections, wrestled with familiar doubts, and encouraged one another to keep listening for the Voice that never left.

When I stood in the pulpit, whether before five people or five hundred—I carried all of this with me. I carried the rejection letters, the bruises from unkind words, the exhaustion of the journey, and the lingering question of whether I was enough. I also carried that whisper, that sacred nudge, that fire shut up in my bones. I could not let it go. And the longer I served, the more I realized I didn't need to.

It is easy to imagine that God's voice should be loud and undeniable. But more often, it is steady and low, speaking to us beneath the surface noise of fear and shame. God does not shout to be heard. God waits to be welcomed. And when you finally quiet yourself enough to hear Him, you realize He never stopped speaking. He just waited until you could listen.

The voice that stayed did not promise ease. It promised presence. And for me, that has always been enough.

I Am Still Tuning My Spirit

There are voices I no longer chase. Some faded with the passing of years. Others were forced on me, loud with shame, wrapped in expectation, choking the breath from my calling. Some I had to release just so I could keep breathing.

The voice that said I had to speak clearly to be called.

The voice that measured my worth by how closely I could imitate a hearing world.

The voice that told me faith comes through the ear, and not through the fire in your chest.

The voice of my own fear, disguised as logic, whispers, "They'll never understand someone like you."

Maybe they didn't. Maybe they still don't. But God never shouted. Not once.

God didn't raise the volume to meet the world's noise. God didn't compete with the chaos. God waited—not in anger, not in impatience—but with gentleness I can still feel in the marrow of my bones.

God knew: I don't need volume to encounter truth. I don't need sound to feel Presence.

What I felt—and what I still perceive—wasn't a "voice" in the way most people mean it. It wasn't an audible word that echoed through the air. It was a knowing. A presence. A vibration beneath the surface of things. It was the Spirit's pressure, gently but persistently pulling me toward something sacred, something unexplainable, something mine.

God met me not in the air, but on the ground.

In the way floors trembled when I stood in a sanctuary and felt the congregation singing—not through their voices but through the soles of my feet.

In the way silence held weight in my chest, not as absence but as space for revelation.

In the way the wind seemed to carry a different kind of language—one that required stillness, not speech.

Most of all, in the way Scripture came alive—not because I heard it read aloud, but because I read it with my body.

The Word became flesh not just in Bethlehem, but in me. In Deaf flesh. In a body that had been told too many times it wasn't built for preaching, for pastoring, for leading. But when I studied the Word—not just the words, but the patterns, the stories, the movement of God in human history—I discovered that every prophet who ever lived had some reason to believe they were disqualified. Moses had a stutter. Jeremiah said he was too young. Isaiah fell to the ground in shame. And Elijah? He ran to a cave and said, "I have had enough, Lord."

But the Lord wasn't in the wind.

The Lord wasn't in the earthquake.

The Lord wasn't in the fire.

The Lord was in the still small whisper—the thin silence. And that's where I found Him, too.

Except for me, it wasn't even a whisper. It was quieter than that. It was stillness. Sacred stillness.

It came to me in the vibrations of memory. In the stirring of my spirit when I was touched by Scripture that spoke to my life. In the pressure behind my eyes when I wept at stories that felt like mine. In the hunger to respond—not because someone demanded it—but because something deeper than language was calling me to say yes.

That is the call I followed. That is the call I still follow.

And when I say "call," I do not mean a moment of clarity. I do not mean lightning bolts or choir music or applause. I mean the slow, aching realization that you cannot not respond. That something in you refuses to let go, even when everything else has fallen apart.

This is not a testimony of triumph. This is a confession of endurance.

The truth is, I have known heartbreak in this work. I have known betrayal. I have known what it feels like to be smiled at in public and crucified in private, as well as crucified in public and smiled at in private. I have known the silence of colleagues who call themselves inclusive but do not lift a finger to help when the systems fail. I have known the exhaustion of having to prove I belong in a space that should have welcomed me already.

Even in those moments, when I was ready to lay the call down and walk away, I felt the same Presence again. Not loud. Not demanding. Just there. Steady. Real.

I do not listen with my ears.

I listen with my memory. With my gut. With the soles of my feet and the tremble in my chest. I listen with my grief, with my hope, with the places in my spirit that still believe something beautiful is possible, even now.

I am not here because I heard a voice.

I am here because I encountered a truth so steady, so insistent, so undeniable, that I could no longer live without responding.

CHAPTER 12

A Life in Motion, a Heart Under Pressure

There was no single explosion, no headline-worthy disaster, no bottom-of-the-barrel moment. Just a season—long and grinding—where every detail of life pressed its weight into my chest like a silent, invisible stone. I was enrolled in graduate school, behind on multiple assignments, and so exhausted I had to reread the same paragraph three times just to absorb its meaning. The professors, brilliant in their own right, rarely noticed whether I had access or not. If my interpreter canceled, or if the captions failed to load, the class moved on without me. My Deafness was never addressed outright, but I could feel its consequences hang in the air like static—interference between me and the education I was fighting for.

At home, we were broke. Not the kind of broke where you cut back on take-out or cancel Netflix. I'm talking about real broke— the kind where your stomach stays tight all day because you're not sure whether the kids will have enough to eat by Friday. The kind where the rent was not just late, but impossible, and the lights stayed on only because the electric company hadn't yet followed through on its final warning. Our pantry had become a puzzle, a shifting equation of canned goods and off-brand cereal that we rationed out like sacred offerings. My wife carried the burden silently most days, her shoulders tight with worry, her eyes always scanning receipts and calendars, trying to stretch what was left into what we needed.

We had four children by the time I was twenty-four. No trust fund, no family inheritance, no cushion. What we had was a faith that flickered but refused to go out, and a marriage that endured not because it was easy, but because we both kept choosing it, sometimes one exhausted hour at a time. During this particular week, all of it was piling on. The babies weren't sleeping, the car had a nail in the tire, we still could not find childcare that took our voucher, and our bank account had a single-digit balance. I still had papers to finish for my professors, most of whom didn't know how much I cared or how hard I worked just to show up with my best. They didn't see the overnight shifts at Walmart from the year before, or the year and a half I spent with sawdust in my lungs and blisters on my hands just to pay a single semester of tuition. All they saw was a tired teacher with high expectations and hearing aids.

At the church, we were navigating tension again. The worship committee had erupted over whether the music was "too contemporary," and several members had voiced concern over "young families not participating enough." Meanwhile, my own family was barely surviving. My children were watching me work myself raw. My wife was holding us together with late-night prayers and dollar store groceries. I was driving to class and lay ministry meetings with one eye on the gas light and the other on the clock, wondering how long I could keep living this divided life—husband, student, father, advocate—without unraveling completely.

That afternoon, I locked the bathroom door—not because I needed privacy, but because I needed a moment where no one needed me. I didn't cry. I didn't collapse. I just sat on the edge of the tub, head in my hands, whispering to a God I wasn't even sure was listening: "Lord, just get me to the end of the day."

There was no thunderous reply. No peace washed over me. Just breathe. Just enough breath to get up. To go change a diaper. To respond to one more email. To cook dinner with whatever was left in the fridge. To rock my baby to sleep and then sit at the dining room table, writing one paragraph of a graduate paper while half my brain begged for sleep. And the next day, I did it again. And again after that.

This is how we lived. Not in triumphant strides or mountaintop breakthroughs, but in the slow, inch-by-inch forward crawl that no one ever applauds. There was no miracle paycheck, no perfect schedule, no church-wide revival that made things easy. There was only movement. There was only staying. There was only the memory of who we were trying to become—held together by whispered prayers, by the sacrament of perseverance, by the kind of grace that doesn't erase exhaustion but walks with you through it.

We never arrived all at once. We didn't overcome by way of epiphany. We endured. We adapted. We survived in spite of systems that misunderstood us, churches that underestimated us, and institutions that ignored us. We kept going because we had to—because the children were watching, because the call to teach and preach and love never stopped, and because somewhere deep inside us, there was still a flicker of hope that whispered, This is not the end of your story.

That flicker was enough.

Marriage at a Sprint – Young, In Love, and Under Fire

We didn't ease into marriage. We ran headfirst into it—young, determined, and already battle-tested. We weren't naive about how hard it would be. What we didn't yet know was just how many people were rooting against us from the start. All we knew was we wanted better than either of us had, and we were going to show people by building a family that was everything family should be.

We came from different worlds—emotionally, spiritually, financially. My wife had grown up with the daily reality of government assistance, navigating the stigma of food stamps and the ache of learning how to go without. Her faith was newer, freshly awakened in a small church where she was finally beginning to feel like she belonged. She had found her place on the worship team and was beginning to build the kind of community she had always longed for. But when we were engaged and we found out we were expecting our first that fall, that church turned cold. Her role on the worship team was taken from her without conversation or kindness. She was made to feel like an outsider in the very space where she'd first believed she might be welcome. It cut deep—and it was only the beginning of the wounds the Church would leave us.

I wasn't baptized in the church I attended in my late teens, but I was there for the years that mattered. My mother was the pastor. That church shaped my worldview during some of the most impressionable years of my life. It was also where I began to wrestle with what it meant to love someone with the kind of intensity that scares people—especially religious people. When our relationship became public, whispers turned into warnings. Some members confronted us outright: we were "living in sin." "Unequally yoked." On a "dangerous path." One even told us that if we didn't separate, we'd be damned. I watched the same people who had embraced me as a teenager now stand at a distance, arms crossed, issuing verdicts instead of grace.

We almost walked away from it all. We were ready to go to the courthouse, just the two of us, with no ceremony and no audience.

No sermons. No drama. No family. Just vows, paperwork, and a quiet "I do." We figured the only thing that mattered was the covenant—not the crowd. But my mother stepped in. She asked me to reconsider. Not because it would make the church happy, but because she believed something sacred still could happen inside the sanctuary among the community.

So, we did it. We stood before God in that church, facing one another with trembling hands, while the air around us pulsed with tension. Both of our parents were in the midst of various divorces—splintered family trees whose broken branches filled the front rows. More than once during that ceremony, I caught someone staring at us with a smirk instead of a smile, as if they had already rehearsed the line they would deliver when it all fell apart: "We told you so." It didn't feel like a celebration. It felt like a trial. But we said "I do" anyway.

Then the adulting really kicked in as the children came – all four of them. No map. No margin. No money. Just faith—and not the clean, glowing kind people preach about. Ours was a dirt-under-the-fingernails kind of faith. The kind that held hands while bills piled up. The kind that whispered prayers between diaper changes and night feedings. The kind that said, we might be broken, but we're not letting go.

We brought our own pain into the marriage. Different families. Different survival mechanisms. Different ideas of what safety looked like. When we fought, it wasn't just about dishes or diapers. It was about our histories clashing. She needed space and silence to process. I needed clarity and conversation. Our coping patterns contradicted each other. Our mental health struggles were like shadows in the room—always there, even when we didn't name them. Some nights we didn't speak. Some weeks we barely looked each other in the eye. There were moments I wasn't sure if we would make it. But we did.

Not because we had it all figured out. Not because things got easier. But because we stayed.

Forgiveness, for us, wasn't a one-time act—it became our spiritual discipline. It lived in our quiet apologies, our decision to lay next to each other even when we were angry, even when we were weak, our choice to hold each other while the baby cried. Forgiveness came in small acts—cooking dinner after a tense afternoon, holding space when neither of us had words, folding laundry when the silence stretched too long. And in those acts, we learned what it meant to love without conditions.

We didn't just survive—we stayed. And that staying, that quiet refusal to leave when it would have been easier, became its own sacred vow.

There were days when the only prayer we could muster was staying in the same room. And God counted that as worship.

Poverty, Judgment, and the Cruelty of the System

Poverty, when it came for us, didn't come as a single dramatic event. It crept in slowly, quietly, like a fog thickening around our daily lives. It arrived in the form of hard choices stacked like bricks on our backs. One overdue bill. One broken-down car. One missed paycheck. And then another. Before long, it wasn't a situation, it was a way of life.

We didn't grow up the same. My wife had known hardship from her earliest memories—state assistance, food stamps, making dinner from whatever was left in the pantry, even if it didn't match or make sense. I had grown up differently. My parents worked hard and made enough to keep us from government aid, which meant I never knew what it felt like to look at a block of cheese and see shame. Until the day my wife gently explained that we couldn't afford deli cheese anymore.

We were standing in the grocery store—tired, both of us carrying babies and decisions, trying to figure out how to stretch fifty dollars across a full week's worth of meals. I had reached for the sliced cheddar I had grown up with—the kind wrapped in butcher paper behind the glass counter, the kind you could fold neatly over a warm sandwich. I didn't think twice about it. That cheese, and the fresh bread beside it, had always just been normal to me. But when she placed her hand over mine and said, "We can't afford that this week," something in me cracked.

She explained what government cheese was. She told me how she had grown up eating thick orange blocks handed out in cardboard boxes. The bread was usually off-brand and dry, but it was what you had, and you made it work. And in that moment, standing under fluorescent lights in the grocery aisle, with our kids reaching for snacks we wouldn't be able to afford, I cried. I cried not because I couldn't have my sandwich the way I liked it, but because I realized how sheltered I had been. Because for the first time, poverty stopped being theoretical. It had become personal. It had settled into my stomach and heart like a stone.

Still, we were judged.

In the church, we were surrounded by people who talked about compassion but rarely practiced it. They told us to tithe faithfully and "God would provide." They gave us long, spiritualized advice about budgeting and trusting—seldom did they ask if we needed a meal. There were no invitations to dinner, except for an older couple who loved us like their own. We were almost always met, more often than not, with tightly folded arms and tighter expectations.

Meanwhile, the state—the very system built to help families like ours—treated us as if we were trying to cheat it. I still remember the day Veronica came home from her appointment with the social worker, shaken and quiet. She had been told, in the clearest terms, that if she divorced me, her benefits would increase. Not just by a little—by enough to actually provide food security, insurance, and support for our children. The message was unmistakable: our marriage was too expensive to keep.

No one considered what that would do to our children. No one asked whether we were stable, healthy, or happy. We weren't treated as a family; we were treated as data points. Algorithms said single mothers deserved help. Married couples? They were on their own.

Then came the jobs—one after the next, like spinning plates I had to keep in the air with trembling hands. I worked wherever and whenever I could. Auto parts. Warehouse labor. CNA shifts that left my back screaming and my hands raw. I worked nights at Walmart, watching the sun rise through dirty windshields on the drive home. I swept up sawdust at the woodshop, lungs aching, skin coated in dust, boots filled with grain from side hustles unloading farm trucks. I clocked in wherever someone would have me, because I knew our children's next meal might depend on it. My heart just wanted to be on a Football field coaching or scouting, my soul just wanted to take care of my family, and my body just wanted to rest. This tautology in my young man's mind wreaked havoc on my personal expectations. When you are told you can never achieve anything and you do not believe it, it makes even the highest dreams as feasible.

Poverty isn't just the lack of income—it's the constant recalculation of whether you can afford to keep working. It's discovering that the cost of gas, childcare, lost sleep, and mental fatigue often outweighed the check I brought home. We did the math again and again. And every time, the cruel equation forced my wife out of the workforce. Not because she lacked ambition, she had dreams of her own, gifts of her own, a calling of her own. But the numbers made the choice for us. She stayed home, because it cost less. And every time she did, it carved out a piece of her future—a thousand silent setbacks no résumé can explain.

Even with her at home, even with me grinding through jobs back-to-back, it never added up. The financial "security" people preached about was always out of reach. As a man, yes, I had more access to work. But access didn't mean safety. I carried with me a body that didn't conform to people's expectations, a body shaped by Deafness, weight, and invisible mental health battles that no boss wanted to understand.

Being Deaf meant constantly navigating confusion and assumptions. If I didn't hear a directive the first time, I was labeled incompetent. If I asked for clarification, I was a burden. I was accused of not paying attention, of being distracted, of lacking motivation. My weight invited judgment before I opened my mouth. My anxiety was read as moodiness. My depression is laziness. I couldn't show struggle, because the world didn't have a language for my kind of work ethic. It only had labels. And if I dared to explain—if I said, "Here's why I'm late," or "Here's why I need to write things down,"—it wasn't met with understanding. It was met with dismissal.

Every effort to tell the truth about my limitations was twisted into an excuse. And we were exhausted.

Not just physically, but existentially. Emotionally. Spiritually. We had done everything the world told us to do—worked hard, prayed harder, stayed married, loved our kids, tried our best. And still, we were barely holding on. Still, we were told we weren't enough.

But we stayed. Not because it was easy. Not because we were saints. But because our children were watching. Because our vows mattered. Because in a world that told us to give up, we decided to keep going.

We gave everything we had.

And still, the world said it wasn't enough.

But we stayed.

And that became our miracle.

Deafness and the Fight for Equity in Education

When I made the decision to return to college as an adult, it wasn't because I had something to prove. It was because I couldn't stomach the thought of staying still. My kids were watching me. My marriage had weathered more than most do in twice the time. I had already worked more jobs than I could count—on construction sites, in retail stockrooms, beside hospital beds, under heavy warehouse lights. And still, I couldn't shake the conviction that I was meant for more than just survival. With my deafness, health issues, and strengths, Education seemed to be the only field, but where I would land did not come until later.

School, for me, wasn't just about advancement. It was about breaking something open—about reaching into the long history of limitations that had surrounded people like me and daring to say, not anymore.

I enrolled in the Special Education program at first. It seemed like the most natural choice. I knew what it felt like to be unseen in classrooms. I understood what it meant to live in the margins—fighting for access, watching others succeed with resources you were denied. I believed I could make a difference. As the semesters passed, and my reality as a Deaf student sharpened under the constant strain of missing accommodations, I found myself questioning everything. Not just my major—but the very system I was trying to join. I changed programs more than once, carrying shame every time I had to start over. I had been told by my assigned mentor that I must not be serious about the prospects of ministry if I am in Special Education. I found this person to be a poor source of advice to me. Not all mentors are mentors for you. Eventually, I found myself in the study of Sociology, drawn to the wider lens—the systems, the roots, the structures beneath the surface. I no longer just wanted to work in the system. I wanted to name it. Confront it. Understand why it kept breaking people like me.

Even as I studied injustice, I lived it in every classroom.

The pattern started early. I'd show up to class with the syllabus printed, the textbook already highlighted, and a hope that this semester would be different. That maybe this time, the accommodations I was promised would actually be delivered. That the interpreter would arrive on time, or the notetaker would show up with a pen that worked, or that someone would remember I wasn't just a student with "special needs"—I was a man with responsibilities, with bills, with a brain built for ideas, not pity.

When the accommodations were provided—when I had a skilled interpreter at my side and clear, accessible notes, I performed at my peak. My GPA soared. My classroom presence was engaged and sharp. I wasn't coasting, I was contributing. I was making connections between texts and experiences, drawing insights that came not just from reading but from living in the world we were analyzing.

When the interpreter didn't show? When no one took notes? When the captions failed, the videos rolled on, and the professors didn't pause? My understanding frayed. My GPA slipped. Not because I was distracted. Not because I was unprepared. But because I was locked out. Shut out. Left to guess at content that had already moved on before I could catch up.

There was a semester when I watched my GPA drop by nearly a full point. And I could track the descent almost week by week— alongside the no-show interpreters, the rescheduled access meetings, the unanswered emails. It felt like trying to run a marathon with a sprained ankle while everyone else sprinted ahead and told you to "just push harder."

When I spoke up about the missing accommodations—when I asked, directly, for what was required by law, I was met with smiles that didn't reach the eyes. Words like "flexibility", "reasonable accommodation," and "patience" were weaponized to excuse neglect. Professors who had once been warm turned cool. One administrator told me, "We're doing our best," as though my expectations were the problem.

I wasn't angry. I was tired. Bone-tired. Soul-tired. Tired of having to be the translator, the advocate, the one who reminded the institution of the promises it had already made.

Eventually, I took the risk of filing formal complaints. I documented every missed accommodation, every class where I sat and nodded while understanding less than half of what was said. I followed the process. I followed the rules. I wrote carefully, respectfully, as if the language of diplomacy could protect me.

But it didn't.

Instead of correction, I was offered containment. I was invited to closed-door meetings where the tone was more about making things go away than making things right. When I didn't back down, when I pushed for structural change—not just for me but for all Deaf and disabled students—I was labeled difficult. The advocacy that should have been celebrated became the reason I was quietly removed from the table.

When I eventually shared my experience with the media, it wasn't because I wanted headlines. It was because the silence was suffocating. I had exhausted the internal pathways. I had watched other students leave in frustration or simply disappear into the cracks. I couldn't do the same. I had children at home who needed to know that silence, when forced, is a form of erasure. I needed them to see that telling the truth—even when it costs you— matters.

When litigation became the last resort, I only stepped into it with hope. Not for vengeance, but for recognition. I wanted accountability. I wanted change. What I received instead was a settlement offer. Quiet. Sterile. With strings attached. The cost of my courage would be future opportunities. I would no longer be allowed to apply at another one of those locations. This has taught me to avoid litigation if at all possible.

I was told—gently, off the record—that my presence was no longer welcome. No formal punishment. Just an unspoken understanding that I would not be hired. That my name would not be put forward. That the places I had once considered home had closed their doors while smiling from the windows. I can remember being fired by a mega-grain conglomerate before working a single day because I had not disclosed my deafness until after I had signed the hiring agreement.

That's what most people never see.

They don't see the way justice can exile you. They don't see the opportunities that dry up because you spoke too clearly. They don't understand how exhausting it is to be brave in systems that reward silence.

I didn't return to school to be an activist.

I returned because I believed education could heal. I believed it could transform not only me, but the world I was trying to raise my children in. But what I found instead was a battleground. A place where access had to be fought for every day, and where truth came with a price.

I didn't want to be a fighter. I wanted to be a student. However, in a world built for ears, I had to shout just to be heard.

Teaching with a Limp – The Battle Isn't Over

It's a strange thing to pour yourself into a profession that was never designed with you in mind.

By the time I became a teacher, most people assumed I had outrun the hardest parts. To them, I had already made it through the storm. I had the degree, the classroom, and the job title. They saw me with a badge clipped to my belt and a whiteboard filled with careful handwriting and assumed the battle was behind me.

The truth is, I entered the classroom already limping.

Not physically—but spiritually, emotionally, systemically.

Even now, with years behind me and a reputation for being the kind of teacher students remember, I still don't have what many would call "full access." Accommodations exist on paper— policies, rights, technical language. But accommodations in practice? That's a daily negotiation. Fire drills, I don't hear. Staff meetings without visual cues. Announcements spoken over the intercom that I miss until someone thinks to tap me. Students asking questions while turned toward the board, voices swallowed in acoustics I can't navigate. Exhaustion seeps in before lunch. And yet, the teaching never stops.

What's changed isn't the system, it's how I'm seen.

I once worked in a school where I felt invisible, or worse, used. Not in any obvious, malicious way—but in that slow-burn sort of way that happens when you're praised publicly while being dismissed privately. They liked that I was "inspiring." They liked the way I made them look progressive. When I asked for real changes—captioned materials, interpreters for training days, basic auditory alternatives—they'd stall. Smile. Say things like, "We'll look into that," knowing full well they wouldn't. I wasn't a colleague—I was a PR asset.

Then came the shift.

It wasn't about new laws or better funding. It was a change in posture—a new school, a new environment, where people didn't just tolerate difference, they respected it. I wasn't asked to prove myself over and over again. I wasn't expected to explain why I needed access—I was simply asked, "What can we do better?"

I still didn't receive more accommodations than before, technically speaking. But the spirit was different. Instead of being treated like a complication, I was seen as someone whose insight mattered. My perspective wasn't a liability—it was a lens. And that subtle change in how I was viewed made the daily burden a little lighter.

Lighter doesn't mean easy.

Teaching as a Deaf adult still feels like running a race with sandbags tied to my ankles. I work harder than anyone realizes just to keep pace. While other teachers casually pick up updates in the hallway, I rely on emails that aren't always sent. While others process verbal feedback in real time, I review transcripts, request written follow-ups, and spend late hours trying to absorb what others heard in seconds.

It's not about wanting special treatment. It's about wanting equal ground.

The truth is—there's no coasting for me. Not ever. I can't afford a bad day. I can't afford to forget a detail. I can't miss an IEP meeting or misunderstand a student's tone or let my own fatigue keep me from showing up fully. If I slip, it's not read as human. It's read as proof. Proof that I shouldn't be here. Proof that Deafness means deficiency. Proof that grace has limits.

So I try my damnest, telling myself like a broken record, "don't slip. don't slip, if you do, you will lose everything."

I stay late. I arrive early. I rehearse lesson plans out loud while the building is still quiet. I overcompensate, overprepare, over function—because that's the price of being taken seriously.

No matter how far I've come, there's still this ache I carry— the ache of knowing that to be excellent, I must bleed brilliance. That for my success to be taken seriously, it has to look effortless. That vulnerability—real, raw, human vulnerability—is a luxury I still can't afford in front of most adults.

But the kids?

They see me differently.

They don't see the limp and call it weakness. They see the presence. The eye contact. The patience. The intentionality. The stories I bring to every lesson. The way I listen with my eyes and respond with my whole being. They don't always know what it took for me to get there, but they know I care. And that, somehow, opens doors the system forgot to build.

They're the reason I stay.

Not the paycheck. Not the praise. Not even the sense of professional duty.

It's the moment a student who rarely speaks raises her hand to share. The moment a struggling teen lingers after class just to say, "Thank you for getting it." It's the quiet nods, the trust that's built over time, the way they start to believe in themselves— because they see someone in front of them who's had to fight to believe in his own worth.

I've yet to find a workplace where I didn't have to outwork the doubt.

I've yet to teach in a building where I didn't have to chase access uphill.

I've yet to stand in a staff meeting where I didn't scan the room for someone who remembered I was Deaf. But I show up. Every day. Because the kids are watching. I want them to know that excellence doesn't always walk with ease. Sometimes it limps.

Changes in Calling, Changes in Identity

I had heard it once before. A calling. Gentle, but clear— something that stirred in me as a child sitting in Sunday school, the kind of voice that settles not in your ears but in your bones. I couldn't have explained it at the time, but I knew it meant something. That God had marked me in some way. I didn't know for what, or when, or how. But I carried that sense quietly through the years—like a buried ember I wasn't sure how to tend.

As life grew heavier, it began to feel like maybe I had imagined it. Like maybe the weight of adulthood—the bills, the children, the long shifts, the self-doubt, the strain of a marriage under pressure—had simply squeezed out whatever hope or imagination I had left. I started to convince myself that I had misheard God, or that I wasn't holy enough to be called in the first place. That God must have moved on to someone more consistent, more disciplined, more worthy.

And yet, the affirmations kept coming.

Sometimes from people I'd known for years—people who had seen the messy parts of me and still said, "You have something special. A calling." Other times it came from strangers, people who'd hear me speak in a casual setting and say, "Are you a preacher?" I would laugh it off, uncomfortable with the suggestion, but something inside me would flicker again, however briefly.

But the moment of surrender didn't come at a revival or during a high mountaintop moment. It came in a place lower than I had ever been.

I can't remember the argument that night, only that it was bad enough to leave me locked out of the house. The kind of moment where nothing feels solid. I remember sitting on the steps in the dark, hearing the sound of my son crying from inside, and feeling like I had failed everyone. My wife. My children. Myself. I had been trying, in my own way, but I wasn't present. I wasn't consistent. I wasn't leading with love. And in that moment, the shame of it all came crashing in like a wave I couldn't stand against.

I didn't have fancy words. I wasn't quoting Scripture or making promises. I just bent my head, shoulders heavy, and cried out: God, please.

Something from my childhood came flooding back—my Sunday school teacher's voice, steady and kind, telling us over and over, "God is always there for you. You just have to look to Him. God is love." It was so simple. I hadn't thought about her in years. But in that moment, I could almost feel her hand on my shoulder. God is love.

I looked up. Not physically—but spiritually. I let go of the pretense and posturing and invited Christ in all over again. Not just as Savior, but as the center of my life. I gave up control—not out of enlightenment, but because I was broken. And God met me there. In the mess. In the failure. In the dark, sitting outside my own home with a baby crying and no answers.

Then the shift began.

Not instantly. Not perfectly. But steadily.

The more I fell in love with God, the more I learned how to love my family. Not just to say I loved them, but to show it. With honesty. With presence. With grace. With patience. With a kind of intentionality that didn't come naturally to me at the time. I began to understand that spiritual maturity wasn't measured in knowledge or status—but in how I showed up for the people entrusted to me.

And with that deepening love, the call came rushing back.

Not as a whisper this time—but as a fire.

It burned in my bones. It lit me from within. I couldn't sit still. I couldn't stop thinking about preaching, about teaching, about coaching. It wasn't ambition. It was calling. And I felt it everywhere. I felt it when reading Scripture, when talking with my kids, when watching someone walk through pain and knowing I was meant to stand beside them. It was like something I had buried was now pounding to be let out.

The fire made people uncomfortable.

I was passionate. Intense. Bold. Some didn't know what to do with it. I was told to tone it down, to be more measured, to stop talking. Truthfully, I didn't have the maturity yet to temper the fire with wisdom. I was all conviction, no filter. All urgency, no patience. The calling was real—but the character to hold it had to be formed.

Over time, through failure and grace and continued growth, I began to understand how to carry the call without letting it scorch everyone around me. I learned that the goal wasn't to be heard, it was to be useful. To be grounded. To be shaped by the same Word I wanted to share.

That's when I realized: God wasn't just calling me to do ministry.

God was calling me to become the kind of person who could sustain it.

He was forming me. Through every painful turn. Through every conversation where I had to humble myself. Through every moment, I failed and asked for forgiveness. Through every job we moved for, every zip code we lived in, every church we visited and left.

The calling was always there. I just had to be broken enough to remember it—and brave enough to say yes.

I didn't embrace my calling because I was qualified.

I embraced it because, when I had nothing left, God still called me by name.

I've been walking in that fire ever since. Not perfectly. But with open hands, open eyes, and a heart that knows this is who I was always meant to be.

Facing Toward Home

I've been sent to serve. Sent to teach. Sent to preach. Sent to the coach. Sent to love people who didn't know my name until I stepped into their sanctuary or stood on their sideline. I've answered God's call every time—packed the boxes, rerouted the bills, shifted the rhythm of my children's lives because I believe in the holy beauty of obedience. I am a Methodist, and itinerancy is part of my vow. I've never needed to be rooted in buildings or titles.

But deep down, if I'm honest, I've always longed for a place that didn't ask me to leave.

A home.

Not a parsonage. Not a short-term lease. Not a rented blessing. A place that is mine. A place that is ours. A place where the front door creaks a little in the winter and the hallway carries the sound of my children's bare feet on Saturday mornings. A place where no one can ask us to move because the Church Board voted otherwise. A place with walls we can paint and a yard we can plant. A place where we can finally—finally—stop holding our breath.

We've lived in more spaces than I can list without pausing to remember. In the beginning, we couch-surfed, bouncing between family members and friends, grateful but exhausted by the unspoken truth that we didn't belong anywhere for long. Then came Section 8, long lines and longer forms, waiting on government phone calls that held our children's safety in the balance. We tried to make those places sacred—hung our kids' drawings on the walls, turned borrowed furniture into story time corners, prayed over rooms that smelled of mold and old paint— but nothing ever quite fit.

Public housing came next. Roaches in the walls. Pipes that leaked for weeks before anyone came. Thin walls that couldn't contain joy or protect our peace. Still, we found laughter. My kids would dance barefoot in the hallway, and we'd blast gospel music on busted speakers just to feel alive. My wife would make dollar- store candles smell like heaven, and we'd host whoever needed a meal, even when we were barely making it ourselves.

Then, we graduated to rentals. Places with names on leases. Spaces that gave us just enough breathing room to imagine staying longer. But even those came with caution. Rent hikes. Sudden repairs. Landlords who didn't know how to spell "accommodation," let alone provide it. Being Deaf added layers— every request for visual alarms or vibrating systems was a negotiation, a reminder that even when we paid on time, our needs were seen as extra.

Still, we held it together. With paint we weren't supposed to use. With dogs that scratched at doors. With cats that curled into warm corners like they'd lived there a thousand years. With kids who built blanket forts in living rooms that weren't really ours, and covered the walls with permanent markers, but that we loved into being. We didn't own those houses, but they were ours in the ways that mattered.

Our home has never been quiet, even to a deaf guy.

There's always someone talking, someone barking, someone slamming a cabinet or chasing a cat or yelling across the hallway to ask where the other shoe went. The dogs beg for scraps and bark at every delivery truck like it's the first they've ever seen. The cats leap from counters like acrobats, knocking over homework and water glasses with equal indifference. There's fur in every corner and crumbs under every couch, but there is also laughter—real, belly-deep laughter. There are hugs in the hallway, chore charts taped to the fridge, apologies whispered at night, and I love you's that never sound rehearsed.

It's not neat. It's not polished. But it is real. It is alive.

It is love, clawed and barked and scribbled and screamed and whispered into every room we've ever occupied.

Yet—beneath the joy, there's still a longing. A deep ache for something more permanent. A place where we can build not just rhythm, but rest. A home that is ours not because we paid the rent on time, but because we signed our names on the deed and dared to believe we belonged.

Ashamedly, if there was a further intent for this book beyond starting conversations and building a world that is led by grace. It is not for pity. Not for applause. But for the possibility to give my children, dogs, cats, and wife a true, stable, forever home base.

Maybe these words—my story, our story—can open a door that's always felt one prayer too far. Maybe this book becomes the bridge between where we've been and where we've always hoped to go. Maybe one day soon, I'll stand on a front porch with paint on my jeans and keys in my hand and say, We made it.

Not for a title. Not for a tax bracket. But for my family.

A place where my Deafness doesn't need to be explained.

Where my children don't wonder what boxes they'll need next year.

Where my wife can breathe without the strain of uncertainty.

Where our dogs can run in the same backyard for more than a season.

Where the cats can grow old in windows they've memorized.

Where love has roots, not just wings.

God has called me to move. And I've moved.

But I also believe God is calling me to stay.

Not to stop serving—but to serve from a place that doesn't shake every time the wind changes. A place where ministry is poured out not from weariness, but from rest. A place where home isn't something we imagine—it's something we live in, every day.

We've moved a dozen times. More. Grace has always known our address. One day, grace will meet us at our own front door.

We Stayed

I used to think that calling meant movement. That to follow God meant to always be going somewhere—preaching, teaching, coaching, serving. That motion was proof of faith. That faithfulness looked like open hands, packed bags, another new address, another new church bulletin with my name printed underneath "Pastor." And for a long time, it did.

We moved more times than I ever wanted to. I became an expert in reintroducing myself. In explaining my Deafness. In adjusting to new church politics, new hallway dynamics, and new cultures wrapped inside small-town sanctuaries. I got good at unpacking boxes before the kids got off the bus. Good at putting the tools back on the shelf just when it was time to take them down again.

And yet, with every move, I carried something deeper than duty—something more than profession or tradition. I carried an ache for stability. A hope that one day, I could give my family what I never had as a child: a place we wouldn't have to leave. A place with a porch and a pantry and picture frames that didn't need to be packed. A place where the walls would know our laughter and hold our grief without having to be repainted for the next tenant.

And so the tension grew: how do you stay when you've been called to go?

How do you raise a family when you can't promise permanence?

How do you answer a God who says, "Whom shall I send?" when your children are quietly wondering if they'll have to change schools again?

This is what I've come to believe: sometimes, the greatest act of faith is not going.

It's staying.

Not staying still—but staying rooted.

Staying present.

Staying committed to a life that doesn't move at the speed of ambition, but at the pace of love.

Staying in hard conversations.

Staying in uncomfortable growth.

Staying in rooms where you've been misunderstood until bridges begin to form.

Staying in your marriage when the heat of an argument makes the door look easier than the table.

Staying with your children long enough to learn how they're wired—not just to raise them, but to know them.

Staying in your own body, even when trauma makes you want to disappear.

Staying with the Church when the Church breaks your heart.

Staying in the story God is telling through your life, even when you don't like the chapter you're in.

We don't own a home yet. That truth still weighs heavy. My wife and I talk about it late at night, when the kids are finally asleep and the silence settles. We talk about what it would mean—to have a yard where the dogs could roam free without a leash, where the kids could bury time capsules under the oak tree and know they'd still be there next year. We talk about paint colors we won't have to paint over, about dinner tables that don't need to be moved again, about closets that hold more than clothes—closets that hold memory.

And yet, even without that address, we've built something permanent.

Our house—wherever it is—has always been full.

Full of barking, meowing, laughter, frustration, forgiveness, spilled milk, raised voices, whispered prayers. Full of kids yelling across the hall, dogs scratching at the back door, and cats knocking over water glasses with Olympic confidence. Full of life. Real life. Loud and lived-in. Noisy and sacred.

There are nights when I feel like we're just barely holding it together.

But then one of the kids curls up beside me on the couch, or the dog lays his head on my lap after a long day, or my wife laughs so hard at something I said that I remember—this is home. Maybe not legally. Maybe not on paper. But in every way that matters.

We stayed.

We stayed through uncertainty.

We stayed through criticism.

We stayed when others walked away.

We stayed when our names weren't called, when our gifts were overlooked, when the support didn't come.

We stayed when grief was louder than hope.

We stayed when staying felt like the harder choice.

And somehow, God met us right there—again and again.

Not because we were strong.

But because we were willing.

Maybe one day—when this book or the next or the next is published, and the keys are handed over, and the address finally bears our name—I'll stand on that front porch and say to my children, to my wife, to every version of me that wondered if it would ever happen:

"This is the house that faith built. This is the home that makes staying possible."

But even if that day takes longer still, I know this:

We've already made it. Because when everything in me wanted to run— We stayed.

And God did too.

CHAPTER 13

Grace Is a Mandate, Not a Metaphor

Grace, in much of contemporary Christian thought, has been domesticated. It has been rendered soft, sentimental, and safe—something whispered rather than wielded. But the grace revealed in Scripture and lived in the body of Christ is not a gentle suggestion. It is a disruptive force. It is the initiative of God not only to forgive, but to free, to heal, and to dismantle systems of injustice. Grace is not a metaphor for divine comfort. It is a mandate for divine action.

The Greek word *charis*, often translated as grace, implies a gift—but not the kind that sits unopened on a shelf. It is a kinetic force, a divine movement toward humanity, an active presence that demands a human response. To receive grace is to be drawn into God's movement in the world. As such, grace is not merely received; it is lived, embodied, and enacted. It cannot remain abstract. If it is real, it must take shape in the body and in the world. It must become flesh, just as Christ did.

I remember standing in a sanctuary as a young Deaf man discerning a call to preach. A respected mentor approached me after I had spoken and said, "You have a powerful message, but you'll need to work on your speech if you want churches to really hear you." I knew he meant well. But the implication struck hard: that my Deafness, my voice, my very body, would be a hindrance to the Gospel. That, unless I sounded a certain way, I could not be the mouthpiece of God.

I carried that wound for years. But grace has a way of turning the wounds we carry into the waters we pour. Not long after, a woman came forward after a small group meeting. Her eyes were tired from years of depression. She had been told by her church that her mental illness was a spiritual failure, something to be hidden. As she shared her story, I didn't know what to say. But I remembered what I had learned through silence. I opened my mouth and said one word: Still. Still loved. Still chosen. Still held by grace.

She broke. Not because I had crafted perfect words, but because I had listened. Because I had not tried to fix her. Because grace flowed through the very place others had dismissed as a deficit. That is when I began to understand that grace is not just for the wounded to receive. It is often the wounded who carry it.

The Epistle of James drives this point home with piercing clarity: "What good is it, my brothers and sisters, if someone claims to have faith but has no deeds? Can such faith save them? ... Faith by itself, if it is not accompanied by action, is dead" (James 2:14–17, NIV). James is not promoting salvation by works. He is denouncing faith that remains theoretical. In the early Christian community—often poor, persecuted, and marginalized—faith was not a luxury of doctrine. It was a matter of survival, of mutual care, of radical sharing. Grace was not abstract. It fed people. It lifted the fallen. It built community across dividing lines.

When Jesus stands in the synagogue at Nazareth and reads from the scroll of Isaiah (Luke 4:18–19), he does not begin with doctrine. He begins with liberation. "The Spirit of the Lord is upon me," he reads, "because he has anointed me to proclaim good news to the poor... freedom for the prisoners and recovery of sight for the blind, to set the oppressed free." This was no poetic flourish. He was invoking the year of Jubilee, the radical tradition in Israel's law that cancelled debts, restored land, and freed captives. Grace, from the beginning, was a justice movement. It was embodied, material, and disruptive. Jesus was not only proclaiming spiritual healing—he was calling for social repair.

John Wesley, one of the founders of Methodism, understood this. His theology of grace was not confined to private salvation. It was public, social, and fiercely practical. He preached in coal mines and alleyways, not because it was trendy, but because grace must go where the people are. He insisted that the "means of grace" were not limited to sacraments and Scripture, but included works of mercy: feeding the hungry, clothing the naked, visiting the sick and imprisoned. To withhold justice was to reject grace. For Wesley, the love of God and neighbor were inseparable. There could be no holiness without social holiness.

The wounded carry this grace because they know what it costs. Scripture does not present the healed as the heroes—it shows the broken as the bearers of God's power. The bleeding woman in Mark 5 reaches out in desperation, and her touch draws healing from Christ. The blind man in Luke 18 cries out above the crowd and is the only one who truly sees Jesus. And in John 20, the resurrected Christ appears—not as a glowing abstraction—but as a man with visible wounds. "Put your finger here," he says. "See my hands." The resurrected body of Jesus still carries the scars. That, too, is grace. Not erasure of pain, but redemption of it.

I have learned to stop hiding my Deafness as a liability. It is the very space where grace speaks loudest. When I couldn't hear, I learned to feel. When words failed me, presence remained. I don't preach in the way some expect—but I carry a message only God could write into this body. Grace is not about overcoming who you are. It's about offering who you are—wounds and all.

So no, grace is not a metaphor. It is not a vague comfort. It is a mandate. It is the compulsion of the Spirit that does not wait for ideal conditions. It calls us to stand where we are unwelcome, to speak when we are told we cannot, to live out the Gospel in bodies the world deems unqualified. Grace is not permission to remain passive. It is the power to act with holy fire.

And this is where we begin—not with tidy theology or poetic gestures, but with the fire of grace that moves through the most unlikely of vessels.

Wesleyan Framework of Grace: A Living Theology

Grace, for John Wesley, was not a static concept—it was a dynamic reality, unfolding across time, soul, and society. He did not divide grace into stages as compartments but described it as a continuous movement of divine love: prevenient, justifying, and sanctifying. Each expression is inseparable from the others, like streams flowing from the same mountain, winding their way into every crevice of human existence.

Wesleyan grace is not merely a doctrine. It is a living theology. It is grace with hands and feet, wounds and wisdom, ever calling the soul to love and the Church to action.

Prevenient Grace. Justifying Grace. Sanctifying Grace. These are not merely theological terms—they are the grammar of God's relentless pursuit of us. They are how heaven bends low into human form and how the Spirit breathes possibility even into places that look abandoned.

Before I knew who I was, before I had language, before I had access, grace was already at work. Before I was diagnosed, labeled, sorted, and segregated, grace was already whispering my name.

Prevenient grace is the divine initiative. It is God loving first. "We love because He first loved us," says 1 John 4:19. Prevenient grace is the reason the prodigal son can return home—it's the whisper in the pigpen that reminds him he's still a son. It is not salvation in its fullness, but the stirring that makes salvation possible. It's the light in the hallway before the door opens.

Wesley described it in Sermon 85: On Working Out Our Own Salvation as the grace that comes before all human response. It is not the result of merit or ritual. It is the unearned invitation of God wooing the soul. As Wesley wrote, "There is no man, unless he has quenched the Spirit, that is wholly void of the grace of God."

That truth lives in my own story. Grace was present when my parents didn't yet know what my silence meant. When teachers mistook my quiet for defiance. When I was sorted into classrooms meant to manage, not nurture. I felt the sting of being "othered" before I could name it. And yet, something in me resisted despair. Something in me—grace in me—believed I belonged. That silent resilience, that flicker of identity before articulation, was prevenient grace.

It is the same grace David invokes in Psalm 139:13–16, "For you created my inmost being; you knit me together in my mother's womb... all the days ordained for me were written in your book before one of them came to be." The language here is intimate, embryonic. God is not waiting for us to become eloquent or educated before He draws near. He is already near. He is the one forming even the parts of us others call broken.

Through a social lens, prevenient grace surrounds the ones society overlooks—children placed in "special ed" without a full understanding of their minds, bodies dismissed as burdens, students tracked downward because their brilliance doesn't conform to standardized molds. Prevenient grace insists they are not problems to be fixed. They are image-bearers already being pursued.

Justifying grace is the pivot. It is the moment—not always dramatic, but always real—when we say yes to the grace that has been chasing us all along. It is not just the forgiveness of sins. It is the restoration of a relationship. Wesley called it pardon, acceptance, and reconciliation in his Notes on the New Testament. It is the healing of alienation and the dawning of peace.

"Since we are justified by faith, we have peace with God through our Lord Jesus Christ" (Romans 5:1). Not tranquility, but reconciliation. The Greek word for justification, *dikaiōthentes*, carries legal weight: acquittal, setting right. But for Wesleyans, it is not merely forensic. It is familial. We are not just acquitted, we are embraced.

In my life, justifying grace didn't arrive like thunder. It crept in, slow and unfolding, through seasons of betrayal, disappointment, and internal collapse. After ministry wounds. After mental health spirals. After trying to earn love in churches that only saw utility. I didn't have a single altar call moment. I had hundreds of mornings where I woke up and decided not to quit. That, too, is grace.

For those on the margins, justifying grace is often defined as less about guilt and more about shame. Less about legal sin and more about internalized worthlessness. For many, especially those told their existence is inconvenient or unworthy—queer bodies, disabled bodies, incarcerated bodies, poor bodies—justifying grace feels like liberation. It is not just, "You are forgiven." It is, "You belong." It is the declaration that no matter what society has named you, God names you beloved.

Sanctifying grace is the lifelong transformation that follows. It is the work of the Holy Spirit in us and through us, refining us in love. It is not the grace that gets us into heaven. It is the grace that makes heaven get into us.

Hebrews 12:1 urges us, "Let us run with perseverance the race marked out for us…"—but that race is not one of performance. It is one of becoming. Sanctifying grace is not perfectionism. It is perfection in love. Wesley's vision, laid out in A Plain Account of Christian Perfection, was not about moral flawlessness but about hearts so full of love that sin loses its grip.

This kind of grace has carried me through seasons of obedience I didn't feel strong enough to choose. Through parenting when I felt inadequate. Through teaching, when I wasn't sure my voice could reach. Through pastoring, when accommodations were denied or misunderstood. Through marriage, when Deafness, trauma, and ministry collided. It has been a refining fire and a sustaining wind.

Sanctifying grace is not polite. It breaks our attachments to ease, to supremacy, to apathy. It dares churches to leave behind comfort and embrace courage. It demands not only the inclusion of the marginalized but the re-centering of their stories. It calls the Church out of respectability politics and into the messiness of justice-making. This is social holiness—not mere niceness or charity, but a holy reckoning with structural sin.

Grace, then, is not static. It moves. It calls. It reforms.

Prevenient grace woos us.

Justifying grace reconciles us.

Sanctifying grace transforms us.

Together, they form not only a theology but a testimony—a way of life, a call to the Church, and a mirror to the world. In my Deafness, my weariness, my persistence, I have not only received grace. I have become a bearer of it. Not because I earned it, but because I stopped trying to pretend I didn't need it.

This is the living grace of God.

Grace Reversed: When the Disabled Carry the Healing

There is a sacred pattern running through the whole of Scripture: the ones the world deems broken are the very ones through whom God chooses to speak, heal, and redeem. The weak confound the strong. The barren give birth to promise. The outcast becomes the cornerstone. In the kingdom of God, the reversal is not the exception. It is the rule.

In Mark 5, we meet a woman whose body has bled for twelve years. She is ritually unclean, socially invisible, economically depleted, and religiously excluded. No priest calls for her healing. No man advocates for her. She reaches—she initiates. This is not passive faith. It is active resistance. She risks being punished, ridiculed, and rejected, yet she stretches through the crowd and touches the hem of Jesus' garment. The power does not flow because she is perfect. It flows because she is desperate—and because she believes healing is not reserved for the unblemished. Jesus turns, not to rebuke, but to affirm: "Daughter, your faith has made you well." The healing is not just physical. It is social. It is theological. He calls her daughter—publicly restoring her place in the community of God.

In Luke 18, it is the blind man who sees most clearly. Though physically unable to see, he perceives Jesus' identity with clarity that others lack. "Son of David, have mercy on me!" he shouts, invoking a messianic title. The crowd tries to silence him. But Jesus stops. And it is this man—dismissed, disregarded, disruptive—who becomes the occasion for a divine revelation. His blindness is not a barrier to faith; it is the context in which faith flourishes. His need sharpens his spiritual vision.

And in John 20, after the resurrection, Jesus returns not with a flawless body but with visible wounds. He does not hide them. He offers them. "Put your finger here," he says to Thomas. "See my hands." The risen Lord bears the marks of crucifixion—not as shame, but as testimony. The resurrection does not erase the trauma of the cross. It transfigures it. The glorified body of Christ includes scars.

What are we to make of this? In each of these stories, the so-called "broken" are not merely recipients of healing—they are its conduit. They carry divine insight. They act in bold faith. They name the Messiah. They preach through wounds. These are not exceptions to the gospel. These are the gospel.

This biblical pattern disrupts our cultural assumptions. We are conditioned to see healing as restoration to "normal," to associate wholeness with able-bodiedness, to equate spiritual leadership with charisma and clarity of speech. But the witness of Scripture turns this on its head. Disability is not a hindrance to grace—it is often its clearest channel.

I know this because I live it. I am Deaf. And I was taught—explicitly and implicitly—that my Deafness was a limitation to be pitied or a problem to be fixed. I was sorted into special education programs not because of my intellect, but because people could not imagine intelligence without speech. I was offered prayers for healing before I was offered equal access. My very body, in some churches, was seen as an obstacle to the Word of God.

In the silence, I heard God.

Not in thunder. Not in applause. Not in the polished homilies of able-bodied preachers. I heard God in the pause between sentences. I heard God in vibration, in stillness, in the spaces where sound had no power but presence did. I encountered God not in spite of my Deafness—but because of it.

I think of 1 Kings 19:11–13, when the prophet Elijah stands in a cave, waiting for a divine word. A great wind rips through the mountains, but God is not in the wind. An earthquake follows, and then fire—but God is not in those either. Finally, Elijah hears the still, small voice. The Hebrew phrase is more literally translated as "the sound of sheer silence." That is where God is found—not in spectacle, but in the quiet space most overlook.

Deafness sharpened my perception. It taught me to see what others missed. It taught me to listen without sound, to watch bodies and movements, to discern truth in the face and hands. My language is visual. My world is embodied. And in that space, grace speaks—not through performance, but through presence.

This grace is not always welcomed. Churches that pride themselves on being biblical often fail to be incarnational. They elevate verbal preaching while ignoring visual-spatial languages. They require accessibility to be earned rather than built in. They measure the power of a sermon by the cadence of the voice rather than the clarity of the witness. But what if the most powerful preaching is done in signs? What if the truest gospel is signed with calloused hands, spoken without words, and carried in bodies like mine?

Nancy Eiesland, in The Disabled God, confronts these assumptions with prophetic clarity. She writes that "the disabled God is not only a symbol of solidarity; it is a real presence in which the disabled know themselves to be truly human, truly valued, truly blessed." The resurrected Christ with wounds is not a temporary image—it is an eternal truth. God does not erase disability in order to redeem it. God inhabits it. Christ rises, still marked.

Isaiah, too, anticipates this vision: "Then the eyes of the blind shall be opened, and the ears of the deaf unstopped" (Isaiah 35:5–6). This is not a prophecy of erasure but of restoration. In the reign of God, the very senses the world disregards are honored, opened, and empowered.

I have preached sermons in classrooms where no microphone was needed, only the movement of my hands. I have stood in pulpits where interpreters bridged two languages. I have advocated for students who were told they didn't belong in honors classes. I have counseled people through trauma using silence as sacred space. I have carried healing, not because I was strong or fluent in spoken language, but because I was present in a way that demanded no performance.

This is what grace reversed looks like. It is when the Church stops seeing the disabled as recipients of charity and starts recognizing us as prophets, pastors, and theologians. It is when the marginalized become ministers. It is when the Deaf do not wait to be heard but speak boldly in the language God has given them.

The pattern of Scripture is clear. The bleeding woman, the blind man, the risen Christ—they do not merely receive grace. They reveal it. And they remind us that grace does not flow from perfection. It flows from presence. From courage. From wounds offered without shame.

If the Church is to be truly faithful to the gospel, it must reimagine who bears the healing. It must learn to see disability not as a challenge to overcome, but as a witness to embody. It must open its eyes, unstop its ears, and repent of the idol of normalcy.

Grace is not always clean. Sometimes it limps. Sometimes it stutters. Sometimes it signs. Sometimes it bleeds.

Always—it heals.

In every age, the Church has faced a temptation: to build its unity by narrowing its welcome, to preserve its holiness by withholding its hospitality. Under the guise of orthodoxy, it has too often practiced exclusion—not of sin, but of people. It has used Scripture not as a scalpel for healing, but as a sword for control. Gender identity, sexuality, relationship status, race, neurodivergence, physical disability—these have become, in many communities, reasons not for embrace but for exile.

The gospel does not begin with purity codes. It begins with incarnation.

The Word became flesh—not ideal flesh, not socially acceptable flesh, not cisgender, straight, neurotypical, able-bodied flesh—but Jewish flesh under empire. Brown flesh in a colonized land. Poor flesh born to an unwed teen mother in an occupied territory. Marginalized flesh. If that is how God chose to come, then it is not a stretch to say that the margins are where God still dwells.

Yet the Church, in so many spaces, continues to confuse holiness with homogeneity. It continues to believe that the path to righteousness must be a narrow road of sameness, not a wide river of mercy. It continues to name as sin what God has not condemned and to silence voices that were born to prophesy. Too often, difference is mistaken for defiance, and conformity for communion.

We must say it plainly: marginalized people—LGBTQ+ people, Black and Brown people, disabled and neurodivergent people, women, single parents, formerly incarcerated persons— are not "issues" to solve. They are not theological problems to be debated. They are not spiritual liabilities. They are prophets with balm. Carriers of wisdom. Bearers of divine image. Not despite their identity—but within it.

Theologians like Gustavo Gutiérrez and Howard Thurman have long called us back to the root of this truth. In A Theology of Liberation, Gutiérrez insists that theology must begin not with abstract concepts but with the lived experience of the poor and oppressed. He writes: "The liberation which is the work of the Spirit is not reducible to a purely spiritual realm. It embraces the whole person: body and soul." Liberation is not just from sin, but from systems that name people as sinful simply for existing.

Similarly, Rev. Dr. Howard Thurman, in Jesus and the Disinherited, asks a devastating question: What does the religion of Jesus have to say to those with their backs against the wall? Not to the privileged. Not to the powerful. But to the disinherited, the disenfranchised, the discarded. Thurman argues that Jesus himself belonged to the disinherited. That his mission was born in solidarity with those whom the world had declared unworthy. And thus, the Church's mission must be measured not by how well it pleases the powerful, but by how deeply it loves the oppressed.

So when the Church builds walls around the communion table—when it polices gender expression more than greed, when it prioritizes respectability over repentance, when it excommunicates gay youth while platforming abusive pastors—it is not following the gospel. It is forsaking it.

True grace reverses the equation. It reorients our vision. It teaches us that the very people the Church tries to exclude are often those through whom the Spirit speaks most clearly. The transgender believer who has survived spiritual trauma and still sings of God's goodness. The Black woman preacher who dares to declare good news in pulpits that once silenced her grandmothers. The autistic theologian whose insights into divine mystery come not in spite of, but through, neurodivergence. The Deaf pastor who signs the Word of God with hands shaped by silence and strength. These are not distractions from the mission of the Church. They are the mission.

God has always chosen the unlikely as messengers: Moses, slow of speech. Mary, unwed and young. Paul, blinded and broken. The woman at the well. The lepers. The demoniacs. The incarcerated apostles. The crucified Christ. The pattern is consistent: God chooses what the world rejects.

I know this truth in my own bones. I have been told I was unfit for ministry because of how I hear. I have been dismissed, pitied, and passed over. But the very thing they said disqualified me—the Deafness, the difference, the struggle—is the thing God uses to deliver the message. It is through my body, through my silence, through my relentless survival, that grace moves.

So I say again: marginalized people are not projects. They are prophets. They carry a word the Church needs to hear. Not a word of rebellion—but of resurrection.

The Church must repent of theologies that treat people like problems. It must lay down the weaponization of sin and pick up the basin and towel. It must stop asking who is pure enough to lead, and start asking who has been wounded enough to speak with authority about healing.

Grace is not a reward for the respectable. It is the language of the rejected.

The Spirit still speaks. In every voice we've tried to silence. In every life, we've tried to sanitize. In every story we've tried to edit. The Spirit still speaks.

Grace as Wesleyan Praxis: Not Just a Belief, But a Task

Grace, in the Wesleyan tradition, is not a passive experience. It is not limited to the soul's private comfort or a person's emotional assurance of salvation. Grace is God's active, initiating, sustaining love—and it always moves outward. It is not just something we receive. It is something that requires a response. John Wesley taught that grace is not a one-time event but a continuous relationship—one that grows, stretches, and sends us back into the world. Real grace, according to Wesley, becomes praxis—a way of living, loving, and laboring that expresses the reality of divine love through concrete acts of mercy and justice.

In his time, Wesley witnessed a Church that had become complacent—ritualistic, wealthy, and indifferent to the poor. So, he stepped outside its walls. Literally. When Anglican pulpits closed their doors to his message, Wesley preached in open fields, in coal mines, and on street corners. He believed that the gospel belonged to those the Church had ignored: the working poor, the enslaved, the sick, and the imprisoned. His commitment was not abstract but embodied. He wore through his shoes traveling on horseback, preached over 40,000 sermons, and gave away most of his income during his life. His message was clear: if grace is real, it must touch the world. If it's divine, it must be lived.

Wesley was not a social worker. He was a theologian. But his theology didn't stay in books. It was expressed in systems: he started free medical clinics, schools for children in poverty, micro-lending circles, and literacy programs for prisoners. He trained laypeople—everyday farmers, merchants, and mothers—to preach and lead. He formed "class meetings," small groups for mutual accountability and encouragement, where believers not only studied Scripture but asked, "How is it with your soul?" These weren't programs. They were expressions of a theology that said grace should shape every corner of human life.

One of Wesley's most radical claims was that acts of mercy—feeding the hungry, visiting the sick, caring for the outcast—were not optional extras for "good Christians." He called them "means of grace." That is, sacred practices in which God becomes present. This stands in contrast to the common idea that grace is confined to prayer, worship, or communion. For Wesley, helping someone in need is as holy as the Eucharist. Sitting with someone in suffering can be as sacred as reciting the Lord's Prayer. Loving our neighbor isn't something we do once we're holy; it's how we become holy.

This conviction echoes the teaching of Jesus, especially in Matthew 25:31–46. In that famous passage, Jesus describes a final judgment scene—not one where people are judged by religious status, but by how they treated "the least of these": the hungry, the stranger, the prisoner, the sick. He says, "Whatever you did for one of the least of these brothers and sisters of mine, you did for me." In other words, the measure of our faith is not what we profess—but what we practice. The presence of Christ is found in the margins, not the spotlight.

If we take Wesley seriously, then the Church today must rediscover grace not just as doctrine, but as duty. Not in the sense of legalistic obligation, but in the way a tree bears fruit: naturally, visibly, rooted in life.

So, what does this "grace fruit" look like in our time?

Fruit like accessible worship spaces, where Deaf congregants have full access to language and liturgy, not as an afterthought, but as a central expression of grace. It means seating that welcomes wheelchairs without awkwardness, lighting that doesn't trigger sensory distress, and preaching that doesn't assume every person in the room can read, hear, or process in the same way.

Fruit like advocating for children in schools—ensuring they get the support they need to thrive, whether they have dyslexia, ADHD, anxiety, or other learning differences. It means Christians showing up at IEP meetings not only for their own kids but for families who don't know how to navigate the system. It means understanding that educational justice is gospel work.

Fruit is like challenging the criminal justice system. Wesley visited prisons not to condemn, but to minister. Today, grace compels us to ask hard questions about mass incarceration, racial disparities in sentencing, and the profit-driven system that treats people as disposable. A Wesleyan Church should be deeply invested in restorative justice, which seeks healing, accountability, and reconciliation—not just punishment.

Fruit like gender equity in the pulpit and leadership. Grace does not discriminate by gender. If God's Spirit was poured out on all flesh—as Acts 2 declares—then we have no right to limit who gets to preach, pastor, or lead. To silence women is to silence part of God's voice. The Wesleyan tradition ordained women long before many others, and it must never turn back.

Fruit like the testimony of lives shaped by grace. My own journey—as a Deaf pastor, a parent, a teacher, and a persistent advocate—has been forged not in spite of my Deafness, but because of it. The world tried to label me as limited. Grace said otherwise. Grace did not remove my limitations; it redefined them. I do not serve the Church as a disabled person who "overcame." I serve as someone whose body, whose silence, whose struggle, and whose persistence is the message.

Grace is not only what we receive when we kneel. It's how we stand. It's how we walk alongside others. It's how we vote, spend, listen, organize, preach, teach, and parent. It's how we treat our enemies, our elders, our neighbors, and ourselves.

In the end, grace is not just about going to heaven.

It is about bringing heaven a little closer to earth—by how we live.

And that is the Wesleyan task:

To let our theology walk.

To let our belief become bread.

To let grace move through our bodies, our buildings, and our budgets.

To let grace do more than comfort. To let it change everything.

Grace as Vocation: From Resistance to Obedience

If grace is real, it does not simply ask for belief—it demands our life. It does not just soothe our wounds; it sends us. Grace, in its truest form, calls. And like many who are called, my first instinct was not to say "yes." It was to run.

Not because I didn't believe in God. But because I did. I knew enough about grace to understand its weight. I had seen it break open the hardest hearts and rebuild lives from ash. I had also seen what it cost.

I watched my mother answer her call to ministry with unwavering conviction—and I watched the Church make her pay for it. I saw her faithful leadership questioned, her qualifications doubted, her spirit worn down by bureaucracy, by bias, by theological smallness disguised as tradition. I saw her carry grace to people who would not receive it from her simply because of her gender. I saw her wrestle with exhaustion that was never called burnout—just "overcommitment." I saw her love people who never called her "Pastor" because she was a woman.

So when I felt the first flicker of call deep in my own chest, I buried it.

I had no desire to inherit that fight.

I wanted to believe that grace could be private. That my faith could stay quiet. That I could serve God without entering the institution that had made my mother bleed.

My wife was reluctant too—rightly so. She had witnessed the grind of ministry from the pew, and she was not eager to see it play out in our own home. She didn't see herself in the cultural mold of a "pastor's wife," a role too often steeped in stereotype and erasure. She knew that answering the call would mean not just surrendering my plans—but ours. And she wasn't sure the cost would be worth it.

Even when I did begin to say "yes," the path was not made smooth. Grace does not promise ease. It promises transformation. And transformation is rarely convenient.

I battled for accommodations in classrooms where professors saw my Deafness as a distraction. I had to advocate for interpreters, captioning, access to theological language in my native visual forms—not as a luxury, but as a right. I encountered spiritual leaders who claimed to welcome "all people," but had no system in place for accessibility, no imagination for Deaf leadership, no framework for understanding that the Word can be signed just as powerfully as it can be spoken.

In ministry settings, I faced assumptions that Deafness meant I couldn't preach, teach, or lead effectively—despite the evidence of my life, my calling, and my fruit. As a seminarian, I was repeatedly reminded—sometimes subtly, sometimes blatantly—that inclusion was tolerated, but not integrated.

Grace does not erase these barriers. But it never stopped calling.

Grace would not let me go.

Even in my fear, grace persisted. Even in my silence, it spoke. Even in my anger, it stayed. It waited through my hesitation. It stayed present through my doubt. When I finally began to say "yes"—even tentatively, even imperfectly—grace became not just the message I believed, but the force I followed.

This is what theologians mean when they say grace is vocational. The Latin root of the word "vocation" is *vocare*, meaning to call. It implies that we are not the origin of our purpose. We are summoned into it.

Wesley would describe vocation not just as a job or profession, but as the outflow of sanctifying grace—God's Spirit continually shaping us and sending us into the world. In his vision of Christian perfection, Wesley taught that our entire lives are meant to become instruments of love. We are not simply saved from sin. We are saved for service.

Grace does not call us where we are comfortable. It calls us where we are needed.

Too often, churches frame calling as a personal achievement. Something to be discerned, announced, and celebrated. But the deeper truth is that vocation is often born in discomfort. It emerges in protest before it becomes peace. The call does not always arrive as inspiration. Sometimes it arrives as an interruption.

I did not want this. I still struggle with it. But I know it is mine.

I know that grace would not let me go. And I believe that what God insists upon, even when we resist, is worth our surrender.

Grace as vocation means understanding that your life is not your own. It means recognizing that your difference—your Deafness, your disability, your trauma, your queerness, your pain—is not something to hide in order to be called. It may be the very place from which you are called.

Calling is not comfortable. It is a compulsion.

It is the divine tug that drags us into places we would not choose, to build things we cannot fully see, with people we are tempted to avoid, in systems we are asked to challenge. It is the slow, costly work of co-creating something new with God— something just, something true, something beautiful.

It is, in the end, the only thing worth building.

Grace in the Church: Accountability and Imagination

The Church cannot afford to speak of grace as a concept divorced from embodiment. Grace is not something we simply believe—it is something we carry, live, and extend. And if we are to call ourselves a people shaped by grace, then we must become a people who confess where we've distorted it, and who dare to imagine what it could become. Grace, rightly understood, compels us not just to personal salvation, but to communal reformation. It is not a soft word. It is a seismic one.

We live in a time when many are not leaving the Church because they've lost faith in God—but because they have lost hope that the Church will make room for them. Grace has been preached from pulpits but withheld at the door. It has been written into doctrinal statements but denied in daily practice. It has been spoken in polished liturgies while being structurally excluded in the very way church life is designed. Grace must no longer be tamed into a theological garnish. It must be returned to its true form: fire, movement, and transformation.

The Church must move—not later, but now. It must move from respectability to repentance, from preservation to reformation, and from charity to solidarity.

Respectability, in many churches, is code for silence. It's the tendency to protect image rather than integrity, to uphold tradition rather than interrogate it. A respectable church may appear healthy on the outside—polished bulletins, growing attendance, strong giving—but beneath the surface, it may be starving for truth. Repentance is not about self-condemnation. It is about turning away from our idols, idols of control, of uniformity, of fear disguised as order. It is the sacred work of listening to those we've harmed and allowing their pain to reshape our theology.

Preservation, though often well-meaning, resists the Spirit. It clings to what has always been, even when what has been no longer reflects the life of Christ. It sees change as a threat rather than an invitation. Reformation, on the other hand, is not rebellion. It is rooted in reverence—a reverence for God's ongoing work in the world. To reform is to trust that the same Spirit who breathed life into the early Church is still breathing, still speaking, still unsettling us for the sake of love.

Charity, though necessary in moments of crisis, is insufficient as a long-term posture. It gives from a place of distance and control. It allows the giver to remain comfortable while the recipient remains dependent. But solidarity demands proximity. It places us in a mutual relationship. It does not say, "You need us."

It says, "We need each other." It recognizes that every person, especially those the Church has historically marginalized—is not only a recipient of grace but a bearer of it.

This means the Church must be held accountable—not abstractly, but systemically. And one of the most urgent areas of accountability is in the Church's treatment of disabled people. Not just Deaf people like me, but those who are blind or low-vision, who live with chronic illness, who use wheelchairs or mobility devices, who have autism, who experience intellectual disabilities, who battle mental health conditions, who have PTSD, who live with invisible pain or fatigue, who were born with disabilities or acquired them later in life.

The Church must confront its complicity in ableism, not merely in individual prejudice, but in the way we have designed theology, worship, leadership, and access around an unspoken assumption: that full participation requires able-bodied, neurotypical, verbal conformity. For too long, disabled people have been seen through the lens of deficit rather than dignity. Too often, disability is named in prayer lists only when healing is the goal, and rarely when wisdom, leadership, or theology is needed.

I have experienced this personally. As a Deaf person, I have been treated as a ministry project rather than a partner. I have been denied access to interpreters, captioning, or full inclusion in theological spaces—while being praised for "showing up anyway." But this is not just my story. I have walked alongside students whose sensory processing differences made traditional classrooms unbearable, yet whose faith was deeper than most adults I know. I've watched friends with chronic pain struggle to sit through worship services designed with no flexibility or empathy. I've spoken with fellow pastors who live with anxiety or bipolar disorder and have been told they are unfit to lead unless they "get healed first."

Yet, grace has persisted. In everybody. In every voice. In every so-called limitation.

The gospel does not erase disability to make people whole. The gospel reveals that people are whole already—because they are loved, called, and made in the image of a God who did not hide His wounds after resurrection but offered them as evidence of His authority.

This is the grace the Church must reclaim. A grace that listens to the lived theology of disabled people—not out of politeness, but out of hunger. Because within our stories are truths the Church cannot afford to overlook.

Accountability alone is not enough. We also need imagination—the sacred ability to see what does not yet exist, and to believe that it can.

The Spirit is already leading us into new expressions of the Church. I have seen worship led entirely in American Sign Language, where silence becomes sanctuary and movement becomes liturgy. I've seen storefront sanctuaries become centers of healing for those recovering from addiction, violence, and shame. I've witnessed faith take root in jail cells, where incarcerated men and women preach to each other with truth and fire. I've seen autistic children welcomed into spaces where stimming is not punished but understood. I've seen queer believers serve communion with trembling hands and radiant dignity.

These are not anomalies. These are altars. These are not second-tier expressions of faith. They are Spirit-ordained, Christ-centered, fully valid manifestations of grace.

So I say this with all the urgency of my calling and all the love I carry for the Church:

If you are a church leader—ask yourself whether disabled people are shaping your theology, or just navigating around it. Ask whether your building welcomes wheelchairs not just through ramps but into leadership. Ask whether mental health is met with prayer and policy. Ask whether your worship space anticipates neurodivergent needs—not as exceptions, but as part of the design.

If you are a congregant—listen for whose voices are missing, and be bold enough to ask why. If you serve on a committee, consider how your decisions affect those whose needs are not your own. If you preach—expand your examples, your metaphors, your imagination. Preach not just about marginalized people, but from their wisdom.

Grace is not always polite. It is not confined. It is not static. It is the living pulse of God's unrelenting love, and it will not wait for us to catch up.

Let the Church be brave enough to follow.

Let the Church be humble enough to repent.

Let the Church be wise enough to listen.

Let the Church be creative enough to imagine.

Let the Church become what grace has always intended it to be—not a monument to the past, but a movement toward healing, justice, and joy.

Grace as Future: Hope for a Wounded World

There are seasons when the structures we inhabit no longer feel like home—when the language spoken in the room no longer fits the shape of our experience, and when even well-meaning people ask us to shrink, to fit, to wait. I have lived through those seasons, and not once or twice, but as a rhythm. I have stood in classrooms designed for hearing but not for Deafness, in conversations where I had to explain my existence before I could offer my insight, in church spaces where welcome was extended— yet the table was already set for someone else.

In those moments, when human understanding ran thin and institutional hospitality wore out, I was not sustained by perfection or certainty. I was carried by grace.

But not the fragile, softly lit version of grace we sometimes reduce to sentiment. This grace did not arrive with polite smiles or easy comfort. It showed up as resilience in silence, as clarity in confusion, as a stubborn fire in my chest that refused to go out. Grace met me not after the pain was over, but right in the center of it. And over time, it became clear: grace is not just what got me through. It is what I now carry.

I carry it into every space that once pushed me to the edge. Into the classroom, where neurodivergent children and disabled youth are asked to prove their value. Into conversations about equity, where stories like mine are too often treated as exceptions or curiosities. Into family dynamics and hospital waiting rooms, into prison visits and protest lines. Into everyday moments where someone is about to give up because they've been told—implicitly or explicitly—that who they are is not quite enough.

I carry grace not because I have mastered it, but because it refused to let me go. And now I see it for what it is: not merely a gift to be received, but a charge to be lived.

Grace is not a church word. It is a human word.

It is not owned by religion. It is animated by love.

It is what restores when injustice has bruised, what persists when policy has failed, what softens us when bitterness threatens to calcify.

It is the unseen current beneath every story of survival, resistance, forgiveness, and hope.

Grace—real grace—does not ask you to erase who you are to become worthy. It asks you to bring your full self to the table: your history, your body, your culture, your silence, your fury, your truth. Grace is not afraid of contradiction. It lives there. It walks with you not only in belief but in doubt, not only in faith but in fatigue. It asks for your honesty, not your perfection.

I say this as someone shaped by faith, yes—but also by experience. By being Deaf in a world designed for hearing. By being different in spaces built for sameness. And what I've come to understand is that my Deafness is not a hindrance to grace—it is a herald of it. It has taught me how to listen beyond noise, how to speak in silence, and how to lead without always being heard. It has opened my eyes to a truth far greater than one community or religion: that our wounds are not what disqualify us from being agents of healing. They are often the very wells from which we draw water to offer others.

So if you're reading this and you do not attend a church—or if you used to, but walked away because it failed to see you—know this: you are not outside of grace. You are held by it. If you are burned out by activism, if you are exhausted by parenting, if you are grieving what the world has stolen from you—know this: grace is not an escape from struggle. It is the courage to live inside of it with tenderness, clarity, and power.

And to all of us, whether we call ourselves believers or skeptics, pastors or parents, poets or policy-makers—this is the moment to recognize that grace is not merely a comfort we carry. It is a burden we bear together. It is not only meant to heal us. It is meant to send us.

When we ignore grace, real people suffer.

Another child is taught to hide their autism instead of celebrate their wiring.

Another single mother is shamed into silence by the institutions meant to uplift her.

Another Black boy is punished for being loud in systems that never asked why he had to be.

Another queer teenager reads a headline and wonders if they will ever be safe.

Another refugee hears "God bless America" and knows it doesn't mean them.

Grace is not an aesthetic. It is an intervention. It breaks the silence. It calls our assumptions into question. It interrupts the normal when the normal is killing us. It rebuilds what the world tells us is unfixable.

So here is the invitation. Not to be religious. Not to be perfect.

But to be open.

To be transformed.

To become a carrier of grace—wherever you are.

Let grace flow through your lesson plans, your courtroom strategy, your protest chants, your hospital rounds, your parenting, your poetry, your service work, your silence, your speech. Let it shape the questions you ask and the policies you write. Let it influence how you treat your employees, your neighbors, your enemies, your elders, and your own body. Let it push you beyond what is convenient into what is faithful. Let it teach you that you do not have to become someone else to belong—you only have to be willing to let love break you open and put you back together differently.

The world does not need more polished institutions. It needs more people marked by grace.

And so, whether you believe or doubt, whether you preach or protest, whether you pray or have not prayed in years:

Let this be your benediction—

Not "Go in peace," but "Go in power."

Not "Hide your pain, "but "Honor your story."

Not "Wait your turn, "but "Take your place."

Not "Return to normal, "but "Build something new."

Because grace has never been the quiet corner of religion.

It has always been the heartbeat of resistance.

The architecture of healing.

The invitation to begin again.

It is already at work—here, now, in you.

CHAPTER 14

Lessons from a Life Unheard

I remember one particular day during high school, a day that has stayed with me not because of any drama or disaster, but because of the clarity it gave me. We were in history class, discussing the causes of the American Revolution. The teacher, energetic and well-meaning, delivered a rehearsed monologue about colonial unrest and British taxation, pacing in front of the board like a performer on stage. Most of the students were barely paying attention, and those who seemed to focus more on whether their own answers might sound clever than on the actual weight of the question.

"What caused the Revolution?" she asked, glancing around the room. A few students shouted back, "Taxes!" "No freedom!" "The Boston Tea Party!" She smiled, encouraged by their energy, then turned to me, tapping my desk. I was sitting quietly, hood pulled up, head laid down, eyes on the interpreter. I looked up and she asked, "Patrick, did you hear the question?"

I nodded. Slowly. I had heard more than the question—I had heard the assumption behind it.

"Yes," I said. "But it depends on who you ask. For the British, it was a rebellion. For white colonists, it was about liberty and control. For enslaved people, it meant a new oppressor replacing the old one. And for Indigenous communities, it was another chapter in a long story of land being stolen."

The air shifted. The noise stopped. The classroom fell into a silence deeper than quiet—one of those sacred stillness moments that appear when truth arrives unexpectedly and asks to be felt before it's spoken about. No one responded right away. The teacher didn't nod or say thank you. She just stared for a moment, then turned back to the board, her expression not offended, but disrupted.

That moment taught me something foundational: silence is not a void to be filled. It is a vessel, waiting to be noticed. It holds weight. It holds a warning. It holds wisdom that the world will miss if it's too busy performing.

That truth came to life in an even deeper way the first time I sat with the story of the prophet Elijah on Mount Horeb. The scene, drawn from 1 Kings 19, has become sacred territory for me. Elijah is not triumphant in this moment. He's not on a stage or winning a battle or declaring a prophecy. He is devastated—tired of fighting, tired of fleeing, tired of being unheard. He hides in a cave and begs God to reveal Himself, not with boldness but with brokenness.

God responds—but not as expected.

First, a windstorm tears across the mountain, the kind that would rattle the stones and shake the bones of a lesser prophet. But Scripture says, "The Lord was not in the wind." Then comes an earthquake, violent and terrifying, rumbling through the foundation of the mountain and of the man himself. But still, "the Lord was not in the earthquake." Then fire—bright, consuming, dramatic. The kind of fire that consumed offerings on altars and carried chariots into heaven. But again, "the Lord was not in the fire."

And then—a pause.

A stillness.

A "sound of sheer silence."

And finally, there—THERE IN SILENCE—is where God speaks.

Not through spectacle.

Not through force.

But through the quiet that lingers when all the noise has given up.

That story is not a metaphor for me. It is a mirror. I know what it's like to search for God in all the places people insist God must be—in the music, in the sermons, in the shouting and the celebration—and to come up empty. I know what it's like to sit in the stillness others mistake for absence and discover instead that Presence has never been closer.

That moment on the mountain is not the exception. It is the rhythm of a God who has always chosen to speak in ways the world tries to talk over.

And so I begin this chapter not by explaining my Deafness, not by defending my difference, but by declaring something holy: Silence is not absence.

It is another kind of presence.

It is not less than sound—it is older.

Not weaker than speech—it is stronger than noise.

Not the failure to participate—but the refusal to pretend.

This is the world I've lived in. This is the world I've learned from.

And if you'll follow me through it, I promise—you won't just hear something new.

You'll begin to feel the Word in ways you didn't know were possible.

Not shouted. Not sung.

But carved into stillness like truth that waits to be seen.

The Misdiagnosis of Difference

It starts early.

Before the ink dries on your birth certificate.

Before you know who you are, the world starts writing its own definition of you—one line at a time, in systems and stares and unspoken rules.

For me, the first marks were made in a preschool classroom where my silence was mistaken for confusion. Where my lack of response was read not as reflection but as delay. I was the child who didn't answer quickly enough. Who stared too long. Who reacted too slowly to instructions barked across the room? The teachers never paused to ask what I might need—they were too busy measuring me against a mold. And when I didn't fit it, they assumed something was wrong.

That's the lie at the heart of every misdiagnosis of difference:

That being outside the norm is the same as being broken.

That if your rhythm is different, your worth must be lower.

For me, that difference was Deafness. But this experience isn't only mine.

Maybe you were the only girl in the room who asked questions that made boys uncomfortable.

Maybe you were the Black student whose intellect was always second-guessed.

Maybe you spoke English with an accent or didn't speak it at all.

Maybe you were too quiet. Too expressive. Too gender-nonconforming. Too brown. Too anxious. Too poor.

Maybe you loved someone your church said you weren't allowed to love.

Or maybe—like me—you lived most of your life not being seen as you are, but as a problem others had to solve.

These misdiagnoses don't happen in emergency rooms. They happen in classrooms and sanctuaries. In kitchens and locker rooms. In offices and social media threads. They happen wherever normalcy is treated like holiness. Wherever performance is mistaken for presence. Wherever sameness is required for safety.

Growing up Deaf in a hearing world meant that I was constantly navigating a double translation—translating the spoken world into a visual one and then translating myself back into a version people would accept. It was exhausting. It was lonely. And it taught me to read people faster than they could read me.

But Deafness wasn't the problem.

The problem was the assumption that communication had only one valid form.

The problem was a system that privileged quick speech over quiet wisdom.

The problem was that my silence made people uncomfortable—and instead of asking why, they tried to fix it.

Schools, especially, were ruthless about this. The entire architecture was built for verbal speed. The students who answered fast were celebrated. The ones who paused to think were left behind. Intelligence was measured by how well you could echo what someone else had already said. There was no room for the student who learned by watching, who processed by drawing connections others couldn't see, who felt the weight of words before speaking them.

In that world, I didn't just fall behind. I became invisible.

And church? Church was complicated.

It was one of the few places I believed God might actually meet me—but the way we designed it often drowned that hope out. Worship was loud. Prayers were long and mostly auditory. Testimonies were shouted. Faith was something you proved with your voice—singing louder, clapping harder, quoting Scripture faster. If you weren't demonstrative, you were assumed to be distant. If you weren't speaking in tongues, you were assumed not to be listening to the Spirit. If you didn't cry on cue or lift your hands at the right lyric, people wondered whether you were truly saved.

But I wasn't faithless. I was processing God in a different language.

Sometimes, I felt the Spirit tremble in my chest during a silent moment—when the room stopped performing long enough for Presence to settle like dew. Sometimes, I saw a child sway gently during a hymn and knew, without sound, that heaven was in the room. Sometimes, I caught a glimpse of someone mouthing their prayer, lips barely moving, and I knew—**knew**—God was listening.

But no one was looking for those signs.

They were listening for volume.

The theologian Lennard J. Davis, in his work Enforcing Normalcy, explains that society doesn't just prefer sameness—it protects it. Normalcy becomes a god. And that god demands sacrifice. Anyone who lives outside the statistical mean must be corrected, erased, absorbed into something more palatable. The Church is not immune to this. In fact, it often sanctifies it. We tell people that their healing is proof of their holiness. That their ability to blend in is evidence of God's favor. That their suffering will be worth it—once they change.

But what if they don't need to change?

What if Deafness, or autism, or chronic illness, or being a woman who preaches, or a man who cries, or a queer teen with a Bible in their backpack—isn't the problem?

What if the problem is our failure to widen the lens?

There is a verse in Isaiah that still undoes me every time I read it:

"In that day, the Deaf will hear the words of the scroll, and out of gloom and darkness the eyes of the blind will see" (Isaiah 29:18).

It's been quoted to me as a miracle promise—as if Deafness were something God would one day reverse. But I don't hear it that way. Not anymore.

I hear it as a reversal not of bodies, but of power.

I hear it as a vision of a world in which those who have been othered—those who have been talked over, left out, and erased—are finally centered. Not just healed but honored. Not assimilated but amplified.

For those who don't share my theology or my reverence for Scripture, I would offer this:

Even if you don't believe in prophets or promises, you know what it feels like to be overlooked.

You know what it's like to be misunderstood on purpose.

You've felt the sting of someone dismissing your difference because it didn't fit their expectation. Maybe you've lived a life unheard, even while speaking perfectly.

Maybe your family never listened unless you were apologizing. Maybe your job only saw your value in numbers, never in nuance. Maybe you learned, somewhere along the way, that the safest way to survive was to make yourself smaller, quieter, more normal.

If so, then we are kin.

Not because we are the same, but because we have been similarly misread. I was never broken. I was never lacking. I was simply different in a world addicted to sameness. The more I've unlearned that addiction, the more I've realized: My difference is not a defect. It is a doorway. A doorway into deeper compassion. Into holy discomfort. Into the kind of listening that transforms not just what we hear—but how we see.

The Theology of Attunement

To be attuned is to be oriented toward the sacred details others ignore. It is not simply to hear, or even to see, but to perceive what is pulsing beneath the visible and the audible. It is to become so present, so aware, that the world's background noise dissolves, and the truth—raw, living, divine—rises to the surface.

Deafness has taught me the theology of attunement.

Not by offering easy answers, but by demanding deeper questions. Not by giving me a shortcut to spiritual wisdom, but by forcing me to slow down enough to notice what most people rush past. Attunement is not a skill—it is a discipline. It is the daily practice of showing up to each moment with humility, of refusing to reduce reality to what can be explained quickly or consumed conveniently. And for those of us who move through the world with a body or mind outside of what society has labeled "typical," attunement becomes a way of surviving—but also, paradoxically, a way of worshiping.

When I enter a room, I do not simply observe it. I read it. I feel the atmosphere long before anyone speaks. I can tell who is holding pain, who is performing politeness, and who is angry but pretending not to be. I notice who looks at me too long and who doesn't look at all. I feel the delay between intention and action in others. I track the micro-movements—the tapping of feet, the hesitation before a word, the slouch of shoulders under burdens no one names. I feel it in my ribs, in my gut, in the hollows of silence.

This is not a mystical ability. It is the wisdom of the edge.

The edge of what's heard. The edge of what's expected. The edge of what the dominant culture teaches us to ignore. And though it began for me in the context of Deafness, I have come to understand that this kind of embodied knowing is not unique to the Deaf community. It is shared, often silently, by people across all kinds of differences.

People who have learned to walk into a room and instantly scan it for safety. People who carry trauma in their nervous systems like ghosts wrapped in muscle. People who know the weight of code-switching just to be accepted. People whose queerness, or Blackness, or gender, or neurodivergence, or accent, or mental health diagnosis has forced them to develop a kind of radar—because the world never gave them the luxury of assuming they belonged.

Attunement is the theology of the overlooked. It is how we read the holy in what others dismiss as noise. It is how we survive—and how we worship.

Scripture is laced with this kind of awareness, though we rarely name it for what it is. When Moses meets God at the burning bush, it is not the fire that changes everything—it is the fact that Moses stops to notice. "When the Lord saw that he had turned aside to see, God called to him" (Exodus 3:4). The miracle is not just the flame. It is the turning. The act of paying attention. Of becoming attuned.

Jesus embodied this kind of divine perception over and over again. He noticed the woman who touched the hem of His garment—not because she screamed, but because her faith moved through silence. He saw Zacchaeus in a tree when everyone else was looking at the crowd. He bent to write in the dust, slowing down the rage of a mob long enough for mercy to enter. His ministry was not just about proclaiming truth. It was about perceiving the people others missed. His life was an act of attunement.

That's where the theology becomes clear:

God is not distant, distracted, or disengaged.

God is attuned.

El Roi—the God who sees me.

Emmanuel—God with us, not generically, but intimately.

The Spirit intercedes with groans too deep for words, Paul writes in Romans 8.

Even in heaven, God is not deaf to silence. God hears what cannot be said.

In my own life, I've come to recognize this theology not just in moments of dramatic encounter, but in the ordinary acts of noticing. When a student's body slumps halfway through a conversation, and I pause class—not because they said they were in crisis, but because I saw it in their posture. When I sit across from someone grieving, and I mirror their breathing, and they say afterward that they felt comforted—even though no words were exchanged. When I am preaching, and I stop mid-sermon because the Spirit has shifted the room, and no one else understands why, but someone weeps in the third pew, and I know: that was God.

This is what it means to be attuned—to the Spirit, to others, to ourselves.

And this is what Deafness has taught me to treasure.

You do not need to be Deaf to learn it.

You need only be willing to listen with more than your ears.

To discern with your presence.

To worship with your attention.

To love with your whole, trembling, noticing self.

Attunement is not a passive state. It is not a gentle form of watching from the sidelines. It is a prophetic form of participation. It demands that we slow down enough to stop consuming each other and start communicating. It challenges the speed of capitalism, the noise of certainty, and the obsession with rightness. Attunement invites us to listen with our wounds, to perceive with our breath, to interpret with our bodies.

In the Eucharist, this is precisely what we are invited to do.

We are not asked to explain the mystery. We are asked to receive it. To take the bread and recognize the body. To take the cup and know, not through argument, but through presence, that God is with us.

That's why Deafness—like so many other embodied differences—is not a problem to be solved but a liturgy to be honored. It slows us down. It quiets the noise. It interrupts our assumptions. And in doing so, it opens us up to the God who was never absent, only unnoticed.

This is the theology of attunement: That the marginalized already carry the map. That the overlooked already hear the music. That the unheard are already tuned to the frequency of God. Not louder. Not faster. But clearer. More deeply. More truly.

Lessons About God

There are truths about God that I could not have learned had I been born hearing. Not because sound is wrong or of lesser importance, but because Deafness placed me at an angle—just far enough outside the cultural center to see what others could not. Deafness became a lens through which the Divine came into focus. It interrupted the default assumptions of both the Church and the world, stripping away performance, noise, and surface-level religiosity, until all that remained was presence.

And presence is where God is found.

This body—this Deaf, resilient, sensitive, attuned body—has not kept me from God. It has introduced me to God more honestly. I do not encounter the Divine as one who listens through sermons alone or who sings in pitch-perfect harmony with the choir. I encounter the Divine in rooms where language breaks down, where silence thickens into meaning, where gestures carry the weight of stories and prayers are offered in glances, in trembling hands, in stillness that refuses to apologize for its depth.

I have learned that God is not obsessed with sound. We are.

We live in a culture that equates noise with importance— where the loudest voice in the room is assumed to be the most correct, where talking fast is mistaken for intelligence, where shouting over others is called leadership. But God does not submit to our obsession with volume. The God I have come to know is not impressed by noise. God listens for truth. God waits for honesty. God meets people not in their projections, but in their presence. And presence does not always speak in words.

Holy presence, I have found, can tremble in a breath. It can reside in a pause. It can stretch across a gesture or rest quietly in a furrowed brow. These are not accidents of communication. They are sacred forms of revelation.

Scripture tells us again and again that God appears in unexpected forms—in burning bushes, in whispering winds, in the cries of exiles, in the bodies of the disabled, in wombs, in tombs, in the margins of society that the empire has tried to forget. But we forget. We keep trying to reduce God to pulpit and podium, to polished theology and pristine pronunciation. We keep building temples God never asked for, while ignoring the burning bushes of our own century—the bodies, the people, the prophets, the communities crying out for acknowledgment.

I have come to believe that Deafness is not only a mode of being—it is a prophetic gift. Not because it makes me special, but because it forces me to pay attention in ways others are rarely required to. Deafness teaches patience in a world addicted to speed. It teaches listening without assumption. It trains the eyes to search for nuance, the spirit to wait before reacting, the body to remain attentive even when the words haven't arrived yet.

These are not deficits. These are disciplines.

Sacred.

Scriptural.

Transferable.

What I've learned through Deafness is not limited to the Deaf community. It echoes across many forms of difference. Black and brown children learn these same instincts in classrooms that were not built for their brilliance. Neurodivergent youth develop this same sensitivity in environments that mistake creativity for disorder. Queer individuals become fluent in this same interpretive listening—knowing how to read a room for danger, for dignity, for welcome. Immigrants, trauma survivors, disabled elders—all become theologians of attunement, because they have had no other choice.

To be different in a world that prizes sameness is to become bilingual in truth and survival. It is to learn to speak in silence. It is to encounter God not in the sound of triumph, but in the sheer silence of persistence.

That is the God I have come to know.

The God who met Elijah not in the fire or the wind or the earthquake—but in the stillness so heavy it could only be holy.

The God who took the Deaf man aside—not to shame him or fix him, but to communicate in a language that honored his body, his culture, his mode of receiving grace. The God who, again and again, chooses to show up in the lives and languages of people whose presence the world tries to overlook. The God who does not require performance, who is not impressed by spectacle, and who is never in a rush. The God who, like a skilled interpreter, matches the pace of the one before Him—adjusting not out of pity, but out of love. I used to think that I had to overcome Deafness in order to be worthy of God. I no longer believe that.

Now, I know that God and I have always spoken the same language.

And if that is true for me, then it can be true for anyone who has been told they are too much, too little, too broken, too complicated, too strange, too slow, too sad, too angry, too far outside the circle to count. If you have ever sat in the corner of the room and wondered whether God knew how to reach you there— let me say this as clearly as I can:

God comes to you.

God has already arrived.

God is not pacing impatiently at the center. God is not waiting for you to move closer, get louder, or become easier to explain. God is already beside you. Already within you. Already listening— not to your volume, but to your truth.

This is what I've learned through the long, beautiful discipline of being Deaf:

That God is not looking for those who sound like Him.

God is looking for those willing to recognize Him—even in unfamiliar form.

When we begin to recognize God in our difference—when we stop asking whether we are worthy and start asking how we might widen the circle for others to see themselves too—then the Church becomes something holy again.

Not a stage. Not a factory. Not a gate. But a table.

CHAPTER 15

The Story Doesn't End Here

The classroom had emptied, but I remained, rooted to the same square of tile I'd been standing on for nearly seven hours. The whiteboard in front of me still bore the faded streaks of the last lesson—smudged red ink from a half-dried marker, words half-legible through the residue of yesterday's erasures. Behind me, the walls hummed faintly with the vibration of the school's old heating system cycling down for the evening, its rhythm familiar and oddly comforting, like the sound of a distant drumbeat reminding me that time had, in fact, passed.

It had been a long day. One of those days where the work of teaching had felt less like planting seeds and more like digging ditches in dry ground. The students had been restless, some disengaged, others distracted by battles I could feel pulsing beneath their skin, even if they didn't have the words or the courage to name them. And I—well, I was tired too. Tired in that particular way only educators, parents, and pastors understand: the kind of fatigue that settles not just in the body, but in the soul, from carrying the emotional weight of others while still trying to keep your own story stitched together.

As I leaned against the edge of my desk, taking in the scattered chairs, the torn corner of a forgotten homework assignment, and the faint smell of Expo marker that clung to the air like dust in a church sanctuary, I noticed the word I had scribbled just before the final bell rang: becoming. No period. No flourish. Just the word, standing there on its own, honest and incomplete.

I hadn't planned to write it. It wasn't in my lesson outline or state standards. But as I stood there, eyes tracing its uneven lines, I realized why it had surfaced. The lesson wasn't about formulas or facts today, it was about the process of staying in motion, of not giving up when the story feels fragmented, of believing that forward is still possible, even when you're moving through the world with a limp, a scar, or a secret.

At that moment, I felt a presence—less like a lightning bolt and more like a quiet clarity rising from the soles of my feet to the back of my neck. It wasn't audible, not in the way others might expect, but it was undeniable. Something in me stirred, deep and steady, like the kind of knowing that doesn't need to be explained or proven.

I was still moving. And I was not alone.

There is something sacred about those moments when the noise fades and you're left only with what you carry and what carries you. For me, Deafness has always shaped how I navigate the world—not just physically, but relationally, spiritually, vocationally. It changes the way I hear a room, the way I read a face, the way I sense tension in a crowd or tenderness in silence. But more than that, Deafness has become the lens through which I see the presence of God—not as distant thunder, but as vibration, as breath, as rhythm moving through the bones of things.

And I've come to see that this way of hearing isn't limited to those with my story. Everyone walks through the world with something that reshapes how they listen and love. Some people carry trauma they can't name. Others carry chronic pain, mental illness, grief that never found its grave, or questions that once masqueraded as faith. Some carry their whole identity as a silent apology, too afraid to take up space in churches that only want the polished and the proper.

Whether your particular burden is visible or invisible, chosen or inherited, this truth remains: if you've made it this far, you are still moving. And if you are still moving, grace is moving with you.

I know it might be tempting to treat this chapter like a conclusion—to read these words as a kind of benediction over what's been. But if you've been paying attention, you already know better. This book was never meant to be a memoir of what happened. It's a dispatch from the middle. It's a sacred interruption. It's an altar made of ash and stubborn hope.

This is not the end of the story.

This is the doorway to the next act.

My story isn't finished—and neither is yours.

Grace didn't stop with survival. It didn't close the book after the fire or the heartbreak or the prayer that went unanswered. Grace kept walking. Grace pressed forward. Grace, as I've come to know it, doesn't wait for healing before it invites you to move.

So, here we are.

At the edge of something holy and unfinished.

If you're willing—if you're brave enough to carry what you've learned into the world that's still unfolding—then you'll begin to see that movement itself is the miracle.

Looking Back So We Can Move Forward

To move forward with clarity, we must first tell the truth about where we've been—not to drown in regret or romanticize the past, but to align our steps with the honest terrain of our story. Because what we carry shapes how we walk. And what we remember determines what we become.

This is not a memoir for sentimentality. It is a map for momentum. These words are for the child who was told they were too loud, too soft, too brown, too pale, too different to belong. For the Deaf kid straining to read lips in a noisy locker room. For the immigrant working three jobs who still wonders if home will ever feel like home. For the woman in the church pew who has swallowed her own voice for decades. For the white man who scoffs when anyone dares name his privilege—because no one saw him crying in the garage after his father left, and no one saw him clawing his way up from poverty. For the white woman who bristles at the word "power" because her scars came from being silenced, dismissed, or expected to be perfect while feeling perpetually invisible.

This is for every person—Black, brown, white, Indigenous, immigrant, queer, straight, Deaf, disabled, neurodivergent, veteran, addict, survivor, lonely father, grieving mother—who has ever felt mislabeled, misunderstood, or misplaced in the narrative of God's world. The pain may look different, but the ache is strangely familiar: the longing to be known, the hope to be seen, the fear of being unworthy, the hunger to be free.

We need to name the hard truth: differences do not disappear as we grow. It simply changes shape. The world will either demand you minimize what sets you apart or shame you into thinking it is a liability. But hear this:

Difference is not disorder.

Identity is not a defect.

Every divergence from a person's perceived norm, whether Deafness, poverty, queerness, whiteness, maleness, femaleness, or any other thread of human story—carries within it the imprint of divine intention.

The grace that threads through these words is not reserved for a select few. It is not conditional on your theology, your political leanings, your success, your failures, or whether you have unpacked your privilege or named your pain. Grace is the one constant in a world of shifting labels and endless arguments. It moves toward the addict and the overachiever, the parent and the prodigal, the skeptic and the saint.

But here's the truth: many of us were never taught, or maybe were taught to fear:

You do not have to be whole to walk in grace.

You do not need a spotless past, a polished faith, or a fully reconciled identity. You do not need to be healed of every wound or have forgiven every enemy. You do not need to feel brave, steady, or even certain. You only need the courage to be honest— the kind of raw honesty that doesn't photograph well, that doesn't sound impressive on a stage, that trembles as it whispers, "God, I'm tired. I'm bitter. I'm bruised. But if you'll have me, I'm willing."

This is the invitation: come with your limp. Come with your stutter. Come with your doubts, your questions, your complicated history, your baggage, your bruised theology. Just come.

Because grace does not wait for you to arrive perfect. Grace meets you on the road. Grace walks with you while you're still bleeding. Grace begins to transform not when you finally feel ready, but in the very act of moving forward while unfinished.

The witness of Scripture screams this holy pattern: Moses stammered, yet God still sent him. Hannah wept so violently that a priest mistook her for drunk, yet her prayers birthed a prophet. Peter denied Christ three times, yet Jesus still built a church on his back. Paul carried a thorn in his flesh that God never removed. Again and again, the Gospel reminds us:

You can be broken and still be chosen.

You can be uncertain and still be sent.

You can be unfinished and still be useful.

And being broken, uncertain, and unfinished is the perfect place to start.

If you are waiting to feel worthy, you may never move. If you are waiting for the pain to end, you may never leave the shore. If you are waiting for someone else to declare you holy enough, you may miss the very invitation pulsing in your chest right now.

Grace is not applause.

Grace is movement.

Grace is not a finish line.

Grace is a road.

Going forward is the act of healing grace in motion.

A Theology in Motion: Grace Is Not a Gate—It's a Path

Friends, we have done ourselves a disservice—perhaps even a quiet kind of spiritual violence—when we've treated grace as though it were a gated checkpoint. Too many of us were raised to believe that grace was a singular moment we had to earn entrance into: a doorway through which only the properly repentant, the theologically aligned, or the morally acceptable could pass. It was presented as a one-time admission ticket—granted when we prayed the right prayer, signed the doctrinal agreement, or wept at the altar with sufficient sincerity.

But I have lived long enough, and limped far enough, to know that grace is not a gate. It is a path—and it is not still. It is not sterile. It is not small.

Grace is alive, moving with fierce tenderness and relentless courage through the broken edges of our lives and the bleeding corners of our world. It winds through addiction recovery centers and Sunday morning sanctuaries alike. It weaves through back pews, courtrooms, living rooms, prison yards, therapists' offices, and ICU waiting rooms. Grace, when rightly understood, is not a passive pardon—it is a persistent presence that refuses to let us stay where we are, even as it welcomes us without condition.

This understanding is not just personal revelation—it is deeply rooted in the spiritual soil of my tradition. John Wesley, the founder of the Methodist movement, did not treat grace as a static object to be received once and for all. He saw grace as an active force, a divine companionship that begins long before we are even aware of it and continues to shape, challenge, and sanctify us throughout our lives. Wesley's theology of sanctifying grace teaches that salvation is not a destination we arrive at, but a journey we *join*—a lifelong unfolding into the likeness of Christ, marked not by arrival, but by continual transformation.

Sanctifying grace means that God is not merely interested in saving us from sin but in forming us for *love*—not just as an internal sentiment, but as a visible, tactile, embodied practice. We are not saved from the world as though creation itself were something to escape; we are saved *for* the world—to become participants in its renewal, ambassadors of divine compassion in the very places we once tried to flee.

This is why Wesley insisted that holiness could never be a private affair. Any notion of piety that does not concern itself with the poor, the excluded, the vulnerable, and the wounded is not holiness; it is spiritual narcissism masquerading as righteousness. Social holiness—the heartbeat of Methodism—demands that we measure our love for God not by the frequency of our prayers or the polish of our beliefs, but by our willingness to enter the pain of our neighbors and become agents of healing within it. Social holiness is living the gospel of grace in real time, like Jesus.

Social holiness does not mean smiling politely at strangers or dropping canned goods in a donation box during the holidays. It means sitting beside someone who is detoxing from heroin and refusing to look away when their body convulses. It means holding the hand of a nonverbal child in your congregation and learning to worship in a language beyond words. It means showing up at city council meetings and school board hearings to advocate for ramps, interpreters, mental health services, and housing protections—not because it's trendy, but because it is *holy*.

Grace in motion means walking with people who have been deemed disposable and staying long after the photo op is over. It means designing sanctuaries where people with sensory processing differences feel at home, not like intrusions. It means building liturgies that make space for those who mourn during worship, who sit with arms crossed and eyes full of unspeakable grief—who need presence, not platitudes. It means resisting the reflex to fix or rescue and choosing instead to remain—to accompany, to learn, to defer, to love.

It is not enough to preach grace. We must practice it. We must embody it. We must live it daily.

Grace that does not move into the margins is not grace—it is empty sentiment.

Grace that does not question systems of exclusion is not grace—it is complicity dressed up in religious language.

Grace that cannot bear to be inconvenienced is not grace—it is comfort with a halo.

True grace is revolutionary.

It unsettles the powerful.

It disorients those who cling to order more than justice.

It refuses to separate spirituality from responsibility.

It does not flinch in the presence of suffering; it draws near.

And here is the most sacred part of this movement: grace never asks us to go alone. It accompanies us. It precedes us. It walks with us in the tension, the complexity, the unknowing. It does not demand perfection, but it insists on presence. It will not let us settle for good intentions when the world is aching for restoration.

This is what I want the Church to remember.

Grace is not an escape from the world.

It is an entrance into its deepest needs. Beginning with the confession that we all have needs.

And if we have truly received it, we will not remain unchanged.

We cannot.

Because grace does not stop at belief.

Grace builds bridges.

Grace dismantles barriers.

Grace walks forward, always forward—toward love, toward justice, toward healing, and toward the ones we were taught to avoid.

Real Change Is Local—and Personal

There is a widespread and deeply seductive myth in our culture. The myth that whispers to us from news cycles, social media feeds, and even from pulpits. The myth says that real change, lasting change, history-making change only happens in the big places, through the big voices, with the big titles. It tells us that unless we are holding microphones, crafting legislation, leading protests, or publishing bestselling books, our actions are too small to matter. It tells us that the work of justice and transformation must be loud, large, and far-reaching to count.

But this myth is a lie. And like most lies, it is dangerous precisely because it is so persuasive.

The truth is this: real change begins in proximity.

It begins not in the corridors of power, but in the ordinary, overlooked spaces we inhabit every single day—spaces that may never be televised or platformed, but which bear the full weight of our calling. It begins in classrooms where the seating chart never accounts for neurodivergence. It begins in sanctuaries where the hymnals are printed in fonts too small for aging eyes. It begins in breakrooms where coworkers grieve silently behind their coffee mugs. It begins at kitchen tables where grace is either practiced or withheld, sometimes without a word spoken.

It begins *on your street*. In your actual life.

I see it in my own story, every day I walk into the building where I teach. The walls are painted with motivational slogans. The mission statements hang in every hallway. There is talk of equity and access. And yet—beneath the well-meaning policies and district-wide initiatives—there are still deep cracks in the floor of inclusion. I feel them when I arrive at a staff meeting and cannot fully follow the discussion because it moves too quickly, faces turned away, words lost in a sea of side conversations. I feel them when fire alarms blare suddenly during a drill, and I am forced to rely not on sound, but on instinct and environment, scanning the reactions of others to know how to respond. I feel them when I see a student struggling to process language in the same way I did, and I watch well-intentioned educators unknowingly interpret their silence as defiance, rather than difference.

Still, I go. Still, I teach. Still, I plant presence like a flag in a land where others like me have rarely stood.

Because I know that accommodation is not charity, it is dignity made visible. And I know that progress is rarely dramatic. It is most often incremental and awkward and full of missteps— but it is progress nonetheless. When a student begins to slow down their speech so I can read their lips, that is grace. When a colleague repeats a key point in writing without being asked, that is grace. When a principal pauses before speaking to make sure I'm facing him, that is grace. Not because it is perfect, but because it is a sign that *someone is moving*.

I see it in the church, too. Each Sunday, I stand behind a pulpit in a rural congregation made up mostly of older adults, many of whom were formed by a very different ecclesial world—one shaped by quiet reverence, traditional liturgy, and a long-standing (often unspoken) hierarchy of who belongs and how. And yet, these beloved saints are learning—slowly, earnestly, and sometimes with holy discomfort—what it means to include not merely in language, but in practice.

They are learning that inclusion means more than opening the door. It means rearranging the furniture, rewriting the expectations, and re-examining the assumptions we've inherited about who counts, who contributes, and who gets to lead. They are learning that diversity is not a political issue but a gospel reality. They are learning that accessibility is not an afterthought but a prerequisite to authentic community. And in this learning, I am witnessing what real church looks like—not a place where everyone agrees, but a place where love makes room.

And I see it at home, perhaps most clearly of all.

I see it in the sacred ordinariness of parenting, where every bedtime routine, every breakfast prepared in silence, every school drop-off is charged with spiritual consequence. My children will not learn about grace from sermons alone. They will learn about grace from how I respond to their meltdowns, from whether I apologize when I'm wrong, from whether I let them see me wrestle with my own wounds and still show up with my whole heart.

Parenting, for me, has never been about producing perfect children. It has been about cultivating a home where imperfection is met not with shame but with welcome. Modeling a love that tells the truth without cutting too deep, a love that holds boundaries without closing doors. Remembering my own childhood—to learn and grow, and heal as I raise my own family.

The daily acts of teaching, preaching, and parenting may never be seen by the masses. But they are not small and do have an impact on society in ways I may never know.

Because actions are not measured by volume. They are measured by sacred weight.

Every time you choose to lean in instead of turning away,

Every time you create access instead of demand assimilation,

Every time you tell the truth when silence would be easier,

Every time you choose mercy over judgment, and dignity over dominance,

You are building the Kingdom of God.

Not in abstract theological theory.

But in flesh and blood. In brick and breath. In human lives.

So do not underestimate the space you already occupy.

Do not discount the sacredness of your own neighborhood, your own dinner table, your own classroom, your own email inbox.

Because real change will not be televised.

It will be embodied and incarnated in you.

Passing the Torch: What Kind of Ancestor Will You Be?

There is a moment—sometimes quiet, sometimes seismic—when you realize that your life is no longer just about you. It is not only about the miles you've walked, but also the scars you've carried and the prayers you've whispered in the dark. Life becomes, instead, about what will remain when you are no longer in the room. What echoes will your voice leave behind? What atmosphere will your decisions create for those who come after you?

This is not a morbid question. It is a sacred one.

Whether we realize it or not, we are all becoming ancestors. Not someday. Not far off in a distant, foggy future. But now. With every choice we make, with every table we set, with every boundary we hold, and every barrier we dismantle—we are forming the spiritual, emotional, and ethical inheritance of the generations that will follow us. We are shaping not only how we will be remembered, but what kind of world others will be born into.

And so I ask you, not as a rhetorical device, but as a holy interrogation of the soul:

What kind of ancestor will you be?

Will you be remembered as someone who hoarded comfort or as someone who risked peace for justice?

Will your legacy speak of a faith that made room for the marginalized or one that kept the doors bolted shut with doctrine and fear?

Will the shape of your life teach your children, your community, your colleagues how to love beyond convenience, how to serve beyond applause, how to tell the truth when silence would've been easier?

These are not abstract questions. They are deeply embodied.

Because your life tells a story—not just with your words, but with your habits, your hospitality, your posture toward power, and your relationship with grace. And whether you are aware of it or not, that story is shaping someone else's theology. Your reactions are teaching. Your patience is preaching. Your decisions are refining you and someone else as well.

So, again—what kind of ancestor will you be?

To become a good ancestor is to choose, again and again, to make space at the table—not just for those who look like you or vote like you or worship like you, but for those whose presence might stretch your comfort zones into compassion. To become a good ancestor is to rearrange the furniture of your life so that others can sit down without shame.

It means disrupting injustice when every voice around you urges you to stay quiet. It means refusing the safety of neutrality. It means learning to recognize the moments when silence becomes complicity—and choosing, in those very moments, to speak even when your voice quivers or your credibility trembles. It means confronting racism, ableism, sexism, homophobia, and apathy not just in the systems around you but in the assumptions within you.

And it means reimagining failure—not as a disqualifier, but as fertile ground. It means turning the compost of your regrets into soil for someone else's flourishing. It means owning the harm you caused so that it does not have to be repeated. It means confessing that you don't know everything, haven't gotten everything right, and still have much to learn—because a legacy rooted in humility is far more transformative than one rooted in image.

I think often about the kind of faith I want to hand to my children—not as a script to memorize, but as a rhythm to inhabit. I don't want to hand them a brittle religion that breaks under the pressure of real life. I want to give them a living, breathing faith— a faith that cries, that doubts, that dances, that disrupts, that repents, that repairs, and above all, a faith that **moves**.

I want them to know that love is not soft. It is resilient. That grace is not passive. It is defiant. That God does not live only in stained-glass buildings, but in the flesh-and-blood encounters of ordinary days. I want them to know that faith is not something you keep to yourself like a secret—it is something you spend like currency, pour out like oil, build with like lumber.

And I want you to know that you can hand down that kind of faith, too.

You don't need to be famous.

You don't need to have a platform.

You don't need to be perfect.

You just need to be *willing*—willing to show up, to stay present, to keep walking even when the road ahead is covered in fog.

Because legacy is not built in one dramatic moment. It is built into the small choices repeated over time.

It is built into how you treat the people no one is watching.

It is built into how you speak about those who have harmed you.

It is built into how you rebuild what others have broken.

It is built into how you love those who do not yet love themselves.

So yes—you are becoming an ancestor. An ancestor who carries a unique and sacred story.

Right now.

With every breath and every act of grace.

The question is not whether you will leave a legacy.

The question is what kind of legacy you will leave.

Whether the fire you carry will burn long enough, hot enough, and holy enough to light someone else's way.

This is your moment.

This is your torch.

Don't drop it.

A Commissioning, Not a Conclusion

This is not a chapter you finish.

This is not the kind of ending that wraps things in ribbon, ties off every question, or gives you the comfort of standing still. No— this is the kind of ending that unsettles you in the best way. The kind that doesn't ask you to applaud, but to act. The kind that doesn't lower the curtain but opens a new door. Because this book, from the first word to the last line, has not been a memoir of conclusions—it has been a story of becoming.

And now the story is about your journey to becoming.

For you are not being dismissed; you are being sent.

You may not feel qualified. You may not even feel ready. But if grace has touched any part of you—if even one line of this journey has resonated deep enough to make you pause, to breathe differently, to see someone in your life with clearer eyes—then you are already moving. Already part of the next chapter. Already holding the torch passed to you, not from me alone, but from every unnamed ancestor who dreamed of a more honest, more inclusive, more merciful world.

Maybe you are a schoolteacher trying to hold space for students whose stories come with jagged edges.

Maybe you are a single parent, giving everything you have to hold your home together with more love than resources.

Maybe you are a grandparent navigating a world your generation didn't prepare you for.

Maybe you are a recent graduate aching to find meaning in a culture obsessed with performance.

Maybe you are Deaf, disabled, neurodivergent, queer, recovering, grieving, deconstructing, disillusioned—or simply trying to remember how to believe again.

Whatever road brought you here, this much is true:

Your story matters.

Your presence matters.

Your next steps matter.

You don't need a pulpit to proclaim grace.

You don't need a seminary degree to live it.

You don't need to be certain to walk faithfully.

You don't need to be unbroken to be useful.

All you need is a willingness to rise—not with arrogance, not with polished answers, but with a heart cracked open wide enough to let love pour through the broken seams.

Because grace—true, holy, revolutionary grace—is not stationary.

It is not a creed to recite or a gate to protect.

Grace is a current. A movement. A daily discipline.

It flows through classrooms where students have stopped pretending to be okay.

It moves through kitchens where family members learn to love again after years of misunderstanding.

It breathes through hospital rooms, prison visitation booths, street protests, church basements, recovery meetings, silent tears, and late-night phone calls where someone finally says, "I need help."

That's where grace goes.

And if you are brave enough to follow it, it will take you places your theology hasn't prepared you for, but your spirit has longed to reach.

This is your commission.

To be the kind of neighbor who shows up.

To be the kind of leader who listens more than they speak.

To be the kind of friend who names the truth with tenderness.

To be the kind of ancestor who leaves more freedom than fear behind.

You don't need to have all the answers.

You only need to say yes to the work love is calling you into—right here, in your own life, in the very place your feet already stand.

So, go.

Not because you're perfect.

Not because you're ready.

But because grace has already gone ahead of you.

Go, and carry what you've received—gently, boldly, humbly—into the places that still feel unfinished, into the people who still feel unloved, into the systems that still feel unmovable.

Let your life be the evidence that grace still breathes.

Let your presence become a doorway for someone else to walk through.

Let your memory become the seedbed of someone else's healing.

And when the world tries to tell you you're too small to make a difference, too broken to lead, too unsure to be trusted— remember this: God has never needed a perfect vessel. Only a willing one.

So go—not to end the story, but to become part of what comes next.

This is your sending. With your name and your story, it is yours to give away.

Not as a conclusion.

But a beginning, made holy by the fact that you said yes.

Carry the fire.

Share the table.

Make room.

Live loud.

Love well.

And go—not because you must, but because the world needs what you carry.

CHAPTER 16

Dare to Dream

Rev. Dr. Martin Luther King Jr once dared to dream, so here is my dream. I dream with my eyes wide open and my heart unguarded. These are not quiet, private dreams; they are loud and holy—too big for me alone, too sacred to ignore. They keep me awake at night with holy restlessness and wake me in the morning with holy fire. I cannot bury them, because they are planted by the hand of God, and they will not stop growing.

Dreams for My Calling

I do not dream safe dreams. I dream the kind that sets your soul on fire, the kind you can't shake no matter how late the hour or how heavy the doubt. These are dreams born in prayer, tempered in pain, and carried in the marrow of my bones. My calling is not something I clock into; it is the fire shut up in my bones, the song I cannot stop singing.

I dream of winning championships—at least seven—not as a monument to my name, but as a living testimony to what happens when faith shapes athletes and character outlasts talent. I do not dream of rings that gather dust, but of young men and women who rise from locker rooms and classrooms knowing they were built for more than scoreboards. I dream of teaching them that discipline is worship, that integrity is strength, and that faith is the only victory worth carrying long after the lights go out.

I dream of teams that learn winning is not just about games but about becoming the kind of people who transform their communities. Every sprint, every play, every late-night talk in the weight room becomes a seed—planted in young hearts, watered by sweat and prayer, and grown into men and women who carry Christ into boardrooms, battlefields, pulpits, and homes. Seven championships are not my ceiling—it is a symbol, a banner, a tangible reminder that when faith and excellence meet, nothing is impossible.

I dream of building an international, self-sustaining network that looks nothing like charity and everything like family. A network born not of pity but of partnership, where grace flows freely and commerce is holy—where rising tides lift every boat that faithfully and with integrity joins the work.

I see this network stretching from rural villages in Zambia to farmlands in Delaware, from the streets of Guatemala to the rebuilding corners of Ukraine, from the highlands of Sudan to bustling cities in South Korea, Germany, and Australia. It is not a pipeline of handouts flowing one direction, but a living exchange—a web of gifts and needs, skills and resources, stories and prayers moving both ways.

Farmers in Delaware can learn soil-restoration practices from growers in Zambia. Educators in South Korea can share literacy strategies with teachers in Guatemala, while Guatemalan artisans teach Americans the lost art of handwoven textiles. Engineers in Germany can design clean-water systems with innovators in Sudan, who in turn help U.S. communities learn how to live sustainably with fewer resources. Pastors in the United Kingdom can share revival practices, while congregations in Ukraine show the world how worship persists under persecution and war.

This is no imperialistic export of Western ideals. This is no savior complex masquerading as a mission. This is reciprocity—a holy commerce of grace, where the Spirit weaves together what the world tried to keep apart. Every partner gives; every partner receives. Every culture brings wisdom, beauty, and strength to the table. The goal is not dependence, but empowerment. The fruit is not controlled, but the community.

In this network, access replaces arrogance. Curiosity replaces condescension. Listening precedes speaking. Partnerships outlast projects. And every deal, every collaboration, every act of generosity is tethered to integrity and mutual respect.

The outcome?

A living embodiment of the Gospel—good news in motion. A Kingdom economy where hunger is met, healing is shared, education is multiplied, and commerce becomes a channel for Christ's love to flood the earth. A quiet revolution that dismantles systems of exploitation and builds bridges of belonging, one faithful exchange at a time.

I dream of becoming a published author, not of one book but of many, volumes that do more than inform minds but transform lives. These would be books born of scars and grace, carrying the voices of the overlooked into spaces where they have long been silenced. They would wrestle honestly with Scripture, history, and culture, unafraid to question, unafraid to proclaim, unafraid to name injustice and point toward healing.

I dream of writing theological commentaries that make the mysteries of God accessible without diminishing their wonder. These works would linger over every word of Scripture, digging through original languages and historical context, yet always arriving in the living heart of grace. They would connect the world of the text to the world we inhabit today, revealing how ancient words still speak into modern wounds.

I dream of penning social commentaries that hold a mirror to both the church and the culture, calling out the sins we would rather hide and summoning us toward the holiness we often fear. These pages would speak with prophetic fire and pastoral tenderness, challenging the proud, comforting the broken, and awakening those who have grown numb.

I dream of chronicling histories that have been neglected or forgotten, histories of the Deaf community, of overlooked saints, of revival movements, and forgotten martyrs. I picture researching archives, walking historic streets, and holding artifacts in trembling hands. I envision narratives where footnotes and facts meet storytelling and soul, where the past becomes a living testimony pointing toward a more faithful future.

These books would be guided by God's prompting. Sometimes the Spirit would whisper softly, sometimes the urgency of the times would stir me, and sometimes inspiration would strike suddenly in the ordinary moments of life. A headline, a hymn, a story told in passing could ignite a chapter, and a prayer whispered in the dark could spark an entire volume.

I imagine these books being discovered in everyday places, a hospital waiting room, a dusty school library, a prison chapel, the back pew of a rural church, and awakening something holy in the reader. I see a young mother, sleepless and scared, finding hope in a line she did not know she needed. I picture a disillusioned pastor discovering courage in a story of someone who stood firm. I imagine a college student wrestling with faith and, for the first time, feeling seen.

I want these books to outlive me, not because of my name, but because of God's name. I long for them to echo long after I am gone, testifying to the truth that God still sees, God still hears, and God still redeems.

My grandfather once told me that the testament of a pastor is not how he arrived or even what was done, but what remains when his time is done. Those words have stayed with me, echoing louder the longer I serve. They strip away pretense and force me to confront the deeper question beneath every sermon, every meeting, every prayer whispered in hospital corridors: When I am gone, what will endure?

I do not want to be remembered for the noise I made, but for the lives that were transformed. I do not want the measure of my ministry to be found in programs or attendance graphs, but in people who discovered they were loved by God and learned to love others in turn. My calling is not to build monuments but to plant orchards—trees whose fruit I may never taste, whose shade I may never sit under, but which will feed and shelter generations to come.

That is why I dream of blessing every church I serve, not with comfort but with courage. I want to leave behind communities that do not depend on me but depend on Christ. I long to leave sanctuaries trembling with praise, altar rails worn smooth from prayer, baptismal waters stirred so often they never settle. I want pulpits braver, congregations bolder, ministries that spill into streets and homes and workplaces, where the Kingdom refuses to be contained.

If my grandfather was right, then the true measure of a pastor is not what he does while standing in the pulpit, but what endures after he steps away. Will faith remain? Will courage remain? Will a fire for justice and mercy remain? Will the children I baptized grow up to baptize their children? Will the hidden seeds planted in another's soil rise long after I am forgotten?

This is the legacy I pray for. Not one bound to my name, but one bound to Christ's name. Not one that crumbles when I am gone, but one that continues to bear fruit in season and out of season, until the Kingdom of God comes in fullness and every tear is wiped away.

Dreams for My Family

I dream of buying my family a home with room enough to grow roots, a place not defined by size or appearance but by the love that fills it. I imagine walls strong enough to hold our laughter during family meals that stretch long into the night. I see hallways echoing with the sound of children running, wide enough to welcome the wandering, quiet enough to give the weary rest. I dream of a home that is not just a house but a sanctuary, where prayer and play flow naturally and where every room speaks belonging.

I dream of raising my children to discover lives that are both joyful and purposeful, not merely by the standards of the world but by the calling of God. I want them to step into the future as people of character and faith, resilient in hardship, humble in success, courageous in leadership, and tender in love. I picture them finding vocations that light their hearts on fire and use every gift God has entrusted to them.

In time, I dream of adopting youth who long for a place to belong. This will not be born of pity but of abundance, an overflow of the love God has already planted in our family. I see sons and daughters welcomed into our home and into our story, their past pain met with patience, their present embraced with joy, and their future rewritten in the language of hope.

I dream of land that restores more than people. I see fields and pastures where rescue animals find safety and purpose, where dogs once chained run free, cats find warm shelter, horses rediscover trust, and goats graze in peace. I imagine a home where creation itself participates in healing, where every creature testifies that redemption is real and that God delights in restoring what was once broken.

This is more than a vision for comfort or stability. It is a vision of the Kingdom planted in soil and wood, lived out in the everyday rhythms of love and welcome. It is a house made holy not by architecture but by the Spirit who inhabits it, a place where anyone who enters—human or animal—leaves knowing they are cherished and seen by God.

Dreams for My Vocation as Educator

I dream of becoming the kind of educator that parents request by name, not because I am the easiest teacher, but because I see their children for who they truly are. I want to be remembered as the teacher who believes in them when others have given up, who draws out their character, and nurtures their curiosity. I long for classrooms that feel like safe harbors, where every child—regardless of reading level, family story, or hidden wound—knows they belong and believes they can grow.

I dream of teaching students not only what to think but how to think. I want them to approach history, past and present, with eyes wide open and a mind willing to ask why. I want them to examine what they believe about God, themselves, and the world—not so they abandon their faith but so they may embrace it fully and authentically. My goal is to raise young people who do not simply inherit ideas but wrestle with them, understand them, and live them out with conviction.

I dream of classrooms where students learn to engage ideas without fear, where disagreement becomes an opportunity to grow instead of a reason to divide. I want them to leave my classroom prepared to step into a complicated world with both courage and humility, confident in their own story yet eager to learn from the stories of others.

I dream of being a bridge between school and home, a source of hope for parents and encouragement for children. I want to help entire communities grow in financial, cultural, spiritual, and literacy competencies, so that no person is held back by ignorance or silenced by lack of access. My prayer is that every mind, body, and spirit has the opportunity to think deeply, wrestle honestly, and discover God for themselves.

The legacy I hope to leave as an educator is not measured by test scores or accolades, but by the lives of young people who learn to think with clarity, live with compassion, and lead with integrity.

Dreams for the Church

I dream of a Church courageous enough to name its sins without fear and humble enough to listen to its prophets without defensiveness. I dream of a Church that does not cling to what is familiar for the sake of comfort but leans into the Spirit's leading for the sake of transformation. A Methodist movement reborn not in polity or property, but in power—the prevenient grace that pursues us before we know we need God, the justifying grace that redeems what sin has broken, the sanctifying grace that perfects us in love and makes us holy.

I dream of Annual Conferences where the cross is heavier than our banners and holy conferencing is more than polite conversation or parliamentary procedure. It becomes the rhythm of our shared life, where we bear each other's burdens, seek the Spirit's guidance together, and leave every gathering more unified in mission than when we arrived. I dream of clergy and laity alike, arm in arm, reclaiming the vision of Methodism as a movement for the world rather than merely an institution to maintain.

I dream of a Church universal that remembers its first love—the Christ who broke bread with sinners, touched the unclean, and called the forgotten by name. I long for a Church that measures its success not by the height of its steeples or the size of its budget but by the depth of its compassion. A Church that opens its doors wide enough for the wounded, the doubting, and the dismissed. A Church where denominations cease to function as dividing lines and become diverse harmonies in one Kingdom song.

I dream of a global Church marked by mercy and fire, a people whose worship does not stop at the sanctuary doors but floods into streets and shelters, classrooms and courthouses. I imagine the world recognizing the Church not by its judgments but by its love, not by its posturing but by its service, not by its self-preservation but by its self-giving.

This is the Church I ache for, the Church I labor for, the Church I believe is still possible through the Spirit's power. A Church that embodies the Gospel so fully that even the most cynical cannot deny the reality of Christ alive within it.

Daring You to Dream

I do not share these dreams to impress you. I share them to invite you. To confront you. To unsettle you until you cannot ignore the holy restlessness rising in your own soul. What is the dream God is planting in you? What injustice keeps you awake at night because silence feels like betrayal? What vision stirs in your chest that terrifies you precisely because it is too big for you to accomplish alone—and that is how you know it is from God?

Write it down. Speak it aloud. Tell it to your children, your spouse, your friends, your church. Whisper it in prayer until it turns into a roar in your bones. Let others laugh at its audacity. Let them call it impossible. Then watch how God delights in taking what seems impossible and turning it into testimony. Watch how He does immeasurably more than all we ask or imagine.

This is not just about me. It is about us. It is about all of us daring to believe that the Spirit is not finished with our lives, our churches, our communities, or our world. Revival is not a memory in the rearview mirror—it is still ahead. The Kingdom of God is not some distant reality we wait to enter—it is already breaking in, nearer than we think.

So I dare you to dream again. Not safe dreams, but bold ones. Not small visions, but holy ones. I dare you to put your shoulder to the plow, your knees to the ground, and your heart in the hands of God, and see what remains after your time is done.

A Prophetic Benediction

My grandfather once told me that the true testament of a pastor is not how he arrived or even what was accomplished in his time, but what remains when his time is done. Those words have followed me into every pulpit, every classroom, every sideline, and every late night spent wondering if what I am building will last. What remains after the applause fades? What remains when my hands can no longer work and my voice no longer carries?

I dream of what I pray will remain. I dream of families rooted in homes where love is louder than fear and hospitality stronger than walls. I dream of children launched into callings filled with purpose and joy, and of adopted sons and daughters who discover belonging not as charity but as family. I dream of athletes whose character is deeper than their talent, whose faith sustains them long after the final whistle. I dream of classrooms where students learn to think for themselves, to wrestle with history and faith honestly, to ask why they believe what they believe, and to walk into the world with both courage and humility.

I dream of churches trembling with praise, altars worn smooth by prayer, baptismal waters stirred so often they never have time to grow still. I dream of pulpits braver and congregations bolder, ministries spilling into neighborhoods and workplaces until love becomes a movement and not just a service. I dream of a Methodist movement reborn, not in nostalgia but in Spirit-led power, and of a Church universal remembering its first love, opening its arms wide enough for the wounded, the doubting, and the dismissed. I dream of networks stretching across nations, connecting Delaware to Zambia, South Korea to Guatemala, Germany to Sudan, and Ukraine, a web of grace where gifts and needs meet and rising tides lift every faithful boat.

But beyond all these dreams, I long for what endures. The Kingdom of God is never built in one lifetime. It is planted and watered by generations, tended quietly in faith, and revealed in glory when Christ comes again.

Like Martin, I have a dream—not of color-blindness but of Christ-centered sight, where every image-bearer is honored and every tear is named. Like Barber, I believe we must rise for the poor and the marginalized, for the least and the lost, for those the world has dismissed yet Christ has crowned. But I am also Rick— pastor and coach, teacher and father, Deaf and hearing by grace, preacher and storyteller, still unfinished and still believing. My dreams are not tidy or easy; they are wild, relentless, and unmistakably born of the Spirit who placed them in me.

So, I dare you to dream with me. Pray with me. Build with me. Weep and rejoice with me. Dare to believe that God still writes impossible stories, still calls unlikely people, still makes dry bones rise in the valley of despair. Dare to imagine a Church that refuses to bow to fear, a people who refuse to settle for small plans when the Kingdom of Heaven is already breaking in.

When my voice and hands are silent and my time has passed, I pray you will keep dreaming. The true testament of a life is what remains after it is done. May faith remain. May courage remain. May holy imagination remain.

Go forward—not with fear, but with faith. Not with hesitation, but with holy boldness. Not with small plans, but with a vision large enough for eternity. And not alone, but together, bound by grace, carried by mercy, sent in love.

May the God who dreamed galaxies into being breathe His dream into your bones. May the Spirit who hovered over chaos hover over your chaos and call it good. May Christ, the author and finisher of our faith, write new chapters through your life that echo long after we are gone.

May we all, someday, stand side by side in the great multitude no one can number, from every nation, tribe, and tongue, and say together with tears of joy, "Worthy is the Lamb who was slain, to receive power and wealth and wisdom and strength and honor and glory and praise."

Until that day comes, keep dreaming. Keep daring. Keep building. The story is not finished, and neither are we.

My name is Rick, and you are…?

ACKNOWLEDGEMENTS

First and always, I give thanks to God. There are no words deep enough to hold the weight of that gratitude. Every moment I survived when I should not have, every breath that carried me from night into morning, every page of this book that made it into the light belongs to the grace of God. Mercy found me when I least deserved it, and grace refused to let go even when I tried to run away.

To my wife: I do not even know where to begin. There were nights when we could have walked away, seasons when the weight felt unbearable, yet somehow, we stayed. We stayed because love was worth more than the fight. Thank you for believing in me when I did not believe in myself. Thank you for raising our children with a fierce devotion that humbles me every day. I will never forget the nights you sat with me in silence when there were no words left, the mornings you encouraged me to keep writing when I doubted my own story, and the quiet ways you loved me when I did not deserve it. You are my partner in everything, my safe place, and my anchor.

To my children: You are my legacy, my hope, and my joy. Each of you carries part of me, and yet you are wholly your own.

Sierra, my firstborn and only daughter. I see so much of myself in you and so much more that I could never be. You used to come to college classes with me when we had no childcare, sleeping on desks or drawing quietly in the corner while I took notes. You dream of earning your bachelor's and master's degrees and leading a nonprofit one day. I have no doubt you will do it, and I will be cheering you the whole way.

O'Rian, my oldest son, is just fifty weeks younger than your sister. I do not always understand your love for soccer, but I admire how fiercely you love it. Your curiosity knows no limits. You read, question, and think in ways that remind me of Einstein and Newton and every restless soul who ever searched for truth. You keep me sharp, and you remind me that wisdom is not found in having all the answers but in the courage to keep seeking.

Tommy, my second-oldest son. Life has not been fair to you. Your health has stolen opportunities you deserved, especially in sports, yet you have never lost your gratitude. I am amazed at how you can find joy in the darkest seasons and teach me what strength and grace really look like.

Blue, my youngest. You are my mirror, my shadow, my mini-me. I will admit that terrifies me sometimes. You shattered the mold set by your siblings. You push boundaries without fear, you try things without hesitation, and you refuse to be anyone but yourself. The world is not ready for you, and I cannot wait to see what you become.

To my mother: You are my confidant and my greatest encourager. You have carried burdens you never spoke aloud and somehow still found the strength to lift mine when I could not lift them alone. You are my sermon-writing partner, the one who listens as I wrestle with Scripture, who challenges me to go deeper, who reminds me to see the people behind the words and the grace behind the command. You are the one who nudges me to finish pages when I want to quit. You remind me that not every hill is worth dying on. Without you, this book would not exist, and neither would the man who wrote it.

To my father: You were my first hero. My earliest memories are not just of you working, though you worked harder than anyone I have ever known. I remember hours on the beach at Assateague, walking the shoreline with salt on our lips and windburn on our faces. I remember driving the countryside with the windows down, the smell of cut grass rushing in, the hum of the truck beneath us steady as your presence. I remember football practices, watching you on the field, your voice cutting through the chaos, teaching me discipline and heart in the same breath.

You taught me to drive before I had a license. I can still see my hands white-knuckled on the wheel, a forty-four-ounce cup of hot coffee balanced on the dash. You said if I could keep the coffee from spilling, I could keep the truck steady. In that moment, you taught me everything about focus and respect for what I was holding.

As I grew older, I began to see the struggles you carried. I still do not know if you were running from something or chasing something, but I know now your restlessness and your drive were two sides of the same coin. From you, I learned we have no one to blame but ourselves, and quitting is never an option. You did not speak much about feelings, but you showed love in the way you provided and protected. Even when you did not always know how to meet me in my silence, you never turned away from it.

To my brothers:

Randy, though you are ten years older, our bond has only grown stronger with time. Our lives are so different, but your love for me has never wavered. I can still hear you teasing me with "Are you going to whine about this all day?" or "Let me Google that for you." Beneath the humor, there is always love. You are good at anything you truly put your mind to, and I believe God is only getting started with you.

Robby, your path has been one I do not always understand, but I respect your tenacity. Life has knocked you down more times than I can count, and every time you get back up. You refuse to stay down. I love you, and I love your boys, my nephews, who carry a piece of you the world needs.

Joseph, my first roommate, my first fistfight, my first interpreter. For many years, I was jealous of you, your friends, your athletic ability, your gift with numbers, your service to our country, your confidence in moving through the world. I regret every burden I placed on you, every time I fought with you, every moment I caused you pain. One of my greatest regrets is not being closer to you. I love you, and I hope for more time to bridge the gap between us.

Special thanks to Rev. Joseph Archie, Rev. Brian Vinson, and Rev. Tim Barth. Our stories go back further than memory, back to a time when we did not yet know how God had already intertwined our paths. I do not see you nearly as often as I wish, but your kinship carried me through some of the longest nights of my soul. You walked with me when I questioned God, life, and purpose. There are others who wish to remain unnamed, and I honor them as well. Their love and grace saved me in ways I still cannot fully name.

To my dogs Duke, Cassie, Maddie, Scooby, Luna, Raven, Starfire, and Duke OG, and my cats Bagheera, Selah, and Skylar. Thank you for the kind of wordless comfort only animals know how to give. You have sat with me in grief, celebrated with me in joy, and taught me loyalty that asks for no explanation.

To classmates, teammates, parishioners, and friends whose names might not appear on this page but whose fingerprints are all over this story, such as those at Kenton and Hartly United

Methodist Churches. Even in seasons of trauma and pain, good people with good intentions crossed my path and left light where darkness tried to settle. A regret I hold is that so many of you, along with me, have yet to see my best. I pray this book gives you a glimpse. Not of perfection, but of grace still working, still shaping, still calling me and all of us forward.

Finally, I give thanks even to those who criticized, doubted, or dismissed me, as my students would say, the haters. The ones who told me to be quiet, who bullied me, who said no one wanted to hear what I had to say. The coaches, pastors, teachers, social workers, and nameless voices who tried to break me, only to teach me to stand. Their challenges became fuel. Their rejection stirred up resolve from within my being. From them, I learned that we are not the sum of our worst decisions, nor are we doomed to repeat the judgments cast upon us. I do not say this bitterly. I mean it with gratitude. You sharpened me in ways I did not recognize at the time.

To every soul who crossed my path, for better or worse, I carry you to these pages. Thank you. If you find yourself in these words, may you also find a holy gift of grace waiting for each of us to embrace.

REFERENCES

As both a teacher and a pastor, I believe that giving credit where credit is due is part of integrity and witness. The following sources shaped the language, theology, history, and ideas throughout this book. Some are quoted directly, others influenced the framing of concepts or metaphors woven into the narrative.

Biblical Translations

Holy Bible, New Revised Standard Version. (1989). National Council of Churches of Christ in the USA.

Holy Bible, New International Version. (2011). Zondervan.

Holy Bible, New King James Version. (1982). Thomas Nelson.

Theological and Biblical Studies

Brueggemann, W. (1978). *The prophetic imagination*. Fortress Press.

Buechner, F. (1973). *Wishful thinking: A theological ABC*. Harper & Row.

Eiesland, N. L. (1994). *The disabled God: Toward a liberatory theology of disability*. Abingdon Press.

Gutiérrez, G. (1973). *A theology of liberation: History, politics, and salvation* (Rev. ed.). Orbis Books. (Original work published in 1971)

Moltmann, J. (1974). *The crucified God: The cross of Christ as the foundation and criticism of Christian theology*. Harper & Row.

Williams, D. S. (1993). *Sisters in the wilderness: The challenge of womanist God-talk*. Orbis Books.

Deaf Studies and Disability Concepts

Bauman, H.-D. L., & Murray, J. J. (2009). Reframing: From hearing loss to Deaf gain. *Deaf Studies Digital Journal, 1*(1).

Eckert, R. C., & Rowley, A. J. (2013). Audism: A theory and practice of audio-centric privilege. *Humanity & Society, 37*(2), 101–130.

Turner, V. (1969). *The ritual process: Structure and anti-structure.* Aldine.

Civil Rights and Social Justice

Barber, W. J., II, & Wilson-Hartgrove, J. (2016). *The third reconstruction: How a moral movement is overcoming the politics of division and fear.* Beacon Press.

King, M. L., Jr. (1963, August 28). *I have a dream* [Speech]. March on Washington, Washington, DC. In J. M. Washington (Ed.), *A testament of hope: The essential writings and speeches of Martin Luther King, Jr.* (1986). HarperCollins.

History.com Editors. (2025, January 31). Florida teen Trayvon Martin is shot and killed. *History.* (Original work published 2013).

Key Biblical Passages Referenced or Paraphrased

Genesis 1:1; 1:27; 2:7
Exodus 2:24
Deuteronomy 6:4–9; 31:8
Joshua 1:9
Isaiah 58:6–7
Mark 7:32–35
Matthew 11:28; 18:1–6
Acts 9:1–19; 18:26
Romans 16:1; 16:7
2 Corinthians 12:9
Ephesians 2:13–22

Hebrews 12:2

Revelation 5:12; 7:9

(All passages cited from the NRSV unless otherwise noted; NIV used for Romans 16:7; NKJV used for Hebrews 12:2.)

Historical and Cultural Influences

Wesleyan Methodist history and figures, including John Wesley and Francis Asbury.

Civil Rights movements of the twentieth and twenty-first centuries.

Deaf community history and cultural narratives.

Broader American historical events referenced

www.ingramcontent.com/pod-product-compliance
Lightning Source LLC
Chambersburg PA
CBHW020915140626
46545CB00015B/48